History as Propaganda

History as Propaganda

*Tibetan Exiles versus the
People's Republic of China*

JOHN POWERS

OXFORD
UNIVERSITY PRESS
2004

OXFORD
UNIVERSITY PRESS

Oxford   New York
Auckland   Bangkok   Buenos Aires   Cape Town   Chennai
Dar es Salaam   Delhi   Hong Kong   Istanbul   Karachi   Kolkata
Kuala Lumpur   Madrid   Melbourne   Mexico City   Mumbai
Nairobi   São Paulo   Shanghai   Taipei   Tokyo   Toronto

Copyright © 2004 by Oxford University Press, Inc.

Published by Oxford University Press, Inc.
198 Madison Avenue, New York, New York 10016

www.oup.com

Oxford is a registered trademark of Oxford University Press

Library of Congress Cataloging-in-Publication Data
Powers, John, 1957–
History as propaganda : Tibetan exiles versus the People's Republic of China / John Powers.
       p. cm.
Includes bibliographical references.
ISBN 0-19-517426-7
1. Tibet (China)—Historiography.   2. Historiography—China.
3. Tibetans—Foreign countries.   I. Title: Tibetan exiles versus the
People's Republic of China.   II. Title.
DS786.P68 2004
951'.5—dc22   2003028121

9 8 7 6 5 4 3 2 1

Printed in the United States of America
on acid-free paper

To Gavin, Kelly, Chet, and Kestrel

Preface

> There are two countries, real and fictional, occupying the same
> space, or almost the same space. My story, my fictional country ex-
> ist, like myself, at a slight angle to reality. I have found this off-
> centering to be necessary; but its value is, of course, open to debate.
> —Salman Rushdie, *Shame*, p. 29

Several years ago I was browsing the shelves in a Sydney bookstore
and saw a small book with a picture of the Potala (formerly the residence of the Dalai Lamas) on the cover entitled *100 Questions about
Tibet*. After perusing a few pages, it became clear that this was a
Chinese government propaganda piece, and it seemed out of place
with the bookstore's very mainstream wares. I asked the owner why
he had decided to carry such a biased book and whether he had any
that presented other sides of the Tibet issue. After looking at the
book he replied that he had not ordered it. He then went to his com-
puter and checked past book orders, and concluded that neither he
nor any of his employees had ordered it, and that the store did not
even do business with the book's distributor. He then laughed and
said, "I've had lots of problems with people stealing books off my
shelves, but this is the first time I've had someone sneak books onto
them." I later found that other bookstores in the area had unordered
copies of this and other Chinese government-produced books on
their shelves, apparently surreptitiously placed there by Chinese officials hoping that these cheaply priced volumes would be purchased

by Australian readers, who would be converted to the Chinese position regarding Tibet.

By contrast, the shelves of bookstores in Australia, the United States, and Europe abound with books published by mainstream presses telling the Tibetan side of the story. In addition, numerous documentaries and magazine articles have been produced that are highly critical of the Chinese version of events and that support the Tibetan view. Big-budget Hollywood movies like *Seven Years in Tibet* similarly present the Chinese as the villains of the story and depict the Tibetan position. While researching this subject, I did a key word search for "Tibet" on the Internet, and among the first 230 URLs found only three that supported the Chinese government position.[1] All three were run by the Chinese government. The rest either explicitly supported the Tibetan position or belonged to Tibetan Buddhist organizations, many of which had messages in support of Tibetan independence. This disparity illustrates the irony of China's complete military victory in Tibet and its poor showing in the ongoing propaganda wars relating to it.

It also exemplifies China's difficulties in convincing foreigners that it has a legitimate right to Tibet and that its rule has been benevolent and beneficial to the Tibetans. Despite its military and economic might—and in spite of the predictable use of its veto power as a member of the United Nations' Security Council to stifle debate on its policies in Tibet—China is regularly castigated in international forums and the press for brutality and denial of human rights to Tibetans. This has become so well known in Western countries that it was even part of an episode of *The Simpsons*. The Simpson family visited the local Chinatown and passed by a section named "Tibettown" that was closed off by chain-link fences and barbed wire, behind which Chinese were brutally—and apparently senselessly—beating helpless Tibetans. No explanation of the reference was given; apparently, it was assumed that viewers were already aware of conditions in Tibet.

China also attempts to use its economic power to stop foreign countries from granting visas to Tibet's exiled leader, the Dalai Lama, in order to deny him an international audience. Despite sometimes strong pressure and heated rhetoric from China, however, he is one of the most recognizable people on the planet and draws huge crowds wherever he goes. Several of his books have become international best sellers, and Martin Scorsese directed a major Hollywood biography of him, entitled *Kundun* (The Presence). He is widely perceived as a charismatic holy man of unimpeachable integrity. In an episode of *Frasier*, when the main character criticized his manager for unethical tactics, she snapped, "If you wanted an ethical agent, you should have hired the Dalai Lama!" Such positive images of the Tibetan leader, and testaments to his in-

tegrity, abound in popular Western culture. His smiling face is instantly recognizable by most people, and was even used in an advertising campaign to
sell Apple computers.

By contrast, China's charismatically challenged leaders attract crowds of
protestors whenever they visit foreign countries, many of them waving Tibetan
flags and shouting "Free Tibet!" This sight has so distressed many of them that
they sometimes cancel appearances when the protestors break through security
and confront them directly. Before visiting a foreign country China's leaders
commonly demand that its leaders physically suppress protestors, and they
dismiss the notion that this is not possible in democratic societies. Moreover,
they tell anyone who is willing to listen that the protests are misguided because
Chinese rule in Tibet has brought unprecedented prosperity and happiness to
its people at a huge expense to the Chinese government. While the Dalai Lama
has become increasingly sophisticated in his use of the international media to
project his image and message, China's leaders tend to look dour and mean-
spirited when they denounce this apparently cheerful Buddhist monk, whose
name is widely viewed as synonymous with wisdom and compassion.

In contrast to the furtive actions of Chinese officials planting their
publications in bookstores, the Tibetan side is well represented by mainstream
presses. There are a number of publishers who specialize in Tibetan studies,
and they uniformly represent the perspective of the Tibetan government-in-
exile headquartered in India and led by the Dalai Lama. Despite Chinese ob-
jections, numerous resolutions have been passed in the UN, the U.S. Congress,
and other legislative bodies condemning Chinese policies in Tibet, and most
Western countries have a number of active Tibet support groups. According
to recent reports, their numbers are growing steadily.[2]

Even when the Chinese government manages to get publications presenting its point of view into Western bookstores and libraries, the results often
fall short of their expectations. When I began this study, I borrowed a number
of Chinese-produced books on Tibet from my university's library, and several
had messages written on the inside covers, apparently by students who had
previously borrowed them. Some of these read: "Don't read this book!" "It's
all lies and Chinese distortions!" Throughout the books messages were written
in the margins proclaiming that certain statements were "lies!" or "bullshit!"
I was struck by the vehemence of these messages, and decided to compare
them to publications by Tibetans or Westerners that follow the Tibetan exile
view of Tibet's history and current status; there I found no such denunciations,
even in those works that had a highly propagandistic tone.[3]

As these observations indicate, the Tibet issue is highly emotionally
charged, and the field of Tibetan studies has been affected by this. When I

entered graduate school in the early 1980s, two or three academic books on the subject per year were being published, generally for the consumption of a small group of specialists. In the intervening years, publications on Tibet have experienced exponential growth, and it is no longer possible to keep track of all the new books. Most of these are produced for Western Buddhists (or Westerners with an interest in Buddhist thought and practice), but many also contain political messages and support for Tibetan independence, along with condemnation of Chinese actions in Tibet. At the same time, the field has become increasingly politicized. My original intention was to concentrate my energies on translation and study of Buddhist philosophical and meditational texts, but during graduate fieldwork I began to recognize that the discipline in which I was working had numerous fault lines of political tension. The Tibetan refugee lamas with whom I read classical Tibetan texts often interspersed their comments with references to the political situation in Tibet, and the very fact that I had access to some of the most respected senior lamas in the refugee community was a result of their present situation.

Prior to the Chinese takeover of Tibet in the 1950s, there would have been no possibility of a foreigner's spending large amounts of time with senior reincarnate lamas (tülku) or abbots of monasteries. But because I arrived in India armed with advanced degrees from North American universities and research grants, I was able to gain access to their considerable knowledge and their limited time. As I pondered this situation, it became clear that part of the reason for my access was that they viewed me as a potential ally in their cause, whose position as an aspiring academic expert could be useful in spreading their political message. When I began teaching in U.S. colleges I began to receive calls from radio and television stations for interviews on the Tibet situation or from newspaper reporters seeking information. Keeping up with the changing (and often murky) situation in Tibet became part of my job, and as a result, I felt it necessary to be familiar with the available information.

The most difficult part of this process was getting beyond interested and biased opinions and finding reliable data on which to base my own conclusions. Publications on Tibet tend to be strongly polarized, and there is an uncompromising tone to those that support the Tibetan exile view and their opponents in the pro-China camp. As I delved deeper into this literature, two things became clear: the two views are mutually incompatible, and both sides sincerely believe what they say. There is little ambiguity or nuance in most contemporary works about Tibet, and some of the most emotionally charged rhetoric is found in studies of Tibetan history. History is viewed by both sides as being crucial to their claims, and both invest a great deal of energy in producing works that purport to tell the "truth" about Tibet's past. Another conclusion I reached during this study is that Tibetan and Chinese writers are operating within a particular psychological context in which certain assumptions guide their inquiry and predetermine their conclusions. Moreover, given their respective—and incommensurable—biases, there is little possibility that they will significantly deviate from the party lines of their communities. Both sides are so thoroughly convinced of the utter rightness of their paradigms that they cannot even imagine that someone might sincerely hold the opposing view, and so they accuse their opponents of deliberately lying and covering up the "facts" and the "truth."

The present study looks at some of the literature on Tibetan history that has been produced in English by Tibetan and Chinese authors, focusing particularly on the mentalities that provide the context of their work. My goal is to reconstruct the thinking within which either the Tibetan or Chinese position appears obvious and inescapable to those who accept it as true. I have chosen texts that are representative of the positions of these two communities and have emphasized the aspects of Tibetan history that are the main sources of contestation. No effort has been made to provide a comprehensive overview of Tibetan history. There are a number of such works available, although most reflect a bias in favor of one side or the other. Certain episodes and periods of Tibetan history are emphasized by Tibetan and Chinese writers, who often attribute to them a significance out of all proportion to their actual impact at the time they occurred, and I have followed their lead by surveying opinions and interpretations of these episodes that either reflect the dominant discourses of the respective communities or are examples of interesting attempts to explain the psychological motivations of historical personages.

As readers will see, the respective narratives tend to be highly consistent, and so there is no need to survey every writer from the two groups on every point; rather, I have decided to choose descriptions that crystallize an aspect of the discourse and the shared imaginings of Tibetan or Chinese authors. Some of these, as we will see, are absurd; others are highly implausible; some are humorous in an unintended way; and both narratives are fraught by internal contradictions and inconsistencies. But they are also deeply believed by people of the communities that produced them, and even the most ridiculous notions are often reflected in works by contemporary Western academics who study Tibet, most of whom evince a bias in favor of one side or the other.

In trying to reconstruct the mentalities of the two communities and highlight their shared assumptions and imaginings, I have also incorporated images from Chinese and Tibetan exile popular culture. These demonstrate the diffusion of "truths" about Tibetan history within the two communities and highlight how the process of acculturation incorporates preconceived conclusions about Tibetan history and the people of the region. These are presented to their respective communities as accurate portrayals of individuals with clear motivations and no significant ambiguities and who have well-defined goals. They are often concordant with how events are presented in traditional Tibetan or Chinese histories, both of which reflect the vastly different cultural myths of the societies that produced them. Chinese sources begin with the notion that China, the "Middle Kingdom" (Zhongguo), is at the center of the world and is the only civilized society, with a mandate to rule over all other countries. Tibetan records composed after the importation of Buddhism are thoroughly infused with Buddhist imagery and presuppositions, and the underlying plot relates to the diffusion and glorification of religion. Chinese and Tibetan authors who use them as source material are inevitably influenced by these notions, which are also reinforced by their cultures and educational systems.

Sorting through this material has proven to be extraordinarily difficult because of the biases in traditional histories, the conflicting claims in modern accounts, and the fact that both sides are guilty of fabrication, distortion, and even invention of historical events that never happened. My hope is that this study will help to clarify the issues and arguments for people who are confused by the competing rhetoric and incompatible claims of Chinese and Tibetans regarding Tibetan history. I have generally focused on the words they use and report what they actually say without attempting to judge their veracity. In each section I have indicated the areas of general agreement—which are often substantial—and then outline how these are overlaid with interpretation. In cases of clear fabrication or outright absurdity, I have interjected a critique, but in general have tried simply to present the discourse they use and allow readers to draw their own conclusions. Moreover, while I have my own biases and presuppositions, I have tried to present the two positions in a balanced way and to let the authors speak in their own words. There is, of course, no way to fully divorce one's own attitudes from such an emotionally charged topic, and readers will probably discern mine as they read, but I hope they will also come to better understand the issues involved in debates about Tibetan history, why apparently arcane vestiges of the past are so important to Tibetans and Chinese, and how they form part of their respective nationalist narratives.

Because of the complexity of the material and the radically polarized paradigms encoded in it, during research on this project I have sought guidance and information from experts in various areas. I wish to particularly thank Chris Berry, who provided me with copies of Chinese-produced films about Tibet and shared his considerable expertise on Chinese minority cinema, and David Templeman, who read over the first draft and provided numerous insightful and helpful comments. I am also grateful to Yan-yan Wang for her translations of the dialogue in Chinese-language films and to Geoff Childs, who provided thoughtful feedback during the early phase of the research and shared his impressive knowledge of Tibetan demography. Chris Forth and Virginia Hooker read early versions of this study and helped shape the methodological aspects of the final presentation. I also wish to thank the Australian Research Council and the American Philosophical Society for providing funding for fieldwork that contributed to the final product and the Faculty of Asian Studies of Australian National University, which gave me sabbatical leave and research funding for the final phase of my work. As noted above, I have been fortunate in gaining access to exceptional informants within the Tibetan exile community, and I greatly appreciate the efforts of Samdhong Rinpoche and Geshe Ngawang Samten in facilitating my research at the Central Institute of Higher Tibetan Studies in Sarnath, India. I am also grateful to H.H. the Dalai Lama for fitting me into his busy schedule for informal talks, most recently in Canberra, Australia, when he participated in a panel discussion in the "Mind and Science" symposium held at Australian National University in May 2002. Finally, I wish to thank my wife, Cindy, for her help and support, as well as her patience as I tried to interest her in the arcana of Tibetan history during the course of my research.

Contents

History as Propaganda

I

Old Tibet

A Clash of Myths

The history which bears and determines us has the form of a war
rather than that of a language: relations of power, not relations of
meaning. History has no "meaning."
—Michel Foucault, *The Foucault Reader*, p. 56

Truths and Facts

The adage that history is written by the victors may once have been
true. In the past, when a conquering force either eradicated its enemies or so completely subjugated them that they were no longer
able to tell their stories to the outside world, effective control over
the production of historical narratives was generally held by governments that had the power to determine what version of history
would be widely circulated and that controlled the means by which
this information might be disseminated. But in modern times, one
of the hallmarks of conflicts between competing groups is an ideological battle over the production of historical "truth" that often continues long after military subjugation has been finalized. Some of
these battles are being waged between recently decolonized states
and their former colonial overlords; in other cases, colonial domination is a current phenomenon. But while the colonial power may
possess the military power to conquer and rule a colony, modern
technology, including the advent of affordable desktop publishing

and the Internet, allows a people that has lost the war militarily to continue the ideological struggle through the production and reproduction of its version of events.

This book examines one such conflict, which is currently being waged between members of the Tibetan exile community and the government of the People's Republic of China (PRC). This conflict is being fought on a number of ideological fronts, only a few of which are considered here. A central issue concerns questions relating to Tibetan history, and both sides clearly believe that this is integral to their respective claims of legitimate ownership of the Tibetan plateau.[1] Briefly, the Tibetan version of Tibetan history is one in which Tibet, prior to the Chinese takeover in the 1950s, is presented as an independent and closed society based on Buddhist principles and ruled by Buddhist monks. The people were both happy and devout, their consciousness was completely derived from indigenous myths and symbols, and Tibet was utterly different from China. According to the Chinese version, China is a multiethnic society in which the Han make up over 93 percent of the population, but fifty-six minorities are also an integral part of the "motherland," coexisting peacefully since time immemorial. Beginning in the seventh century, Tibet came into China's cultural orbit, and since the establishment of formal Chinese sovereignty in the thirteenth century, Tibet has continually been under the direct rule of the Chinese central government.

Each side views its version of Tibetan history as an essential part of its national identity. Tibetan histories generally construct a narrative in which China played at most a peripheral role until the mid-twentieth century, while Chinese sources paint a picture of Tibet in which the region was completely under the administrative and political control of various Chinese central governments from at least the thirteenth century and in which Tibetan culture is largely derived from China.

There is a growing corpus of works in Western languages that explore this contested history, and debates about Tibet tend to be highly emotionally charged. Many Western writers on Tibet—including academics, who commonly claim to adhere to "the facts" in making their assessments—are no less passionate than Tibetan and Chinese writers trying to persuade readers to their respective points of view. A number of Western academics who write about Tibet advocate for either the Chinese or the Tibetan position, and they often present the issues in absolute terms, as conflicts between truth and falsehood, good and evil, oppression and freedom (this is particularly true of pro-Tibet authors).

The main sources I have examined in this book are written in English by Tibetan and Chinese writers who base their presentations either on Tibetan or

Chinese records. All the Tibetan writers use only Tibetan or English sources, and all of the Chinese writers use only Chinese or English sources. None indicates that he or she reads the other's language.

Surprisingly, no study I have seen to date compares the works of these contemporary Tibetan and Chinese authors. This may be because the obviously polemical tone and often hyperbolic rhetoric used in most English works on Tibet by Tibetans or Chinese cause many readers to dismiss as propaganda those with which they do not agree. Yet, if read carefully, they are rich sources for understanding Tibetan and Chinese notions of identity and alterity. Although they leave much to be desired as historiography, they reveal a great deal about how Tibetans and Chinese view themselves and their countries, and how their divergent versions of history help to form their respective national narratives.

The main sources for this essay are thirteen works by contemporary Chinese authors, thirteen works by contemporary Tibetan authors, two Chinese government Web sites devoted to Tibet, and the Tibetan government-in-exile's official Web site. The printed works can be further subdivided according to whether they were published in a mainstream Western press or by either a Chinese government body or a Tibetan exile body. Three of the Chinese sources were published by mainstream Western presses (C4, C5, and C9),[2] whereas most of the rest were published by the Foreign Languages Press in Beijing or other Chinese government-sponsored presses. On the Tibetan side, most were published by mainstream Western presses, although three (T2, T3, and T9) were published by the Tibetan government-in-exile or by Tibetan exile organizations.

This division is significant, because the language used in books published by mainstream Western presses is generally more circumspect and restrained than what one reads in works published by Tibetan exile presses or Chinese government bodies.[3] The latter all contain highly emotive language and stake out extreme and uncompromising positions. In these sources, there is no ambiguity, and issues are presented in black-and-white terms. Despite the differences in language and style of presentation, however, the positions of Chinese and Tibetan writers respectively tend to be highly uniform, and there are few substantive differences within either group regarding their respective core historical narratives. For this reason, I believe that it is legitimate to consider each faction's texts as a whole for the purpose of this study, because the shared historical narratives of each group are multifaceted, and each source contributes to understanding the shared assumptions and worldviews of the two communities to which the authors belong, as well as the range of discursive strategies that are employed in presenting their cases.

In analyzing these sources, I use a modified version of the model developed by M. A. K. Halliday, which examines texts in terms of three topics, which he calls "field of discourse," "tenor of discourse," and "mode of discourse."[4] Halliday's model looks at texts in terms of their social contexts, focusing on the interaction between texts and social situations. The field of discourse is the nature of the social action that is occurring; it describes the activity in which the participants are engaged. The tenor of discourse identifies the participants and their status and relationships. The mode refers to the language used and what the participants expect the language to do for them (whether it is expository, didactic, persuasive, etc.). Halliday's approach focuses on key words, that is, words that are repeated or that crystallize an aspect of the discourse.

Tenor of Discourse

I have decided to alter Halliday's order and begin with the second heading, because identifying the participants is crucial to understanding the discourse of these two groups of texts. The first striking feature of all of them is that they were written in English by non-English-speakers. Thus, they are not intended (or at least not primarily) for indigenous consumption. Indeed, if one compares them to contemporary Chinese- or Tibetan-language materials on Tibetan history, there are striking differences in tone and content. Contemporary Chinese and Tibetan sources generally assume that their readers accept a particular conclusion (for instance, either that Tibet was an independent country prior to the Chinese military incursion of 1950 or that it was not), and they often use a sort of shorthand to describe events that are well known to Tibetan or Chinese readers. Similarly, they tend to omit events that could potentially undermine the integrity of their respective historical narratives, presumably because both writers and readers are primarily concerned with reaching a particular conclusion rather than engaging in a detailed examination of historical records and events.

A second notable feature is that most of these sources (as well as others that I have examined but that are not included among the texts cited in this study) are written in American English and use American spellings. Thus, they are apparently primarily directed at an American audience, and several sources indicate why this is so: in the Chinese texts, the United States is seen as the dominant power in the world today and as the main source of misguided denunciations of Chinese policies in Tibet, and it is hoped that Americans who read these works will be persuaded that China has a "historical right" to Tibet and that its rule has been benevolent. On the Tibetan side, the hope is that

American readers (and other foreigners) will become advocates of the Tibetan cause.[5] Many Tibetans continue to hope that the United States will deliver them from Chinese rule, despite the fact that successive U.S. governments have consistently upheld Chinese claims of sovereignty over Tibet and have never seriously questioned them. The tone of many Tibetan works indicates that the authors apparently believe that the historical analysis is so persuasive that if only U.S. policymakers were to read and comprehend it they would reverse their position and support Tibetan independence. Thus, these texts are not merely academic exercises (although several Tibetan writers indicate that they engaged in research and writing only out of curiosity): they are clearly intended to be persuasive, and it is hoped (and often assumed) by the authors that if the intended audience reads and considers the historical analysis it will certainly conclude that Tibet was an independent country prior to 1950 and that China's rule is illegitimate.

The stakes are equally high for the Chinese writers. As with the Tibetan sources, the Chinese works are mostly written in American English (although most published in China are replete with odd sentence constructions and grammatical errors), and they generally state their aim in writing in the introduction. Most indicate that they believe that there is much "misconception" regarding Tibet and that this has been created by the Tibetan exile government (and the Dalai Lama in particular). Moreover, the process of misinformation has been aided and abetted by Western "reactionaries" and "imperialists."[6] The main opponents of the Chinese writers are commonly referred to as "the Dalai clique," "splittists," or "reactionaries."[7] The Chinese sources fall into two main groups: those published by mainstream Western presses and those published by Chinese government bodies. As with the Tibetan works, the former tend to be more restrained in language, whereas the latter use emotionally charged rhetoric. This group can be further subdivided into two sections: those that were written during the Cultural Revolution (1966–1976) and those written either before or after it. The former are characterized by extensive use of often incomprehensible Marxist terminology and a highly aggressive and anti-Western tone; the latter use far fewer Marxist buzzwords and are more restrained in their rhetoric. Despite these differences in language, the historical narratives in all these works are highly consistent, and there are few significant differences.

In addition to presenting their respective histories, each group attacks the other, and certain writers are singled out for either praise or censure. Several Chinese sources specifically attack Tsepon Shakabpa's *Tibet: A Political History*,[8] an extended historical analysis that claims to demonstrate that Tibet was independent prior to the Chinese takeover. Others attack Western academics whose conclusions are concordant with Shakabpa's. Tibetan sources criticize particular aspects of the Chinese historical narrative, and several take issue with A. Tom Grunfeld's *The Making of Modern Tibet*.[9] These attacks reject many of Grunfeld's conclusions, commonly impugn his integrity, and also deny his authority to write about Tibet by labeling him a "sinologist" who does not read Tibetan and so has no standing to write about Tibetan history. Several of the Chinese works, by contrast, shower praise on both Grunfeld and his work.

This sort of reflexivity is one of the striking features of contemporary literature about Tibet. Most of the Chinese and Tibetan authors considered in this study indicate that they are aware of both the other side's positions and works by Western authors, and often directly reply to them. Western authors who write about Tibet are also generally aware of the emotionally and politically charged nature of the field and often attempt to distance themselves from the often vitriolic polemics of Tibetan studies by claiming that their analyses are based on authoritative historical records and that their conclusions are determined by the facts presented in them. Despite these claims, as we will see, the results of their narratives are often as polarized as those of the Chinese and Tibetan writers, and many employ the same rhetorical strategies and language.

Field of Discourse

The general parameters of the field of discourse have already been indicated. These are mostly persuasive works, and some are probably more accurately characterized as propaganda. Their Chinese and Tibetan authors obviously intend to convince their English-speaking (or at least English-reading) audience of the correctness of their respective versions of history and the conclusions they draw from them. Chinese authors indicate that their goal is to make their readers understand that Tibet is an integral part of China and that therefore any criticism of China's actions in Tibet is illegitimate because these are "internal affairs." Tibetan writers want to internationalize the issue of Tibet's historical status and indicate that they hope their works will convince readers that Tibet was an independent nation that was brutally and illegally invaded by its imperialist neighbor and that this will spur readers to join the Tibetan cause and agitate for their country's independence.

On the Chinese side, the editors of *Tibet: Myth vs. Reality* state that they hope to "counter false charges against China concerning Tibet and explain the real situation in the region," which will "help bring about a better understanding of the Tibetan people—their history, their relations with other people in China—and the major events and changes that have taken place on the 'roof of the world.' "[10] The editors of *Tibetans on Tibet* inform readers that there is currently a great deal of interest in Tibet worldwide, but most foreigners have misguided notions about the region. They indicate that their work will correctly inform readers about "the attitudes of the Tibetan people."[11] This will be accomplished by presenting unsolicited, uncoerced statements of Tibetans from all walks of life ("the Tibetan people themselves").[12] In *The Historical Status of China's Tibet*, Wang Jiawei and Nyima Gyaincain assert:

> The historical status of China's Tibet is clear as clean water and the blue sky—a fact known to the world. In the last few decades, however, certain forces in Europe and the United States have supported a small number of people led by the 14th Dalai Lama to concoct a theory of "Tibetan independence," blurring the vision of many people who are not clear about the facts. . . . One loves clean water and a clear, blue sky. This book has been compiled to allow readers to clearly witness the historical status of China's sovereignty over Tibet through settling the muddied waters and sweeping the mist from the sky.[13]

These statements indicate the sort of actions in which Chinese authors believe themselves to be engaged. Their writings are intended to persuade a Western audience that claims of Tibetan independence are false and that an unbiased examination of "historical facts" will reveal that Tibet has been an integral part of China since time immemorial. Further, current misconceptions are the result of the sinister machinations of disaffected elements among the Tibetan exile community (generally referred to as "Tibetans in self-exile") and Western "imperialists" who have spread misinformation to undermine China's national unity and weaken it politically.

The Tibetan works also indicate that their presentations are intended to combat misinformation and reveal the "truth." The Tibetan government-in-exile's Web site contains its official "White Paper," entitled "Tibet: Proving Truth from Facts," which states that it "is intended to respond to the new demand for concise information on key points of the Tibetan question, and at the same time, to serve as a response to the Chinese propaganda. . . .Truth being on the side of the Tibetan people, we feel the need from time to time to restate the facts plainly, as they really are, and trust that this will serve the cause of truth and justice."[14]

Several Tibetan sources propose to get to the truth of the Tibet question by examining the lives of Tibetans who are portrayed as representatives of a particular type (most often, peasants and workers) or as emblematic of the Tibetan people as a whole. In the introduction to *Tibet*, Colin Turnbull asserts

that the book provides "an account that represents . . . Tibet as seen by a Tibetan."[15] It contains the reminiscences of the Dalai Lama's brother, Thubten
Jigme Norbu, on the Tibet of his youth and early adulthood, and is notable for
the fact that China is virtually absent from his recollections. The myths he
recounts, the symbols he employs, and the historical narrative he paints are
mostly of indigenous origin, although he also stresses the influence of India
on the formation of Tibetan religion and culture. China, of course, lurks in the
background of his narrative, but he avoids mentioning it wherever possible,
thus underlining his vision of Tibet as utterly separate from China.

Dawa Norbu, author of several works on Tibetan history, dedicates his *Red
Star over Tibet* "to my family and the Tibetans in and outside Tibet, who have
been patiently waiting for their 'rightful rangtsen' [independence]." In the preface to the first edition, he asserts that he wanted to produce a work that accurately details Tibetan history and civilization because "Tibetan explanations
are quite inadequate, and the Chinese views too one-sided." In the preface to
the second edition, he states, "My only hope is that I have managed to tran-
scend polemical and didactic inclinations." Norbu is frequently critical of certain aspects of the common Tibetan exile historical narrative, but his book still
follows its main outlines. He paints a picture of Tibet in which the Chinese
were not a part of Tibetan consciousness prior to the entry of People's Liberation Army (PLA) troops into the region in the 1950s, and in which they are
portrayed as utterly alien and even incomprehensible. He stresses the animosity and alienation felt by ordinary Tibetans toward their self-proclaimed
"liberators," and uses anecdotes to demonstrate the vast cultural gap between
Tibetans and Chinese. In one story, he tells of how some Tibetans clapped
their hands and cursed in an attempt to drive away a group of Chinese soldiers,
but the Chinese believed that the Tibetans were welcoming them:

> Some labourers carrying manure met the Chinese near the Dolma
> Palace. The most effective ritual that the Tibetans could perform
> against the enemies of religion was *dogpa*, which consisted of clap-
> ping the hands and cursing simultaneously. So the labourers
> clapped their hands. The Chinese were plainly pleased. Parting their
> chapped lips, they smiled and joined in, clapping vigorously. We
> thought they were being craftily deceitful, but later we learnt that
> clapping was a way of welcoming and congratulating comrades.[16]

In the preface to *Tibet: The Road Ahead*, Dawa Norbu indicates that part
of his claim to greater objectivity than other Tibetan writers is the fact that his
family was poor, and so his views are not colored by the biases of the monastic
or aristocratic elites: "I felt that I should try to write a book that simply unfolded

what really went on in Tibet. The fact that I was neither a lama nor an aristocrat helped such an attempt."[17] Similarly, in *Red Star over Tibet* he emphasizes that his account is based entirely on the recollections of "ordinary Tibetans" and that no lamas or aristocrats were consulted. These statements are apparently intended to counter the common Chinese assertion that "the broad masses of the Tibetan people" supported their claim to sovereignty over Tibet and eagerly welcomed the troops of the PLA. At several points in both books Norbu distances himself from Tibetan elites and claims that his sources speak for the masses. Like most of the other writers considered in this study, both Chinese and Tibetan, he declares that *Tibet: The Road Ahead* is the result of a quest to locate and accurately present the "truth," and he states that "if it promotes a better understanding of the Tibetan Question or serves the bipartisan cause of the Tibetan people, then my labour would not have been in vain."[18]

Tsepon Shakabpa (an official in the Tibetan government that was overthrown by China in the 1950s) declares that he wrote his book because "I realized that the world stood in need of information on Tibet's historical and political status."[19] The tone of the work indicates that he is confident that the truth of Tibetan independence will be made clear to his readers and that they will thus be able to see through the distortions created by the Chinese government and its supporters. A similar sentiment, though written in highly emotive language, is found in the publisher's note to *Tibet: The Facts*, which was compiled by the Scientific Buddhist Association. It asserts that the book is

> a challenge to the lies churned out by Beijing's propaganda machinery and a reminder to the silent world that all is not well on the Roof of the World and that what happened in Tiananmen Square had been happening in Tibet all along. If nothing else, *Tibet: The Facts* will serve as a record of China's crime of GENOCIDE in Tibet. It will also serve as a tribute to the courageous Tibetans who struggled against all odds and sacrificed their lives in the struggle for freedom and in defence of their country, their faith and their homes. But more urgently, it is hoped that *Tibet: The Facts* will help to stir the conscience of the free world and to arouse international indignation against China's imperialist policies and her brute suppression of . . . the Tibetan people . . . who, among others, are struggling for freedom from Chinese colonial rule.[20]

This book contains the most emotionally charged rhetoric of all the Tibetan sources examined in this essay (although its language is still quite tame in comparison with many works written in Tibetan for indigenous consumption). It is a vitriolic indictment of Chinese policies in Tibet and an attempt to deny any shred of validity to China's historical narrative. The authors frequently use italics and capital letters to highlight particularly strong words and assertions, and the Chinese takeover of Tibet is equated with a number of atrocities, the main ones being the Nazi invasion of Poland and the Holocaust. As the above passage indicates, they hope that their account of "the facts" will spur the world to action on Tibet's behalf and that direct pressure will be put on China to release its hold on the country.

Most of the Chinese and Tibetan sources considered in this study clearly indicate that they are attempting to overcome misinformation regarding Tibet and to present a factual account of its history. Several also assert that it is hoped that readers will react in certain ways: the Tibetan sources expect to sway world opinion in favor of the Tibetan cause, and the Chinese sources believe that their accounts will convince readers that Tibet has always been an integral part of China and that its culture is part of the vast mosaic of the motherland. In addition, they indicate that their "accurate" account will counter criticisms of Chinese rule in Tibet and cause readers to realize that since the 1950s Tibet has "made rapid progress," resulting in unbounded joy and gratitude on the part of Tibetans. The words they choose are intended to spark positive associations for a Western audience. Tibet today is described variously as "prosperous," "free," and "happy." All of the Chinese government-produced sources refer to the changes that China has made in Tibet as "democratic reforms," a term that has positive associations for people who live in democratic societies and who are raised to believe that democracy is the best of all possible social systems, but it is odd in this context because at minimum, democracy requires that free and open elections be held from time to time, and no such event has ever occurred in Tibet.

Several of the Chinese works indicate that they were originally written in Chinese and later translated into English. The translators are not mentioned, but the censors who cleared the language and content are. Given the preponderance of awkward phrasings and grammatical errors, it is clear that ideology was considered more important than readability. Due to the extreme sensitivity of the Tibet issue, there is little if any room for deviation or individual interpretation. In contemporary China, the Communist Party strictly controls the presentation of history, and several formal "Resolutions" have been issued by the Central Committee, which are intended to guide historians in the "correct" interpretation of historical events and actors.

The overarching ideology of Marxist-Leninist conceptions of history pervades the works of contemporary Chinese historians. According to the standard periodization, societies progress from a state of primitive communism to a slave society, which is oppressive and thus foments peasant rebellions. These result in its overthrow and lead to the formation of a feudal system. Feudalism in turn contains inherent contradictions that foster conflicts between classes, a situation that results in further rebellions and the establishment of a capitalist system, in which the means of production are controlled by an elite, who exploit the workers and profit from their labor. Their alienation from the products of their work leads to another round of rebellions, the outcome of which is the founding of a socialist state, in which the means of production are owned by all and which will in time progress toward communism. One core element of all presocialist states is the use of religion by the ruling elite to keep the masses in line. Religion was denounced by Karl Marx as "the opiate of the masses," a theme that was echoed by Mao Zedong. This doctrine is found in a number of Chinese works on Tibet, which portray religion as a tool of control cynically deployed by the ruling class of lamas and aristocrats in order to routinize their control over the peasantry and suppress potential rebellion. According to Huang Hongzhao, who teaches in the History Department of Nanjing University, "Many regulations, taboos, and commandments were prescribed to inhibit the followers' mind, such as giving alms, forbearance, prudence and deep in prayer [sic]. All this was intended to deceive and benumb the people, so that they would be meek and obedient under the rule of the religious authority of serfdom."[21]

The focus of most contemporary Chinese historiography is class struggle and peasant rebellions. Guided by Mao's version of Marxism, Chinese historians often ignore dynastic struggles and instead focus on how peasant revolts weakened regimes and forced their successors to make "concessions." They also detail how "feudal contradictions" remained unresolved, sparking further revolts and concessions.[22] They chart China's progress along standard (and often highly contrived) Marxist-Leninist lines, and several of the writers we are considering insert peasant rebellions into Tibetan history to construct a narrative that conforms to the standard periodization of Chinese Marxist historiography.

An integral aspect of the Chinese version of history is that the inevitable progression of Chinese society from a slave society to feudalism and then to capitalism was derailed by imperialism, which is blamed for all of China's woes. According to Albert Feuerwerker, "The study and writing of modern Chinese history . . . is primarily an ideological exercise and emotional release, repeated over and over again, the function of which is to harness and channel the real political and economic frustration encountered in China's nineteenth- and twentieth-century experience in the interests of a new historical integration under the auspices of the Chinese Communist Party."[23]

As a number of scholars have noted, there is a pronounced "monotony" in these works, which present a highly uniform version of events with little individual creativity or analysis.[24] History is written to serve current propaganda purposes, and major policy shifts are often accompanied by adjustments in how historical figures are evaluated. China's peasants are uniformly presented as hardworking, brave, and patriotic, their exploitive masters as venal and brutal, and the imperialists as devious and despicable. Readers are expected to understand that China has always been great and strong and that whatever problems it currently faces are the results of the machinations of foreigners and not of errors by its present leaders.

This approach reflects Mao Zedong's dictum "Make the past serve the present" (*gu wei jin yong*), according to which the purpose of historical writing should be to serve the Party's current political goals. "History for history's sake" is virtually unknown in China, and historians are prevented from engaging in research that might call the orthodox viewpoint into question. Most academic historians work in departments of Marxism-Leninism and were trained in Party history and appointed on the basis of their loyalty to the Party. Only the most senior historians, people with a long record of service to the Party, are allowed access to traditional historical sources. The rest rely on their researches and on the Party's official Resolutions. All Chinese historians are expected to produce works that serve the Party's current aims and that exactly mirror the official version of events.

One of the central debates in the field is the relation between theory and facts. Since the Cultural Revolution of the 1960s and 1970s, the official policy has been that "theory must take the lead over facts" (*yi lun dai shi*), which means that being ideologically correct is far more important than critically examining the past. Contemporary Chinese historians are mainly concerned with the "contributions and mistakes" (*gong guo*) of historical figures, that is, how they contributed to Chinese civilization and the furthering of the historical process as conceived by Marxist ideology, and what their class identity was. Because of this orientation, historical circumstances are generally not discussed in detail, because what is important is the Marxist moral of the story. As Suzanne Weigelin-Schwiedrzik puts it, "Learning about Party history meant learning to write in the way that the Party wanted future members of the bureaucracy to publicly think."[25]

History and Truth

Both the Chinese and the Tibetan authors we are considering make similar claims regarding history. In many of these works, history is conceived as an independent voice of truth, and the authors frequently make reference to "historical facts" and answer rhetorical questions by indicating what they consider "history's verdict" to be. For example, 100 Questions about Tibet asks, "Q: An American newspaper said that Tibet did not become part of China until 1950, and only in the late 1970s did the Carter administration officially recognize China's sovereignty over Tibet. Does this accord with history? A: History says No."[26] Similar language—and similar appeals to the final authority of "history"—are found in both groups of texts, but are particularly prevalent and strident in the Chinese sources.

To illustrate their claims, all of the Chinese works published in China accompany their assertions about the nature of old Tibet and the improvements subsequent to the Chinese takeover with pictures that either claim to represent the brutal system of old Tibet or the current happiness of its people. The covers of Great Changes in Tibet and Tibet: No Longer Mediaeval, for example, juxtapose these cheery titles with photographs of smiling Tibetan women; the implication appears to be that they are smiling because Tibet has leaped forward and because they are no longer medieval.[27] Other images include an elderly Tibetan woman fervently praying near the Jokhang, one of the holiest pilgrimage sites of Tibet, "on the 20th anniversary of the Tibet Autonomous Region." The authors imply that her prayers are not motivated by religious fervor, but rather by her joy at the transformations brought about by Chinese rule. Similarly, Tibet: The Facts contains a number of pictures that depict the brutality of Chinese rule and support Tibetan claims to independence, and on the inside of the cover of Tibet: A Political History there is a copy of an official Tibetan government seal that was affixed to documents. All the writing is in Tibetan scripts, and the inscription indicates the indigenous sources of Tibetan government authority. China is never mentioned, nor is the authority of the emperor invoked or even tacitly acknowledged, which implicitly indicates that it was irrelevant to the exercise of power in Tibet.

Western studies of Tibet, particularly those written by academics, are generally more restrained in their language than are those of Chinese or Tibetan authors, but here, too, one finds emotionally charged rhetoric and often passionate advocacy for one side or the other. This is particularly true of pro-Tibet works, whose authors are often trying to persuade their target audience of the illegitimacy and barbarity of China's occupation of Tibet. Many of them indicate that they have personal connections with Tibetan refugees and are deeply concerned about their plight, but they also state that their analyses are balanced and authoritative and that their conclusions are derived entirely from the facts of Tibetan history and not from bias or personal feelings. Some claim to possess authority to tell the truth of the situation because of direct contact with

Tibet and their own eyewitness experiences; others have not visited Tibet or Tibetan refugee settlements, but assert authority on the basis of extensive study of available written sources on Tibetan history. An example of the first group is Hugh Richardson, who headed the British Mission in Lhasa during the 1930s and 1940s. He states in *Tibet and Its History* that he decided to write an introduction to Tibetan history after listening to debate regarding Tibet's status during the fourteenth session of the General Assembly of the United Nations in 1959: "I was struck by the need for a guide to Tibetan history which had regard not only to its continuous development over thirteen centuries but also to the Tibetan background and character and to the Tibetan point of view. That is what I try to offer in this book."[28]

Richardson indicates that he is uniquely qualified to report on what really happened in Tibet because he lived there for a number of years prior to the Chinese takeover and had extensive contacts with Tibetans from all walks of life, from the most senior government officials to peasants. It is also clear that he believes that he is telling a story that Tibetans themselves are unable to tell and that he perceives himself to be advocating on their behalf. He adopts an academic tone in most of the book, straightforwardly reporting the main events of Tibetan history, but in a number of places he heaps contempt on what he characterizes as Chinese fabrications and distortions, and when he describes the Chinese takeover and its aftermath he employs highly emotional language that is apparently intended to convince his readers of the utter illegality of Chinese rule in Tibet and its brutality.

Western authors who mainly support the Chinese view of events, such as Grunfeld, are no less certain that their accounts are written to dispel misconceptions and reveal the truth of Tibetan history and the real nature of the Chinese takeover. In his introduction to *The Making of Modern Tibet*, Grunfeld indicates that he is aware of potential criticisms of his book, but he rejects them, stating that his analysis is balanced and authoritative, a "search for a middle ground. . . . I have made every effort to use materials from most, if not all, contending points of view. I therefore choose to call this book 'disinterested and dispassionate history,' and I present it as an attempt at historical interpretation without political, religious, economic, or emotional commitments to either side, but rather with a commitment to furthering historical understanding and even 'truth.' "[29]

Despite these claims, as we will see, Grunfeld's book evidences a clear pro-Chinese bias, and it contains a number of historical inaccuracies and distortions.[30] The same is true of other Western sources on Tibet, a number of which are also examined in this study. I have chosen a few works that are representative of particular genres and points of view; these are juxtaposed with the Chinese and Tibetan sources to highlight how the biases of the pro-China and pro-Tibet factions are reflected in the works of Western authors, all of whom indicate that they are concerned with presenting "truth" and "facts" in an unbiased and objective manner. In addition to Grunfeld's book, I consider Melvyn Goldstein's monumental study *A History of Modern Tibet*, a massive work that in my opinion is the most balanced treatment of modern Tibetan history, a richly documented study that in its author's words attempts to be "neither pro-Chinese nor pro-Tibetan in the current senses of the terms. It does not set out to support the Dalai Lama's government-in-exile or to support the People's Republic of China. Rather, it attempts to explicate a dramatic historical event: the demise, in 1951, of the de facto independent Lamaist State. It examines what happened and why, and it balances the traditional focus on international relations with an emphasis on the intricate web of internal affairs and events."[31]

Goldstein succeeds in his purpose to a large degree, but in both this work and his subsequent study, *The Snow Lion and the Dragon*, he betrays a bias in favor of the Chinese position in a number of places. For example, he portrays the fourteenth Dalai Lama as a devious but inept politician who continually exasperates China's leaders with his duplicity, intransigence, and bungling.[32] The Chinese, by contrast, are portrayed as being exceedingly patient and as forgiving the recalcitrant and foolish Tibetans time and time again before finally reaching the end of their forbearance and initiating military action.

The most vehemently pro-China text considered in this study by a Western author is *Tibet Transformed* by Israel Epstein (a naturalized Chinese citizen of Polish descent), a lengthy book published by the New World Press in Beijing that uses the sort of rhetoric found in works by Chinese authors on Tibet and reflects the Chinese government's party line. On the pro-Tibet side, I examine Richardson's *Tibet and Its History* and Warren Smith's *Tibetan Nation*,[33] both of which are academic works published by Western presses. Grunfeld, Epstein, Richardson, and Smith all present highly polarized versions of Tibetan history, despite their claims to objectivity and concern with truth. Epstein asserts that his book is based on his own observations during three visits to Tibet and that it reports the truth of what he saw and was told by ordinary Tibetans, "given largely in the words of hundreds of people who were there all along—mainly Tibetans, within a frame of historical background from many sources, and of comment. . . . I believe that the reader will find this account a true reflection of the essential nature and historically-determined direction of the great and basic process of change that has occurred, and is continuing, in Tibet."[34] Whereas Richardson's claim to authority is based on his personal contact with

Tibet prior to the Chinese takeover, Epstein asserts that he is uniquely qualified to report what really happened in Tibet because of his extensive travels there in the immediate aftermath.

Mode of Discourse: The Use of Language

As indicated above, most of the works used in this study are intended to be persuasive, and the language they use is clearly chosen to convince readers of the correctness of their authors' respective historical narratives and the conclusions they draw from them regarding Chinese rule in Tibet. Some of them could also be considered propaganda, though the line between persuasion and propaganda is often drawn on the basis of whether a particular person agrees with the conclusion or not. In both groups, the language is highly specific and distinctive. Certain words come up time and again in each group of texts, both in those published by academic presses and by those published by the Tibetan exile government or PRC bodies. In addition, when one side refers to key words used by the other, they are generally dismissed with the term "so-called" and framed in scare quotes (for example, Chinese sources frequently refer to "so-called 'independence' " and Tibetan sources to "so-called 'peaceful liberation' ").

In Chinese sources, the words "motherland," "unity," "prosperity," and "happy" occur over and over again, while in Tibetan sources such terms as "alien," "invasion," and "brutal" predominate. The most contentious focus of this war of words is the nature of pre-1950s Tibet. Chinese sources uniformly describe it using the terms "feudal," "serfdom," "backward," "cruel," "brutal," and others. Tibetan sources refer to it as "peaceful," "happy," "religious," "deeply Buddhist," and so on. Table 1 contains some of the terms used in the works considered in this study. Those that are distinctive phrasings of a particular text are cited according to source and page number; words that are used by all or most of the works in one of the two groups are not cited.

As Table 1 indicates, the contrast between the two groups could hardly be more pronounced. There is no common ground for their respective visions of Tibet. What the Chinese sources portray as a dark, brutal feudal serfdom governed by despotic lamas and aristocrats who casually tortured the miserable serfs for their enjoyment and profit, Tibetan sources describe as a poor but idyllic land isolated from the outside world in which the people were united in their common devotion to Buddhism and their respect for their lamas, and in which most were basically happy and content. It was a land all admit had "some problems," but they agree that there was no significant gap between

TABLE I. Keywords: Tibet Prior to the Chinese Takeover

Chinese Sources	Tibetan Sources
torture (C1, 40)	content (T6, 144)
persecuted (C1, 41)	happy (T11, 302)
bitter life (C2, 16)	poor (T8, 52)
miserable lot (C2, 16)	peace (T8, 345)
incredibly barbaric (C2, 16)	pleasant (T8, 347)
cruel (C3, 26)	good (T8, 347)
savage (C3, 26)	warmth (T8, 345)
nightmare (C2, 16)	satisfied (T11, 13)
hell on earth (C7, i)	beautiful country (T8, 345)
enslavement (C3, i)	free (T8, 345)
darkest, most reactionary (C7, i)	enlightened (T6, 192)
dark, cruel, and barbarous (C3, i)	immutable tranquility (T1, 10)
inhuman political oppression (C1, 42)	benevolent (T6, 192)
lived worse than animals (C3, i)	lived without haste (T8, 345)
worked like beasts (C13, 51)	worked leisurely (T6, 252)
feudal serfdom (C3, i)	no class system (T8, 324)
theocracy (C2, 15)	deeply religious
dictatorship (C3, 26)	Dalai Lama's government
serf owners (C1, 42)	no superiority or inferiority complex (T6, 174)
blood-sucking exploitation (C3, 21)	left us alone (T6, 182)
rampant disease, premature death (C1, 42)	starvation was nonexistent (T11, 9)
backward economically (C13, 7)	poor
Chinese overlordship (C5, 89)	independent
Tibetan local government	central government
central government	Chinese government

rich and poor and that the government mostly left the populace alone to their simple religious lives. According to Tibetan works, this tranquility was shattered by the Chinese "invasion," which resulted in massive loss of life and cultural genocide on a vast scale.

Chinese sources portray their takeover of Tibet as a "liberation" that freed the "serfs" from their feudal oppression and that has resulted in dramatically increased prosperity for the Tibetan people. From a state of "Medieval extreme backwardness"[35] Tibet has "leapt forward" in all significant areas, and now its grateful people happily celebrate their full (re)integration into the motherland. Much of this is strikingly reminiscent of Western colonial discourses that justified invasion and colonization on the basis of the purported cultural benefits that colonial rule brought to the natives. The Chinese claim to legitimacy has two main components: first, Chinese writers assert that China has an indisputable legal claim to overlordship of Tibet, one that goes back at least seven hundred years; second, they state that their direct takeover in the 1950s was justified by the appalling conditions in the region. They admit that the Tibetan government based in Lhasa and headed by the Dalai Lamas (which they refer to as the "Tibetan local government") exercised authority over most internal affairs in the central Tibetan provinces, but during the period when Tibet became estranged from China conditions there steadily worsened, demonstrating that the Tibetans were incapable of managing their own affairs without the aid of the "advanced Han nationality." These points are crucially important to Chinese writers, because if Tibet was an autonomous state prior to the Chinese takeover, then China would be guilty of colonialism, and if the Tibetan claims regarding the generally happy nature of old Tibet and the brutality of the Chinese "invasion" are correct, then Tibetan charges of genocide and imperialism would be justified.

This, of course, is exactly what Tibetan exile writers contend is the case, and a number of Western authors share this conclusion. But Western authors are no less polarized than the Chinese and Tibetans, and there are two distinct points of view among them also. Among the authors considered in this study, Israel Epstein and Tom Grunfeld enthusiastically endorse the Chinese version of events and use much the same language as do Chinese writers to describe conditions in Tibet prior to the 1950s.[36] Grunfeld paints a picture of a brutal, exploitive, and primitive society whose people were "powerless" but "resigned" to their "difficult and harsh existence." Tibet was highly stratified, with the nobility inhabiting an environment of "opulent splendor" while the vast majority endured lives of desperate poverty and misery. Most of the people were "serfs," and many lived in slavery. In Grunfeld's version of old Tibet, the country was a "rigid and ossified feudal society" in which torture was widespread. He provides lurid descriptions of "brutal forms of punishment" and states that "a British resident of two decades reported seeing countless eye-gougings and mutilations."[37] He does not, however, indicate who this British resident was nor what sadistic curiosity led him to witness so many torture sessions.

Grunfeld is contemptuous of the view that old Tibet was a pleasant place in which to live. While he acknowledges that many travelers to old Tibet reported that Tibetans were generally friendly and smiled a great deal, this does not mean that they were happy, but rather, that they were resigned to their sufferings: "Witnessing the smiling faces and friendly people, which literally every traveler did, could as easily have been an indication of Tibetan stoicism." Those Tibetans who lived in that society who claim that they were content or who assert that most people were generally happy "were simply unable, or unwilling, to face the realities."[38]

Grunfeld's book contains many harsh judgments about old Tibet, but he gives no indication that he has ever visited the country (either before or after the Chinese takeover), nor that he has ever personally interviewed Tibetan refugees. He admits that he does not read or speak Tibetan and does not cite any fieldwork experience among his subjects. Despite these apparent limitations, he indicates throughout the book that he is confident of having ascertained the reality of conditions in old Tibet. He achieves this mainly by rejecting accounts of Tibetans who lived in Tibet and Western travelers who paint a positive picture, and by privileging Western accounts that portray Tibet in a negative light. In Grunfeld's calculus, a negative account always trumps a positive one, and a Western visitor to Tibet (with a negative view) always has more authority than a Tibetan who lived there. Thus, for example, he cites a highly idealized version of old Tibet in Marco Pallis's *Peaks and Lamas* and Thupten Jigme Norbu's positive image of his country. Both claim that the populace was generally law-abiding and that crime rates were very low, but to counter their claims, Grunfeld cites "a frequent visitor to western Tibet," "a former resident," and "yet another" who reported encounters with thieves or fears of robbery. Grunfeld concludes that "there is no evidence to support these images of a utopian Shangri-la."[39]

In Grunfeld's view, those Westerners and Tibetans who reported positive impressions of Tibet were either blind to its squalid realities or deliberately obfuscating. He also frequently excoriates Western journalists who paint a positive picture of old Tibet or who report that the Chinese committed human rights abuses. The Chinese, however, are said to be "honest" and are considered by Grunfeld to be generally reliable informants: "The emerging evidence tends to substantiate China's view of events . . . when events were depicted for public consumption, China appears to have fabricated the least."[40]

A more nuanced perspective is found in Melvyn Goldstein's *A History of Modern Tibet* and *The Snow Lion and the Dragon*. Unlike Grunfeld, Goldstein is fluent in Tibetan and has extensive fieldwork experience all over the Tibetan plateau; he also used a wide variety of Tibetan-language sources in preparing his studies. Unlike Grunfeld and Epstein, Goldstein is adamant that prior to the Chinese takeover in the 1950s Tibet enjoyed de facto independence, but like them, he asserts that it was a feudal theocracy, and he portrays most of its rulers as corrupt, venal, and inept. Moreover, in *A History of Modern Tibet*, the overall thrust of his analysis indicates that the weakness and isolation of old Tibet, coupled with the bungling and corruption of its leaders, created a situation in which the Chinese takeover was inevitable.

In Goldstein's view, "The Tibet Question is about control of territory— about who rules it, who lives there, and who decides what goes on there." He claims that he is taking a "realpolitik" stance that is free from the sentimentality of the pro-Tibet faction and also avoids the obfuscation and propaganda of the

Chinese side, but it is clear in both books that his sympathies lie with the Chinese. While he acknowledges the "terrible sufferings" that the Tibetan people have experienced in recent decades, he also indicates that the Chinese people have suffered. Like the Chinese writers cited above, he refers to the changes imposed on Tibetan society as "democratic reforms," and while he admits that there was "loss of life" and "food shortages," his choice of language indicates that he rejects claims that Tibetans have been subjected to genocide and widespread starvation, as pro-Tibet writers claim. Moreover, like Grunfeld and Epstein, he asserts in a number of places that the Chinese pursued a "gradualist policy" in Tibet and that they showed tremendous patience and "moderation" despite the prevarication and mendacity of Tibetan officials who tried to hold on to their positions and privileges in an attempt to delay what he apparently views as an inevitable process of historical change.[41]

The picture of old Tibet painted by Epstein, Grunfeld, and Goldstein stands in marked contrast to Richardson's version. He admits that the country was poor and technologically backward, but he contends that the populace was generally happy and content, and he agrees with the Tibetan authors examined in this study that it was a deeply religious land with little difference between rich and poor. Richardson reports that there was a traditional aristocracy that, along with the monasteries, controlled most of the land, but the land itself was poor, and most landowners were only slightly better off than the peasants who did most of the work. Many aristocrats also engaged in manual labor, and if a particular landowner became too exploitive it was relatively easy for workers simply to move somewhere else.

Throughout his book Richardson takes issue with Chinese writers who assert Chinese sovereignty over Tibet and who characterize its society as brutal and exploitive. He admits that it lacked modern technology and that it was poor, but his descriptions indicate a sense of nostalgia for a generally pleasant country and its religious and friendly inhabitants.[42]

While Richardson and other Western and Tibetan writers freely acknowledge that Tibet was by no means perfect, Robert Thurman's characterization of Tibet is distinctive in that he appears to recognize no flaws in old Tibet. Thurman, the Jey Tsong Khapa Chair of Tibetan and Buddhist Studies at Columbia University, was formerly an ordained Tibetan Buddhist monk and has published extensively in the field. He never visited old Tibet, but has worked with Tibetan lamas in exile, and this appears to be the main source for his conclusions about it.

In Thurman's version, old Tibet was an idyllic land of spiritual adepts. He refers to them as "psychonauts" and claims that while the West invested its resources in the pursuit and development of external technologies, the Tibetans invested just as heavily in the pursuit of spiritual perfection. The West's astronauts, in a marvel of technological advancement, were able to reach the moon and to send probes into the far reaches of the solar system, but Tibet's psychonauts chose to explore the outer limits of human consciousness: "The essence of Tibetan culture is defined by this experience of real Buddhas dwelling among them."[43]

While other writers portray Tibet's relative poverty in a negative light, Thurman contends that Tibet's people freely chose to reject materialism to better pursue their religious goals. The economy was deliberately "minimalist" because Tibetans wanted to produce only enough to feed everyone and provide a small surplus to guard against any shortage. They realized that greed and corruption result from excessive materialism, and so they consciously decided to limit themselves to a "small is beautiful" economy. Thurman's Tibet was "a place of unprecedented opportunity for the individual intent on enlightenment: maximum low-cost lifelong educational opportunities, minimum taxes, no military services, no mortgages, no factories of material products, no lack of teachers and realized beings."[44] It was a "spiritual civilization,"[45] a country in which the people had a deep sense of the interconnectedness of all life that resulted in an attitude of stewardship of the environment and in which the government unilaterally chose to demilitarize the country, creating a "zone of peace" that is a model that should be emulated by other nations.

The final Western author considered in this study, Warren Smith, uses a wide variety of sources to counter Chinese claims of legitimate sovereignty over Tibet and to debunk the Chinese historical narrative. He adopts a strongly polemical tone and uses highly emotive language in his denunciations of Chinese actions in Tibet. He indicates that his decision to write was a result of his extensive contacts with Tibetans in Nepal, Tibet, and India, and that a five-month trip to Tibet allowed him to see the reality of Chinese rule: "The experience that most altered my life and set me on a path of devotion to the study of Tibetan history and politics was my five months in Tibet in 1982. One would have to be spiritually, not to mention politically, blind not to see the evidence of Chinese oppression and cultural destruction in Tibet." Smith is adamant that prior to the 1950s, Tibet was an "independent country" and that China's takeover was an "invasion" that violated international law. He contends that Chinese and Tibetans are two distinct ethnic groups and that despite Chinese attempts to destroy their culture and to assimilate them into their own, Tibetans remain convinced of their distinctiveness. Smith portrays the Chinese as thoroughgoing cultural chauvinists who implicitly believe that they are both racially and culturally superior to their minority populations, including Tibetans. These attitudes result in constant friction and resentment among conquered minorities who seek to maintain their traditions and cultures despite assimilationist pressures. Smith employs particularly harsh language in his characterizations of the Chinese takeover and subsequent rule, which he refers to as "foreign domination." He claims that the Chinese have used torture, physical and psychological coercion, and starvation to subdue the Tibetan populace and that their actions have led to "suicides, despair, and hatred."[46]

Table 2 indicates the distinctive language employed by the Western writers examined in this study. They are divided into two groups: the ones on the left are generally pro-China, and the ones on the right are strongly pro-Tibet. I suspect that the writers on the left would reject my characterization. As seen above, all indicate that they consider their works to be objective and fact-based, but all share certain biases that set them apart from the pro-Tibet writers. The most important of these is a conviction that China has brought democratic reforms to Tibet and that it has pursued a gradualist policy that is characterized

TABLE 2. Western Writers on Tibet Prior to the Chinese Takeover

Epstein, Grunfeld, Goldstein	Richardson, Smith, Thurman
powerless (W4, 13)	easy-going (W5, 27)
slavery (W4, 15)	social inequalities (W5, 27)
bitterness (W1, 12)	kindly, cheerful, and contented (W5, 27)
resigned (W4, 33)	active contentment (W5, 27)
primitive land (W4, 121)	minimalist (W11, 111)
very little class mobility (W4, 14)	simple and somewhat spartan (W9, 20)
rigid and ossified feudal society (W4, 129)	inner modernity (W11, 113)
feudal theocracy (W4, 9)	Religious State (W5, 129)
theocratic state (W3, 35)	sacred society (W11, 113)
highly stratified society (W4, 15)	relaxed and flexible (W9, 21)
feudal economy (W3, 45)	economy well organized (W11, 111)
serflike peasants (W3, 35)	nobility virtually expropriated (W10, 9)
serfs, slaves, outcastes (W4, 9)	relatively happy land (W10, 10)
low productivity (W4, 16)	"small is beautiful" economy (W11, 113)
filthiness . . . garbage (W4, 17)	arts flourished explosively (W11, 113)
brigands, thieves, burglars (W4, 23)	peaceful and secure (W11, 110)
open corruption (W4, 23)	tolerant of diversity (W9, 21)
torture and mutilation (W4, 24)	cheerful (W11, 113)
brutal forms of punishment (W4, 24)	unilaterally disarmed society (W8, 40)
human sacrifice (W4, 29)	fun-loving and playful cheerfulness (W9, 21)
cannibal system (W1, 141)	nonviolence (W10, 9)
internally disunified (W3, 37)	nationalist consciousness (W1, 398)
local autonomy in domestic matters (W4, 59)	de facto independence (W5, 185)
distinct and independent (W3, 1)	deeply conscious of separateness (W5, 240)
Tibetan oligarchy (W4, 99)	Tibetan government
population decline	balanced population (W9, 21)

by extreme patience in the face of Tibetan obtuseness and obstruction. They also agree on the use of the term "serf" to characterize the majority of the Tibetan population prior to the 1950s.[47] The Western writers on the right side, by comparison, all use highly emotionally charged language and strongly denounce China's actions in Tibet. Most admit that China has brought some benefits—such as schools, roads, hospitals, and telecommunications—but these are generally dismissed as mechanisms of control and indoctrination or as means of supplying Chinese troops and transporting Han Chinese settlers to the region. All agree that old Tibet was a generally pleasant but backward society and that Chinese rule has been an unmitigated disaster for the people and the land of Tibet.

The words employed by these authors indicate that the Tibet issue is as contentious for Western authors as it is for Tibetans and Chinese. The language on either side is as polarized as in Table 1, and several of these authors use the same terminology as Tibetan and Chinese writers. Epstein and Grunfeld utilize emotional rhetoric in their characterizations of old Tibet, which they view as a brutal and exploitive system with no apparent redeeming features. Goldstein is more reserved in his terminology, but he also paints a picture of a backward and internally corrupt state. While he acknowledges that the Chinese takeover has resulted in suffering for many Tibetans, he also appears to believe that democratic reforms have brought change for the better and that the Chinese showed great patience in their policy of gradually introducing these reforms.

As the language employed by writers on the right side of the chart indicates, the pro-Tibet faction tends to adopt polemical and uncompromising rhetoric and strongly denounces Chinese policies. All but Thurman admit that old Tibet was far from perfect and that it was economically stagnant and technologically backward, but these features are offset by the unhurried lifestyles of Tibet's inhabitants and their general cheerfulness and contentment. Richardson and Smith adopt often vitriolic language in describing the Chinese takeover and the sufferings it has brought to Tibetans, and they are particularly concerned with rebutting what they regard as Chinese fabrications and propaganda.

In the next chapter, I examine the background of the current battles over Tibet's histories, focusing on some of the key areas of contention. Chapter 3 looks at modern Chinese history and how it contributes to the nationalist narratives underlying the works of our Chinese authors. The fourth chapter is concerned with the Chinese takeover of Tibet in the 1950s and its aftermath, focusing on the sort of language employed by Chinese and Tibetan writers to make their respective cases.

As we will see, the assertions and conclusions of each group rely heavily on their respective historical narratives. Both factions believe that history can be used to "prove" their assertions, and to this end they highlight certain key points in Tibetan history. The most important of these are: (1) the marriage of the Chinese princess Wencheng to the Tibetan king Songtsen Gampo (ca. 618–650); (2) the surrender of Tibet to the Mongols in the thirteenth century and Tibet's subsequent annexation into the Mongol empire; (3) relations between China and Tibet during the Ming and Qing dynasties and the Nationalist period (1911–1949); (4) the Chinese takeover of the 1950s; and (5) the anti-China riots of March 1959 in Lhasa.

Interestingly, both sides agree completely on the main events: that the Tibetan king Songtsen Gampo married a Chinese princess named Wencheng, and that in 1247 the Tibetan lama Sakya Pandita officially ceded sovereignty of Tibet to the Mongol ruler Godan Khan. They further agree that Tibet became a part of the Mongol empire and that Sakya Pandita and his successors were regents of Tibet who managed its internal affairs; that following the decline of Mongol power, the Yuan dynasty (1279–1368) was replaced by the Ming dynasty (1368–1644), during which imperial interest in Tibet diminished. During the Manchu Qing dynasty (1644–1911), imperial interest increased, and several of the Manchu emperors supported Tibetan Buddhism. When the Nationalists replaced the Qing in 1911, they asserted Chinese sovereignty over Tibet, but Tupden Gyatso, the thirteenth Dalai Lama (1876–1933), responded by officially declaring that Tibet was independent, and all Chinese officials were expelled from the country. Following this, there were few contacts between China and Tibet until 1950, when the recently inaugurated People's Republic of China sent troops of the People's Liberation Army into eastern Tibet. They subsequently marched to Lhasa, the capital of Tibet, and established direct Chinese control over Tibetan domestic affairs. The Tibetan government continued to function alongside the new Chinese administration until March 1959, when a series of anti-Chinese riots erupted in Lhasa. They were suppressed by the PLA, and Chinese authorities then abolished the Tibetan government. The Dalai Lama subsequently fled to India, where he later established a government-in-exile.

There is general agreement on all the above events in the sources considered in this study, but the two groups' interpretations of "what really happened" are diametrically opposed and mutually incompatible. The core differences between the two groups are found in the *reasons* they posit for why things happened as they did and the psychological motives they ascribe to historical figures. The amount of writing dedicated to each of these events and the often highly emotional or propagandistic language used demonstrate how important their interpretation is to the respective groups. In the following chapters, I examine some of the key points of dispute, focusing on the sort of language used by the writers to argue their points.

As we will see, a key reason for their differences lies in the sources on which they rely. The Tibetan authors cite as evidence ancient Tibetan chronicles, written by Buddhist clerics whose main interest was in charting the spread of Buddhism and enhancing its prestige; many were also concerned with exalting the power and influence of the early Tibetan empire, which later became an important cultural symbol for Tibetans.[48] The ancient Chinese records were written mainly by authors directly employed by the dynastic governments, and they extolled the morality and culture of their employers and of China in general and praised its military might.[49] Because contemporary Chinese and Tibetan authors accept much of what these chronicles say at face value and retrospectively insert their respective culture's current interpretations of historical events, they arrive at radically different conclusions.

In the following three chapters, I begin each section with an outline of the general historical context in which debates take place. These are not intended to be "objective" presentations of what really happened, but overviews of the period in question that set the scene for understanding the rival interpretations. These are primarily drawn from traditional Tibetan and Chinese accounts, which generally agree on the main outlines of the historical periods in question. They are followed by an analysis of the fault lines in rival interpretations that highlights the contentious aspects of Tibetan history and how they are conceived by Tibetan and Chinese authors.

2

Characters, Plots, and Motivations in Tibetan History

Peace through matrimony has proved a stupid plan;
Our princess was lost, not to return.
Who has now taken our Kokonor?
The western barbarians are like falcons,
Well-fed and soaring.

—"Emergency," *Tu-fu, China's Greatest Poet,* p. 197

Tibetan Origin Myths

According to Michael Aris, Tibetans "by comparison with many other peoples of the east or west . . . maintain a high level of historical consciousness and a deep sense of the vitality of the living past. . . . Mythical events were remembered and recorded as 'history' . . . to serve as the basis for their re-enactment as ritual."[1] Histories of Tibet by Tibetan exiles generally begin with ancestral myths that stress the central role of Buddhism in the early development of Tibetan civilization. According to one popular story, the Tibetan race began thousands of years ago when a monkey who was a physical manifestation of Avalokiteśvara, the buddha of compassion, mated with an ogress living in the mountains of Tibet. Their progeny were the forbears of modern Tibetans. From their father they inherited the qualities of gentleness and compassion, while their mother's passionate and violent nature also became a part of their psychological makeup.

For Tibetans, this legend provides an explanation for why they have fervently embraced Buddhism but also often engage in negative actions. According to the story, Avalokiteśvara consciously chose to take the form of a monkey to begin the process of creating a Buddhist country on the Tibetan plateau, and as Tibetan civilization developed, he continued to intervene to prepare the people for the introduction of Buddhism. This required that Tibetans be gradually civilized to counteract the violent tendencies that they had inherited from the ogress. He worked in tandem with other buddhas and bodhisattvas to nurture the spiritual inclinations of the Tibetan people, helping them to suppress their negative tendencies and develop their culture. The first stage of this process culminated in the initiation of the "first dissemination" (*snga dar*) of Buddhism during the reign of King Songtsen Gampo, who is also characterized by several traditional Tibetan histories as an incarnation of Avalokiteśvara.

According to another Tibetan origin myth, the earliest settlers on the Tibetan plateau were refugees who escaped the conflicts described in the Indian epic poem *Mahābhārata*. The Indian connection is important in this context because contemporary Tibetan histories develop a narrative in which India, particularly Indian Buddhism, was the main source of the development of Tibetan culture, and China played at most a peripheral role. Shakabpa, for example, cites both of these origin myths and states that some anthropologists believe that Tibetans are related to Mongoloid races. He admits that this might be possible, but he adds that they are a separate race and clearly different from the Han in terms of biology, culture, and language. He does not concede any connection between early Tibetans and Chinese and consistently emphasizes Tibet's connections with India.

Not surprisingly, most of the Chinese histories considered in this study downplay Indian influence and do not even mention these two origin myths. Wang Furen and Suo Wenqing do state that many Tibetans consider their progenitors to have come from India, but contend that "this presumption . . . is again opposed to truth." The truth, as they perceive it, is that Chinese tribes settled in Tibet and so the Tibetans are related to the Han. They assert that Neolithic human remains "are free from such physical features of the Indians of the Aryan race as prominent noses and deepset eyes" and that "the Neolithic culture of these areas was closely related to that of the interior of China."[2]

The Marriage of Songtsen Gampo and Wencheng

Contemporary Tibetan histories state with considerable national pride that from the seventh to ninth centuries Tibet was a major military power in Central

Asia. During this period, Tibet attacked China a number of times, and at the height of its territorial expansion conquered and annexed large portions of Chinese territory. Under the kings of the Yarlung dynasty (so called because its headquarters were in the Yarlung Valley of central Tibet), a significant empire was created, and Tibetan fighters enjoyed a fearsome reputation among their neighbors. During the early period of expansion, Songtsen Gampo's forces attacked and defeated several Chinese tribes, and as a sign of his growing power, in 634 a mission was sent to the Chinese emperor Taizong (r. 627–650) requesting a marriage alliance. This is described in Tang dynasty chronicles as a tribute mission, but the message it delivered was an ultimatum and not a gesture of subservience by a vassal. When the request was denied, Tibetan troops attacked and defeated the armies of tribes affiliated with the Tang in 637 and 638. In 638 an army (reportedly comprising 100,000 soldiers)[3] camped on the border with China, and again envoys were sent to the Chinese capital to request that the emperor give Songtsen Gampo a princess of the royal family in marriage. The envoys were attacked by Chinese troops, but because of the size of Songtsen Gampo's army, the emperor subsequently changed his mind, and in 640 agreed that the princess Wencheng would marry the Tibetan king.[4]

Chinese historians downplay the military angle: they portray the marriage as a calculated move by the emperor to bring the belligerent Tibetans within the Chinese political and cultural orbit and indicate that he was in no way pressured by Songtsen Gampo; he freely gave the princess in marriage, and this is presented as the beginning of a long process of sinification of Tibetan culture.[5] According to several Chinese writers, Wencheng was almost single-handedly responsible for introducing Chinese culture to the backward Tibetans, who eagerly adopted Chinese technology and customs. Wang and Suo state that she was "a pioneer adherent to unity and friendship between Hans and Tibetans and an enthusiastic disseminator of Tang culture."[6] They describe her retinue as cultural ambassadors, experts in various fields who were brought to Tibet not to care for the princess, but as cultural missionaries. According to *Tibet: Myth vs. Reality*, the "local kingdom of the Songtsan Gambo ruling house" was "a state based on a slave system,"[7] but Songtsen Gampo recognized the superiority of Chinese culture and longed to transform Tibet in its image.

> An admirer of the Tang civilization, Songtsan Gambo made several matrimonial approaches and finally asked the emperor for the hand of one of the imperial daughters,[8] hoping thus to cement closer economic and cultural ties with the Tang Dynasty. In 641, the favour was granted, and Princess Wen-cheng and Songtsan Gambo were

united in holy matrimony. The princess brought with her dowry
many books in the Han language and a retinue including craftsmen
and experts in pharmacology and calendrical science. All this had
much to do with Tibet's subsequent economic and cultural development. . . . The marriage between the king of Tibet and the Tang
princess brought the Tibetans and the Hans together.[9]

According to Chinese histories, the marriage created a blood bond between
Tibetans and Han Chinese, and in the following centuries this was supple-
mented by increasingly close cultural and economic ties. It implicitly acknowledged Chinese superiority, and effectively initiated Chinese dominance over
Tibet. This narrative reflects traditional notions about the power of Chinese
civilization: the implication is that the barbarian Tibetan king was able to put
military pressure on China and annexed some of its territories to his growing
empire, but as a result of his contact with its superior culture decided to become a vassal of the Chinese emperor and to abandon his own culture by
remaking it in China's image. Wang and Suo portray him as a barbarian who
stood in awe of China's advanced civilization and who was keenly aware of the
backwardness of his own country:

> While a representative of the slave-owning class [he] was not
> conservative-minded. He felt drawn to the time-honoured, advanced
> culture of China's hinterland. Unlike his compeers in general, he
> was not bent on consolidating his rule by safeguarding the reigning
> backward mode of production. Instead, he used his powers to intro-
> duce the more advanced culture from other peoples, first and fore-
> most the Hans, to help promote the productive forces of his . . . soci-
> ety.[10]

The notion that a successful military commander would be so overwhelmed by the cultural superiority of enemies he had defeated in battle that
he would renounce further expansion and strive to emulate them is, of course,
highly implausible, but it is widely accepted in China. The ability of their culture to entice barbarians to adopt their ways is also assumed by contemporary
Chinese, and it is a core part of the mythology of the imperial period.[11] The
notion that Wencheng converted the Tibetans to Chinese culture has a very
long pedigree in China. The earliest example is found in the Tang chronicles,
which state that "[since] Princess Wencheng went and civilized this country,
many of their customs have been changed."[12] Neither Chinese nor Tibetan
writers appear to recognize that traditional accounts indicate that she was quite
young when she came to Tibet, perhaps only eleven or twelve years old, and

so it is unlikely that she would have had the authority to sinicize Tibetan culture or to preach Buddhism.

It is also reported in traditional Chinese sources that Wencheng convinced the king to outlaw the common practice among Tibetans of putting red ochre on their faces, which she considered barbaric, and that at her urging he began wearing Chinese silk brocades instead of felt and skins.[13] According to the Tang annals, he "praised the costume of the great empire, and the perfection of their manners, and was ashamed of the barbarism of his own people."[14]

Several of the Chinese writers we are considering also contend that she convinced Songtsen Gampo to develop a written script for the Tibetan language.[15] She advised him to send the scholar Tönmi Sambhota to India and to use Indic scripts as his model, which is curious because it is highly unlikely that a Chinese princess would have any knowledge of Indic languages or that she would advise the king to use them as a model when she was purportedly a missionary for Chinese culture. It also conflicts with the assertions of Wang and Suo, Li An-che, and Li Tieh-tsung that, following the marriage, there was constant communication between Tibet and China and that this took place in Chinese. If Wencheng had the sort of influence over Songtsen Gampo that they imagine, and if cultural and diplomatic contacts were as extensive as they believe, it is likely that he would have turned to China, and not India, for the source of a written script.

Despite these difficulties, Grunfeld comes to the same conclusion as these Chinese authors: "Princess Wen Cheng brought with her religious artifacts and is credited with having introduced to Tibet the use of butter, tea, cheese, barley, beer, medical knowledge, and astrology. She is said to have encouraged . . . the sending of a minister, Thonmi Sambhota, to Kashmir . . . to bring back a written script for the Tibetan language based on Sanskrit."[16]

This motif of Wencheng as a cultural ambassador continues to be popular among Chinese today; an example of its pervasiveness is a Hong Kong martial arts film entitled *The Emperor of Tibet*, which centers on the story of Songtsen Gampo's marriage to Wencheng.[17] It opens with large Chinese characters across the screen announcing "Princess Wencheng spreads our culture in Tibet!" The central plot portrays Songtsen Gampo as a barbarian ruler obsessed with importing Chinese culture and enticing China to assimilate his country into its empire. He has to contend with evil and ignorant advisors who try to prevent the marriage in order to retain Tibet's traditional (and inferior) culture and its territorial sovereignty. After much martial arts mayhem and intrigue, the evildoers are vanquished, and the film closes with the marriage ceremony. It is clear that from this point onward Tibet will be increasingly sinicized until its culture is advanced enough for it to be annexed to the Chinese empire. As

FIGURE 2.1. Image of Tönmi Sambhota, minister of Songtsen Gampo, who is credited with creating a written script for the Tibetan language, at Songtsen Gampo's burial tumulus in Chonggye Valley, central Tibet. Photo by John Powers.

with Chinese histories of Tibet, there is no mention that the marriage was the result of military pressure by Tibet on China.

In Chinese histories of Tibet, the fact that the Chinese emperor was apparently forced into giving away the princess is either flatly denied or not mentioned. Not surprisingly, it is strongly emphasized by Tibetan writers. Shakabpa states that after capturing the Chinese city of Songzhao, Songtsen Gampo "asked for an imperial princess in marriage as an alternative to war ... the Chinese gave battle but were defeated so the Emperor finally agreed to give a princess in marriage." He also stresses the fact that the Chinese emperor accompanied Wencheng "as far as the Tibetan border," which Shakabpa implies indicates both that he was in the inferior position and that he was clearly aware of the physical demarcation between his country and Tibet. Shakabpa, along with several other Tibetan writers, also points out that according to early chronicles, prior to his marriage to Wencheng Songtsen Gampo had already married a Nepalese princess named Bhṛkutī and that he later married three Tibetan women from aristocratic families.[18] Shakabpa's conclusion is that Tibet was no more a part of China as a result of the marriage to Wencheng than it was of Nepal, and that all of Songtsen Gampo's weddings were politically motivated. His intention was not to subordinate himself to the Chinese emperor, but to extend his power and influence.

In contemporary Tibetan historical narratives, the role of China in the formation of Tibetan culture is minimized, whereas Chinese sources highlight every communication by either government to the other, official gifts, diplomatic missions, and cultural contacts. For Chinese authors, every sign of contact between the neighboring states is viewed as evidence of Chinese overlordship. Tibetan authors, however, uniformly assert that the decisive foreign cultural influence on Tibet was India. They emphasize the role of Buddhism in transforming Tibetan culture, and they view the importation of Buddhism as being almost exclusively connected with Indian teachers and institutions. Most of the Tibetan writers also put a Buddhist spin on the marriage and assert that Songtsen Gampo's intention in marrying Wencheng was to bring a Buddhist princess to Tibet and thus facilitate the importation of Buddhism.[19] This notion appears to relate to the claim found in several traditional Tibetan histories that Songtsen Gampo was both a devout Buddhist and a physical manifestation of Avalokiteśvara and that the two foreign princesses were also phys-

FIGURE 2.2. Images of Songtsen Gampo and his two foreign wives in his burial tumulus in Chonggye Valley, central Tibet. Photo by John Powers.

ical manifestations of Tārā, whose purpose in life was to facilitate the transmission of the dharma to Tibet.[20] Dawa Norbu cites unnamed Tibetan chronicles which assert that Songtsen Gampo's intention had nothing whatever to do with politics, but was solely motivated by religion:

> When I was at the Chinese school . . . the Chinese teacher would say, patronisingly, "Ever since Princess Wencheng married Sontsen Gampo, the Chinese and Tibetans have been blood relations." In one way it was an example of an equal if not weaker sovereign offering his daughter to a stronger one, as Tibet was militarily superior to China at the time. However, Gampo's was not a politically motivated marriage. The Tibetan chronicles emphatically state that the king married the two foreign princesses in order to get the two most venerable images of Buddha for Tibet.

According to Norbu, "That Tibet was a greater military power in Central Asia from the seventh to the ninth centuries is an indisputable historical fact."[21] He and the other Tibetan writers also emphasize that Tibetans were strongly aware of their cultural and religious differences with the Chinese and never considered themselves to be part of China.

Just as the conclusions of Chinese writers are influenced by their cultural assumptions and their reliance on Chinese dynastic sources that portray neighboring countries as barbarians and exalt Chinese culture as the apex of civilization, the views of Tibetan writers are shaped by indigenous histories, which were generally written by Buddhist clerics and were intended to glorify Buddhism and enhance its influence on Tibetan culture. When describing Tibet's relations with other countries, their primary interest is the story of the importation of Buddhism and the role played by Indian teachers, and they generally show little interest in politics or commerce.[22] Because he relies on these as his main sources, Dawa Norbu does not question the notion that the leader of an expanding military empire with no prior interest in or knowledge of Buddhism would marry princesses from two neighboring countries solely to secure Buddhist images. Although traditional Tibetan histories portray Songtsen Gampo as both a devout Buddhist and an incarnation of Avalokiteśvara, records of the period do not indicate that he actually showed any great interest in religion. He is said to have sponsored the building of two temples to house the buddha images brought by his Nepalese and Chinese wives, but beyond that there is little reliable evidence that he was interested in propagating Buddhism, and when he died he was buried according to the protocols and rituals of the pre-Buddhist royal cult.[23]

While Chinese historians, both ancient and modern, emphasize Wencheng's Han ethnicity and her role as an ambassador for Chinese culture, early Tibetan chronicles focus on the notion that she was a physical emanation of Tārā. In *The Blue Annals* (*Deb ther sngon po*), for example, this identification is stressed, and Chinese Buddhism features only as a heterodox system that the Tibetans rejected in favor of normative Indian models. Wencheng plays a minor role in this account, but as an advocate of Buddhism and not of Han culture.[24] Gö Shönnubel, the author of *The Blue Annals*, is primarily concerned with the transmission of the dharma and with describing the glory of the empire of the "religious kings" (Songtsen Gampo and his successors Trisong Detsen and Ralpachen) and pays little attention to Chinese cultural influences in Tibet. Similarly, *The Mirror Illuminating the Royal Genealogies*, a fourteenth-century Tibetan chronicle, discusses Songtsen Gampo's marriages at length, but it emphasizes the king's power and his identity as a physical emanation of Avalokiteśvara. It reports that when the marriage proposal was first made by the minister Gar to the Chinese emperor, the latter roared with laughter and belittled the Tibetan king and his country. Only after realizing the great power of the Tibetan army did the emperor relent. Wencheng is said to have begged her father and relatives not to force her to go to Tibet, but the emperor replied that if he refused, the Tibetans would invade and devastate his country. She is credited with divinatory powers, but nothing is said about her efforts to import Chinese culture. Instead, the chronicle reports that she was distressed by the barbarism of the Tibetans and attempted to escape and return to China.[25] In several places, this account accuses the Chinese of chauvinism and high-handed behavior toward Tibetans, but Wencheng is said to have been less guilty than other Chinese.[26]

Chinese authors, as we have seen, portray Wencheng as a pivotal figure in the history of Tibet and as the primary source for the dissemination of Chinese culture. In Tibetan accounts, however, she plays at most a peripheral role and is briefly mentioned along with Bhṛkutī but never accorded any significance in shaping its history. In a study of these accounts, Richardson concludes that she was "a dim figure . . . who made no mark on either Tibetan or Chinese history in the remaining thirty years of her life [following Songtsen Gampo's death] and whose religious affiliation is uncertain."[27] Similarly, pro-Tibet Western sources emphasize Songtsen Gampo's key role in Tibetan history, but view Wencheng only as one of several wives whose importance begins and ends with her importing of the buddha image popularly known as Jowo Rinpoche.[28] Robert Thurman, for example, appears to endorse the traditional Tibetan notion that Songtsen Gampo was a manifestation of Avalokiteśvara and portrays him as a deeply religious man intent on remaking his country into a "spiritual civilization":

He began transforming the civilization from feudal militarism to something more peaceful and spiritual, based on the people's culti- vated moral outlook. . . . He began a systematic process of cultural adaptation. He sent a team of scholars to India to learn Sanskrit, create a written language for Tibetan, and begin to translate the vast Buddhist literature. He married nine princesses from different sur- rounding countries, including Nepal and T'ang China, requesting each to bring Buddhist artifacts and texts with her to Tibet.[29]

Thus began a "multigenerational drive to import Buddhism from India."[30] In Thurman's view, Songtsen Gampo enthusiastically embraced Buddhism and used it as a source of imperial legitimization. His marriages to Wencheng and Bhṛkutī were intended to import Buddhist culture, and were not in any way motivated by political or strategic concerns.

Trisong Detsen and the Great Debate

While there is doubt regarding Songtsen Gampo's level of interest in Bud- dhism, it is clear from Tibetan sources that some of his successors became ardent Buddhists. In the eighth century, King Trisong Detsen (ca. 740–798) devoted considerable resources to the importation of Buddhist culture (mainly from India) and the building of Buddhist monasteries and temples. Like Song- tsen Gampo, he is regarded by Tibetan tradition as an incarnate buddha and is characterized as the second of Tibet's religious kings (chos rgyal).

In traditional histories, Trisong Detsen is said to have invited a number of Indian Buddhist teachers to Tibet, the most prominent of them being Śantar- akṣita, the abbot of Vikramaśīla, one of the great seats of Buddhist learning in India. Shortly after he arrived, however, a number of natural disasters occurred in Tibet, and traditional histories attribute them to the actions of indigenous demons who supported the native Bön religion and opposed the importation of Buddhism. Several of the king's ministers, also reportedly proponents of Bön, advised the king to expel Śantarakṣita, which he reluctantly did. Before he left, however, Śantarakṣita advised Trisong Detsen to invite the tantric mas- ter Padmasambhava to Tibet because his magical powers could subdue the demonic opponents of the dharma.

When the invitation arrived, Padmasambhava agreed to the king's request. As he reached the border, however, Tibet's pro-Bön demons created a huge snowstorm that prevented him from advancing into the country. He responded by retreating to a cave and meditating; the power of his meditation caused the

FIGURE 2.3. Jowo Rinpoche, a statue of Śākyamuni Buddha as a young prince; according to Tibetan tradition, it was brought to Tibet by Princess Wencheng and is today housed in the Jokhang. Photo by John Powers.

snowstorm to stop, and he was able to proceed. As he traveled toward the Tibetan capital, demons continued to attack him, but he defeated them all with powerful mantras and magical power. The Tibetans who witnessed the spectacle of a single man announcing that he was battling all of the assembled demons of the country were so impressed that Trisong Detsen was then able to win over most of his advisors and the aristocracy. From that point on, Tibet began a wholesale importation of Buddhism, primarily from the great monastic universities of northern India and tantric lineages that mainly derived from Bihar and Bengal. Records of the time indicate that Chinese Buddhist masters were also involved in missionary activity in Tibet, but they do not appear to have had the same level of imperial support or to have enjoyed as much success as Indian Buddhists.

According to Tibetan histories, in 767 Trisong Detsen, Śantarakṣita, and Padmasambhava officially consecrated the first Buddhist monastery in Tibet, which was called Samye and located in the Yarlung Valley. After this, the first group of Tibetan monks was ordained, and in the following decades Buddhism began to attract increasingly large numbers of adherents. The government allocated significant funds for the importation of Buddhist literature, teachers, and artifacts, and increasing numbers of Buddhist missionaries traveled to Tibet to spread their various versions of the dharma. This led to a confusing situation in which competing messages were being propounded in various areas of the country, and traditional histories report that Trisong Detsen decided to stage a debate between two of the main doctrinal rivals: proponents of Indian gradualist Buddhism and the Chan master Hashang Mahāyāna (Hva shang Ma hā yā na; Chinese: Heshang Moheyan), who advocated "sudden awakening."

According to Hashang Mahāyāna, buddhahood is a sudden flash of realization in which one awakens to one's innate buddha-nature. It results from meditative practices in which one halts the flow of thoughts and allows the

FIGURE 2.4. Statue of Padmasambhava, who, according to Tibetan tradition, played a pivotal role in the "first dissemination" of Buddhism to Tibet, in the Jokhang, Lhasa. Photo by John Powers.

buddha-nature to manifest spontaneously. Religious activities and rituals, prayer and ascetic practices, and moral behavior are irrelevant to this objective, and even constitute obstacles if one believes that they are a legitimate part of the path.

The opposition was headed by Kamalaśīla, a student of Śantarakṣita who followed the traditional Indian Mahāyāna paradigm, according to which sentient beings suffer because of the results of their previous actions, which were motivated by ignorance. This ignorance is primordial and has been cultivated and reinforced during countless lifetimes, and so it is impossible to eradicate it all at once. He likened the process of attaining buddhahood to climbing a mountain, which must be done step by step. The path to awakening also proceeds in stages, and the successful attainment of each stage is necessary before one can move on.

According to the most popular account of the debate, composed by the fourteenth-century scholar Pudön Rinchendrup (1290–1364), the Chinese faction was unable to counter Kamalaśīla's arguments and remained silent.[31] Trisong Detsen declared that the Indian side was victorious and that the doctrine preached by Hashang Mahāyāna was heretical and should be banned in Tibet. In accordance with the ground rules of the debate, the Chinese faction returned to China in disgrace, and Pudön reports that many of them committed suicide. Hashang Mahāyāna was so enraged by this turn of events that he later sent Chinese assassins to Tibet, who murdered Kamalaśīla by squeezing his kidneys.

Interestingly, there is also a Chinese account of the debate, composed by a monk named Wangxi, who asserts that the Chinese side was in fact victorious, but that Hashang Mahāyāna and his followers returned to China after the debate, and many of them were so upset about the degeneration of Buddhism in Tibet that they committed suicide. This version sounds rather dubious, because presumably, if they had won, they would have remained to spread their teachings, and they would have felt victorious rather than suicidal.[32]

This debate has been the subject of a wealth of scholarly research, much of which has focused on discrepancies in the various chronicles.[33] Pudön's classic version, which is the most widely accepted account among Tibetans, reports a grand debate held in Lhasa and presided over by Trisong Detsen, but Giuseppe Tucci contended that it was more likely to have occurred at Samye, the main center of Buddhism at the time. Later studies questioned whether the debate ever really took place because of the fundamental discrepancies between the purported accounts of the event and the fact that dossiers of the doctrines and practices of Kamalaśīla and Hashang Mahāyāna fail to mention many of the core teachings of their opponents, which raises doubts about whether they actually met in public debate. Added to these problems is the fact that neither spoke the other's language, and their respective religious environments were fundamentally different. Luis Gómez concludes that although there was probably a series of informal confrontations between Chinese and Indian Buddhist factions, the debate story is likely to be a later fabrication that summarized the many complexities of this process into a single winner-take-all contest with a decisive outcome.[34]

Despite these problems, there is no dispute among Tibetan Buddhists regarding either the historicity of the debate or its outcome. It is universally believed that the Chinese faction was soundly defeated and that its teachings were proscribed.[35] From this point onward, the Indian Mahāyāna gradualist paradigm reigned supreme in Tibet. The moral they derive from this story is that Chinese Buddhism in general is heretical and was banned by the religious king Trisong Detsen and never again exerted any significant influence in Tibet.[36] The importation of Buddhism continued, but there was no longer any question that India was to be the sole source. According to the fourteenth Dalai Lama, "Thus, the Buddhist teaching that spread to Tibet is just the stainless teaching of India and nothing else. The Tibetan lamas neither altered it nor mixed it with another religion."[37]

Because of the pervasiveness of Buddhist culture in Tibet, another implication for Tibetans is that the debate created a rift between their country and China and that this continued to widen as Indian influence in Tibet grew. Shakabpa indicates that the debate led to "the defeat of the Chinese system of Buddhism," following which it never again exerted any significant influence.[38] Thubten Jigme Norbu tells much the same story and states that "the Indian victory was resounding, and the Chinese left. From that moment all Chinese hopes of exerting religious influence were lost." He concludes that "the fact that Tibet looked to India rather than China for spiritual and intellectual guidance was most important."[39]

Chinese historians tell a different story. Most of the writers considered in this study fail even to mention the debate, but those who do allude to it only briefly and underplay its importance for Sino-Tibetan relations. Li Tieh-tseng asserts that during the reign of Trisong Detsen "a Chinese sage named Ho-shang Mahayana arrived in Tibet and converted the ignorant masses." He does not mention the story of the debate, but rather states that when Kamalaśīla arrived in Tibet, "he met with a great deal of opposition from Mahayana."[40] Li An-che does refer to the debate and admits that the Chinese side lost, but he explains away the defeat by asserting that it was not a fair contest because Hashang Mahāyāna's school focused solely on meditation and eschewed debate and involvement with language, and so it was "bound to lose; for by the

FIGURE 2.5. Monk in costume in 'cham dance, Phyang Monastery, Ladakh. Photo by John Powers.

logic of the school it does not indulge in verbal communication."[41] He does not attempt to explain the discrepancy between this stance and their participation in a public debate.

In Chinese sources that accept Wangxi's account, Hashang Mahāyāna is declared the winner of the debate, and the aftermath is characterized as a time of increasing Chinese influence in all areas of Tibetan society, including religion. As an example of this theme, a Chinese government publication entitled *China's Tibet* carried a description of Tibetan religious dances (*'cham*) in which a Hashang Mahāyāna character appears, accompanied by a group of disciples. It states that "the portrayal of these Han monks . . . signified that their enduring contribution is not forgotten in Tibet and the desire that all ethnic groups live in unity."[42] This interpretation is somewhat bizarre, however, because the Hashang Mahāyāna character is a comical figure with a large round face and exaggerated Chinese features and wearing Chinese brocade robes. He is clumsy and prone to injuring himself, and his disciples try to protect him while secretly laughing behind his back.[43] He and his disciples interject themselves into the performance from time to time, and their antics are hugely entertaining to the audience. For the Tibetan spectators, he is a symbol of the great rift between normative Tibetan Buddhism and Chinese Buddhism, while Indian Buddhist figures are portrayed as paradigms of authentic dharma.

The Fall of the Yarlung Dynasty

Trisong Detsen's successors continued to patronize Buddhism, and imperial dedication to the dharma reached its apogee during the reign of King Ralpachen (r. 815–836). He is regarded by Tibetan tradition as the third of the religious kings and as an incarnation of the buddha Vajrapāṇi. According to traditional accounts, he devoted huge amounts of money to the construction of temples and monasteries and sponsored Tibetans who traveled to India for religious instruction. He also invited Indian masters to Tibet. He is said to have displayed his devotion by having Buddhist monks sit on his outspread hair braids, indicating his subordination to religious authority. This affront to the royal dignity and his largesse in funding Buddhist activities led to a revolt among his advisors, who successfully plotted his assassination.[44]

After his death, his cousin Lang Darma (r. 838–842) ascended the throne. Traditional sources portray him as a devout adherent of Bön who viciously persecuted Buddhism, but early records indicate that the extent of his persecution was ordering some monks and nuns to return to lay life and withdrawing royal sponsorship for Buddhist institutions and practitioners. His reign was cut short by a Buddhist monk named Belgyi Dorje, who disguised himself as an actor in a performing troupe. He rode into the palace on a black horse and wearing a white cloak. During the entertainment, he performed a dance in which he placed an arrow in a bow and aimed it toward the king. Believing that it was part of the act, Lang Darma did not react, and Belgyi Dorje delivered a fatal shot. Belgyi Dorje escaped by riding the horse (which was white but had been covered with black soot) through a river and reversing his cloak, which was black on the other side. Thus, when the king's guards went looking for a man wearing a white cloak and riding a black horse, they passed by Belgyi Dorje, who was wearing a black cape and riding a white horse.[45]

The "Second Dissemination" of Buddhism in Tibet

Following Lang Darma's assassination, the dynasty crumbled, and for the next few centuries no single person or group was able to gain control over the whole Tibetan plateau. With the withdrawal of royal support, Buddhism declined, but there were still many adherents in Tibet. A revival began in the eleventh century when the kings of western Tibet invited the Indian scholar-monk Atiśa Dīpaṃkara Śrījñāna, 982–1054) to travel to Tibet in order to restore Buddhism and reform degenerate practices that had arisen there. At first, he was reluctant to accept, but in 1042, at the urging of his tutelary deity Tārā, he arrived in Guge in western Tibet. Although he initially intended to stay for only three years, he ended up remaining in Tibet until his death, and his mission exerted a profound and lasting influence on the character of Tibetan Buddhism. According to Thubten Jigme Norbu, "Atisha, perhaps more than anyone, gave Tibetan Buddhism, and the Tibetan people, the character they have today."[46]

Atiśa was an adherent of both traditional Indian Mahāyāna gradualist Buddhism and of tantra,[47] and he taught his Tibetan disciples a path that combined the two. He also stressed the need for intensive study and meditation and held that cenobitic monasticism is the ideal lifestyle for a person intent on liberation. Together with his disciple Dromdön he founded the first Tibetan order, the Kadampa. This school was later absorbed into the Gelukpa, which became the dominant tradition in Tibet.

In the accounts of traditional and contemporary Tibetan historians, Atiśa is a towering figure who transformed their country's religion and whose influence on their culture is incalculable. For modern authors he also represents the move toward Indian Buddhism and a corresponding rejection of Chinese traditions. He is credited with initiating the "second dissemination" (*phyi dar*)

FIGURE 2.6. Mural on cliff face near the outskirts of Lhasa, memorializing a spot where Atiśa is reported to have stepped on the way to the city. Photo by John Powers.

of Buddhism to Tibet and with firmly fixing its dominant paradigms. Whereas Shakabpa and Thubten Jigme Norbu devote five and six pages respectively to his mission and its impact, he is generally ignored by the Chinese historians we are considering in this study. Li Tieh-tseng only mentions in an endnote that Atiśa "visited" Tibet, but says nothing about his activities or influence.[48] Li An-che does not mention him at all, but does allude briefly to the second dissemination. He admits that Indian Buddhists played some part in this, but attempts to imply that Han monks were far more significant: "Buddhism was revived by Tibetan monks who took refuge in A-mdo through cooperation with Han monks there, and much later with scholars from India again. It was in commemoration of the Han contribution that Tibetan monks still wear a badge of Han monastic garments."[49] This is a curious assertion, and it is not entirely clear exactly what he is trying to imply. His comment is typical of Chinese authors writing about Tibet: even in cases in which there was no Chinese influence at all, they either try to twist events to make it appear that there was or invent historical events. Li provides no references, but he appears to be referring to a story in the *The Blue Annals*, in which three Tibetan monks fleeing Lang Darma's persecution of Buddhism were sheltered by an Uighur Buddhist monk, but this minor incident is not presented as being particularly important, whereas the role of Indian monks is discussed at great length.[50] As we saw above, from the ninth century onward, Tibetans rejected Chinese forms of Buddhism and accepted Indian Buddhism as normative. When the rulers of western Tibet attempted to revive Buddhism, they looked to India, and Atiśa's reputation as a great Indian scholar was central to the success of his mission. Moreover, anyone who has ever seen Tibetan monastic robes will know that they do not wear badges of any kind, and the configuration of their robes is derived from Indian texts on monastic discipline (vinaya), which are also normative for Chinese Buddhist monks.

Tibet and the Mongols

Tibet's state of political disunity persisted into the thirteenth century, when the country was annexed by the Mongol empire. Under the leadership of Genghis Khan (1162–1227), the Mongols emerged from the grasslands of their country and began a remarkable campaign of conquest. As their power grew, their soldiers gained a reputation for brutality and invincibility, and many rivals simply surrendered without a fight to avoid the massacres that commonly followed Mongol military victories. Beginning in 1207, Tibet began paying tribute to Genghis Khan; in exchange, he did not invade Tibet or interfere in its administration.

This situation changed after the death of Genghis in 1227, when Tibetans stopped paying the yearly tribute. His successor, Ogedai, sent a cavalry force under the command of his son Godan (d. 1251), which looted several monasteries and killed a number of monks. During this campaign, Godan gathered information about the military and political situation in Tibet; his field commanders' reports indicated that there was no central political authority and that the various regions of the country were ruled by relatively weak local hegemons. The greatest concentration of power lay in several major monasteries, and so Godan summoned a senior lama of the Sakya order named Sakya Pandita Günga Gyeltsen (1182–1251) to his court in Liangzhou (modern-day Gansu province) to formally submit the country to Mongol overlordship. Realizing that he had little choice, Sakya Pandita obeyed, and in 1247 arrived at the Mongol capitol with his nephews Pakpa Lodrö Gyeltsen (1235–1280) and Chakna and agreed that Tibet would become a part of the Mongol empire. He also gave religious teachings to the khan. In exchange for his obedience Godan appointed him viceregent of Tibet under ultimate Mongol authority. To convince his fellow Tibetans to accept this state of affairs, Sakya Pandita sent a letter back to Tibet in which he argued that the country had no chance of withstanding an assault by the Mongol armies and that the khan had expressed an interest in converting to Buddhism:

> The Prince has told me that if we Tibetans help the Mongols in matters of religion, they in turn will support us in temporal matters. In this way, we will be able to spread our religion far and wide. The Prince is just beginning to learn to understand our religion. If I stay longer, I am certain that I can spread the faith of the Buddha beyond Tibet and, thus, help my country. The Prince has allowed me to preach my religion without fear and has offered me all that I need. He tells me that it is in his hands to do good for Tibet and that it is in mine to do good for him.[51]

According to Tibetan accounts, this was the beginning of an arrangement referred to as the "priest-patron" (*mchod yon*) relationship, in which the Mongols agreed to leave Tibet fully under indigenous Tibetan control, and the Sakya hierarchs became the religious preceptors of the khans and rulers of Tibet. All of the Tibetan writers cited in this study who discuss this period agree that this was a special and religiously based association that developed from their shared religious convictions. They further assert that Tibet did not cede overlordship to China, because at that time the Mongols had not conquered China. This occurred in 1279, when Kubilai Khan added China to the already substantial Mongol empire. When Mongol power waned in the fourteenth century, Tibet regained its independence from Mongolia, although some elements in Tibet continued to have close ties with various Mongol tribes. China also regained its independence from Mongolia, several decades after Tibet and by different means.

The Tibetan exile government's official version of Tibetan-Mongol relations is outlined in a publication entitled *The Mongols and Tibet: A Historical Assessment of Relations between the Mongol Empire and Tibet*, which claims to be based on Chinese-language sources, although a number of its assertions are found only in Tibetan chronicles. According to its version of events, Godan does not appear to have been particularly concerned with military expansion; rather, his primary interest was in religion. After encountering Tibetan Buddhism during his military incursions, he "decided to seek a spiritual teacher to lead the Mongolians in a desirable moral direction. . . . [Godan] was convinced that no power in the world exceeded the might of the Mongols. However, he believed that religion was necessary in the interests of the next life. Thus he invited Sakya Pandita to Mongolia."[52]

This presents the Tibetan counterpart to the Chinese belief in the attractiveness and transformative power of Chinese culture. In the Tibetan version, a Mongol warlord with no previous interest in Buddhism developed a concern with the afterlife as a result of his contacts with Tibetans and decided to invite Sakya Pandita to his court, not to acquire new territory, but to beg him to become his religious preceptor and convert his people to Buddhism. The text also indicates that this turn of events had been predicted by Sakya Pandita's uncle, Sakyapa Jetsün Drakpa Gyeltsen, who had told him that in the final years of his life Mongolians would visit him and that he should accept their invitation because it would be an opportunity to benefit all sentient beings and promote Buddhism. Thus, Sakya Pandita's visit to Mongolia was not a desperate attempt to save his country from invasion prompted by a command by the Mongol khan, but a religious mission motivated by compassion and a selfless desire to spread the dharma.

After meeting Godan, Sakya Pandita gave him teachings on "Generating the Bodhisattva Mind" and other topics, following which he became "even more devoted to Buddhism and his teacher." The lama was invited to travel to other parts of China and spread his message, and when he was in Liangzhou, "many people . . . dreamt that Lord Manjushri . . . was giving teachings at Liangzhou."[53]

A central aspect of the Tibetan version of events is the claim that China was merely a part of the Mongolian empire and that the Mongols and Chinese were entirely separate and mutually antagonistic races.[54] Contemporary Chinese histories, however, assert that the Mongols are a nationality within China and that their empire was a Chinese one. In the Chinese accounts considered in this study, the brutality of the Mongol conquests is downplayed. Instead, their acquisition of territory is portrayed as a nationalistic program to unite the various races of China, who are said to have eagerly welcomed their incorporation into the motherland: "In the brief space of half a century, they succeeded in subjugating the independent regimes and local forces, thus bringing the people of all nationalities under a central government. This unification of the whole nation conformed to the advance of history and the desire of the nationalities."[55]

Not only did they eagerly embrace the inevitable advance of the Mongol armies into their territories (nor, apparently, did they mind the slaughter and destruction that generally followed), but the various nationalities (*minzu*) also benefited enormously due to the importation of Chinese culture and commerce with the central provinces. Wang and Suo also believe that Sakya Pandita saw himself as contributing to the process of unifying China's nationalities (which included Tibetans, who had come to view themselves as Chinese due to centuries of close contacts). Although they indicate that he was a member of the exploitive class who sought "to safeguard the interests of his own class," he is also portrayed as a Chinese patriot who "played a great role in unifying China. . . . Despite the fact that he was over sixty, he braved a thousand miles of hazardous journey and worked hard to forge direct political connection between Tibet and the Mongol royal house. . . . [He] was a man of firm character. Adhering to his political stand, he went to great pains to overcome what he considered mistaken ideas. Until his death . . . he devoted a good part of his life to the cause of national unification."[56]

Whereas Chinese writers assert that the territories of the Mongol empire were inherited by the succeeding Ming dynasty—and continued to devolve to succeeding dynasties and to China's current government—Tibetan works maintain that the agreement ceding authority was made between the Mongol khans and Tibetan lamas who served as their personal preceptors and that these relationships were not continued during the Han Chinese Ming dynasty, which succeeded the Mongol Yuan dynasty. The main problem with Chinese claims that later dynasties inherited Mongol lands is that the Mongol empire included vast areas of Asia and eastern Europe which were not in fact controlled by the Ming or Qing dynasties. The Mongols conquered most of Eurasia, and their territory extended from Lithuania in the west to Persia in the south. But although contemporary Chinese histories emphatically state that Tibet became part of Chinese territory as a result of Mongol conquests, they do not attempt to claim that Lithuanians are a minority nationality of China or that the Crimea is an inalienable part of Chinese territory.[57] Moreover, while Korea, for example, was administratively incorporated into neighboring Chinese provinces and ruled directly by the central government, Tibet remained an autonomous region whose internal affairs were administered by Tibetans.[58] By the same logic with which China later annexed Tibet, India could claim Australia as one of its provinces because both were once parts of the British empire, though under separate administrations, as were Tibet and central China during the Yuan dynasty.

According to the Chinese sources, however, the precedent is unambiguous: "The already multinational realm of China was re-unified, with Tibet organically included." Godan Khan's successor, Kubilai Khan, appointed Sakya Pandita's successor, Pakpa, as the "regional ruler under the court of Beijing."[59] In an attempt to explain away the religious dimension of the priest-patron relationship, Li Tieh-tsung asserts that the arrangement was a pretense by the khans to subjugate the Tibetans:

Kublai Khan found the warlike Tibetans a difficult people to rule, and resolved to reduce them to a condition of docility through the influence of religion. Buddhism was selected as the religion best cal-

culated to tame the wild tribesmen of Tibet. . . . The extraordinary
tolerance that the court extended to the lamas had the effect of ena-
bling the latter to sap the resistance of the bellicose Tibetans. Eventually the Tibetan bloodthirstiness was converted into a passion for
spiritual satisfaction. Thus, through the religious link between
China and Tibet, China was able to exercise a dominant influence
over her vassal state.[60]

Thus, it would appear that the Tibetan sources are mistaken in thinking
that Sakya Pandita and his successors converted the Mongols to Buddhism; in
fact, the Mongols—who, interestingly, were not Buddhists themselves at that
time—decided that of all available religions Buddhism would best serve to
render the Tibetans docile, and so they actually converted the Tibetans, even
though they were already Buddhists.

All the Chinese sources considered here agree that from this point onward
China exercised unbroken sovereignty over Tibet. Some admit that during
short periods in later centuries Tibetans may have occasionally acted indepen-
dently in internal affairs, but this was due only to the forbearance of Chinese
emperors, who sometimes "left the Tibetans alone to manage their affairs so
long as [their] authority was not challenged." Even during the reigns of the
powerful fifth and thirteenth Dalai Lamas, "after all, the Dalai Lama's authority,
even if it resembled or suggested sovereignty, was given by the emperor." During the Mongol period, the "figurehead Sakya priest-kings" may have exercised
limited local authority, but ultimately they danced to the Mongols' tune.[61]

Not surprisingly, the Tibetan historical narrative reads quite differently. In
their discussions of this period, Shakabpa and Dawa Norbu carefully distin-
guish between Mongols and Chinese and cite instances in which the two
groups were at odds. An example cited by Shakabpa is Sakya Pandita's lobbying
of Godan Khan to desist from throwing large numbers of Chinese into a river.
This was being done to reduce the Chinese population so as to negate the
potential Chinese threat to Mongol power.[62]

According to Dawa Norbu, Sakya Pandita was "invited" to visit Godan, and
he "converted the emperor to Lamaism, and became his personal Lord of Refuge." He does not mention that he also submitted to Mongol control, nor that
his successors became rulers as a result of being appointed by Mongol khans.
Instead, he states that Pakpa became the "national mentor of the Imperial
Court" and that this post was inherited by his successors, who "ruled over
Tibet." There is no indication in Dawa Norbu's account that the Tibetans acknowledged Mongol overlordship, and he asserts that during this time, "Tibet's
cultural relations with India were stronger than those with China." He further

cites a number of internecine Tibetan political disputes that occurred during this time without any intervention by the Mongol Yuan government, and he concludes that "the emperors at Peking did not intervene in these political struggles, because Tibet was not under their domain."[63]

The Mongols and Tibet is even more emphatic: it asserts that the priest-patron relationship was established exclusively between the Mongol khans and their Tibetan preceptors, and that Chinese subjects of the empire played no role in it:

> An analysis of the nature of the Mongolian empire and of relations between Tibetans and the Mongols reveals the uniqueness of the relationship that developed between the Mongol Khans and Tibetan spiritual leaders. It also refutes any contention that the Tibeto-Mongolian relationship could in any way be interpreted as being a relationship between China and Tibet, much less that it constituted an annexation of Tibet by China. In the first place, the Mongolians were and are a race distinct from the Chinese; and their empire was a Mongol empire, not a Chinese empire. . . . Relations established between Mongol rulers and Tibetans pre-dated those established between the Mongols and the Chinese by the conquest of the latter, and were entirely unrelated. This, the review of history contained in this paper . . . conclusively demonstrates.[64]

Thubten Jigme Norbu, like other Tibetan authors who discuss this period, skirts the issue of Mongol overlordship and ignores the role that the Mongol military had in establishing the relationship between the Sakya lamas and the Mongol khans. He also characterizes Sakya Pandita's summons to the Mongol court as an "invitation": "So great was his learning and his reputation for spiritual attainment that he received an invitation from the Mongolian chief Godan. . . . While at the Mongol court, the Sakya Grand Lama won ready recognition by the force of his personality and the power of his teaching. . . . The establishment of friendly relations with their powerful northern neighbors put Sakya's supremacy beyond question."[65]

Thubten Jigme Norbu characterizes the Mongols as a culturally and religiously backward people who were uplifted by their friendly contacts with Tibet, and views Kubilai Khan as a man who examined various religions, but was converted by Pakpa, who "won him over to Tibetan Buddhism, not once admitting that he was anything but the Emperor's equal."[66] He states that Kubilai "established him as the political ruler of Tibet," but gives no indication that Tibet had ceded ultimate sovereignty to the Mongol empire. Rather, he asserts that the Mongols provided Tibet with "protection," while the Sakya lamas reciprocated by serving as their religious preceptors. Both sides saw their relation as one of "political equality," and neither had political authority over the other.

Norbu's version of the Mongol-Tibet relationship is contradicted by both Chinese and Tibetan accounts of the period, which clearly indicate that the Sakya hierarchs ceded sovereignty over Tibet to the Mongol khans and that Tibet's subordination continued with their respective successors. Shakabpa, however, does acknowledge that Sakya Pandita surrendered sovereignty over Tibet, but he also emphasizes the special bond between the Mongol rulers and the Sakya lamas, who "won the hearts of the Mongols." In common with Dawa Norbu and Thubten Jigme Norbu, he cites the story that Pakpa requested that Kubilai always occupy a lower seat than he on public occasions to demonstrate his inferior status; Kubilai responded that this would diminish his authority with his ministers and vassals, and so both agreed that when he was receiving religious instruction he would occupy a lower position, but in public ceremonies Pakpa would sit on a lower throne. For Tibetan writers, this arrangement implies a roughly equal status between the two, but Dawa Norbu believes that the religious dimension took precedence and that both recognized Pakpa's ultimate superiority. Shakabpa, however, appears to believe that the two were equals. Throughout his discussion of this period, he states several times that Tibetans exercised full control over internal affairs and that the Mongols recognized their authority and did not interfere with their administration. Ultimately, it was "a relationship based on mutual cooperation and respect," a "unique central Asian concept" that "cannot be defined in Western political terms."[67]

Shakabpa stresses the notion that China and Mongolia were separate entities that were involved in a bitter conflict for control of territory, and not two Chinese ethnic groups who perceived themselves as part of the Chinese motherland. He also asserts that during the Mongol Yuan dynasty, "the actual administration of Tibet remained in Tibetan hands."[68] The Mongol khans never asked the Tibetans to give up their autonomy, and the Tibetans never offered to do so. Rather, the Tibetans entered into a special and religiously based association to avoid conflict and to ensure that they would be left alone to practice their religion in peace. Moreover, it was founded on common religious beliefs, which were not shared by the Han Chinese Ming rulers who overthrew the Mongols. So, although they may have occasionally maintained the "fiction" of continuing as patrons, their claims were not legitimate. The priest-patron relationship was revived by the Manchu Qing rulers, who succeeded the Ming dynasty and who patronized Tibetan Buddhism, but all Tibetan sources agree that the connection definitively ended when the last Qing emperor was overthrown by the secular Nationalists in 1911. Because they were not Tibetan Buddhists, they could not participate in this arrangement.

The Tibetan authors' belief in the equality of the two parties in the priest-patron relationship reflects their assumptions about the role of Buddhism in Tibet's interactions with its neighbors. Because of the importance they ascribe to Buddhism and the profound effect it has had on their society, they tend to view the world through a lens colored by Buddhist perspectives. All the Tibetan writers we are considering in this study agree that the Mongol khans and their preceptors, the Sakya lamas, were engaged in a religious affiliation that worked to the advantage of both and that the two parties were ultimately interested in the promotion and dissemination of Buddhism. The Mongols benefited by receiving religious instruction from their court chaplains, and the Sakya lamas were able to gain influence in Tibet and Mongolia and to spread the dharma. What Tibetans generally ignore is the fact that the arrangement may well have benefited the Sakyapas—it certainly brought them enormous wealth and political power—but it left ultimate authority over Tibetan affairs in the hands of foreigners.

This pattern persisted during later centuries, particularly during the period when Tibet was ruled by the Dalai Lamas. Following the unification of Tibet under the authority of the fifth Dalai Lama, Ngawang Losang Gyatso (1617–1682), in 1642, every subsequent Tibetan ruler relied on foreign patronage and military protection to support and maintain his power. The "Great Fifth" Dalai Lama was installed as sovereign of a unified Tibet by the Mongol ruler Gushri Khan, who used his armies to defeat the Dalai Lama's rivals. Throughout his life he continued to rely on Mongol power to support his reign and keep his enemies at bay.

As Buddhist monks, the Dalai Lamas (like the Sakyapas before them) were generally reluctant to maintain powerful armies or personally order the use of force, although they were happy to have others do their fighting for them. So, under their regime, Tibet became militarily weak and thus vulnerable to attack. From the time of the Sakya regency, no Tibetan ruler held power without at least the implicit military backing of a foreign supporter. As a result, Tibet became dependent on the kindness of strangers and unable to defend itself. The most important of Tibet's patrons was China, which was called on on several occasions to send its forces to defend Tibet against foreign aggression. When China itself was weak, instead of building up its own armies Tibet looked to other foreign saviors in times of need. Because of this situation, even though Tibetan governments generally controlled Tibet's domestic affairs with little outside interference, they were reluctant to gainsay China's claim to sovereignty over their country. This created a murky situation in which indigenous Tibetan governments led by the Dalai Lamas or their regents were effectively rulers of their country but were unable to officially declare their independence from China and risk losing its military support. Thus, China could continue to proclaim its overlordship on the international stage without fear of being contradicted by Tibet, and, not surprisingly, other foreign governments accepted China's assertions. Tibetans commonly characterize the priest-patron arrangement as an agreement between equals, but in fact it was a relationship of dependence and subordination. It may have been beneficial to the Sakya lamas, but its legacy was a state of weakness and dependency on foreign patrons. When, in the twentieth century, Tibet was no longer able to find a military savior to rescue it from military aggression by its former protector, it easily fell to China's army.

In Tibet's dealings with its more powerful neighbors, the priest-patron relationship became the model for its foreign affairs policy, and later governments also sought China's protection from their enemies and its financial support, believing that this was freely offered and had no strings attached. The Tibetans assumed that the gifts and military aid they received were acts of devotion by their religious clients that did not imply that the recipients were in an inferior position. But Chinese records indicate that the emperors and those who chronicled their reigns had a different view. They conceived of China as the cultural and military center of the world; tributary states came to the emperor's court overwhelmed by its grandeur and received gifts from him in exchange for their submission to imperial authority. According to Thomas Heberer:

> These self-images not only constitute a self-contained sense of identity, they serve also as a transethnic cultural consciousness that considers all groups who lie outside the cultural "center" to be, according to such logic, culturally inferior. Because Chinese central power and culture have continued for two thousand years, traditional ethnocentric notions dominate the patterns of behavior toward non-Han people and the expectations of how they should behave toward the central power. Imperial China understood itself as the cultural center of the world and its culture as the culture of all humanity. Accordingly, in traditional perceptions it was acknowledged that numerous other people had settled well-defined areas, but only one people was entrusted with the mandate of ruling humanity. This people inhabited the earth's epicenter, the "Middle Kingdom."[69]

There was no possibility of any foreign ruler engaging China in a relationship of equality, and the emperor's largesse was conditional on his vassals' acceptance of his overlordship. The Tibetans chose to ignore this aspect of Chinese imperial policy, and assumed that the priest-patron relationship conferred no rights of sovereignty on the patrons who supported them militarily and materially. The conflict between these two irreconcilable views is still evident in the discussions of this arrangement by contemporary Tibetan and Chinese authors, and neither side appears to understand or acknowledge the perspective of the other.

Relations with China during the Ming Dynasty (1368–1644)

As we have seen, Sakya hegemony over Tibet was dependent on Mongol armies. When Mongol power waned in the fourteenth century, the Sakyapas were unable to retain their position of authority, and in 1358 were overthrown by Jangchup Gyeltsen (1302–1364) of the Phakmo Drupa branch of the Kagyu order, who had been one of their governors. Within a short time he extended his authority over most of the Tibetan plateau. The Mongols were unable to do anything about this because of their own military weakness; ten years later they were conquered by Han Chinese, who subsequently founded the Ming dynasty. In an attempt to assert an authority they were unable to exercise in fact, the Mongol court recognized Jangchup Gyeltsen as their viceroy in 1351. During his reign, he attempted to reverse the dependence on foreign powers that had characterized Sakya rule. He instituted a program of protonationalism that hearkened back to the traditions of the Yarlung dynasty's religious kings, although he refrained from openly antagonizing the Mongols by declaring that Tibet was no longer a vassal state. After the Ming dynasty was founded, he also refused to acknowledge subordination to it, but the Ming rulers still claimed Tibet as a part of their territory. As Goldstein notes, however, the Ming emperors "exerted no administrative authority over the area," but still sought influence by giving presents and titles to prominent Buddhist teachers.[70]

One way the Ming emperors attempted to influence Tibetan affairs was by encouraging powerful Buddhist leaders to participate in the Chinese tribute system. According to Chinese imperial mythology, everyone who was a tributary explicitly acknowledged subservience to the emperor and vassalage to China, but in reality, the system was a sophisticated bribe that was designed to purchase loyalty. Assuming that their superior civilization and technology were attractive to their "barbarian" neighbors, Chinese rulers invited them to come to the imperial court and acknowledge their inferiority and subservience;

in exchange, they received gifts and grandiose titles. In this process, the barbarians would "come and be transformed" (*lai hua*), that is, they would naturally be drawn to Chinese culture and manners and be impressed by the superior morality of China's leaders.[71] Through such contact they would become more and more sinicized and eventually come to view themselves as Chinese. At this point, they would no longer pose a threat to the Middle Kingdom and could be integrated into it. They would adopt the Chinese language and script and begin performing Chinese rituals. In traditional Chinese views, the main difference between Chinese and barbarians was not race but culture, and once barbarians became assimilated they ceased to be barbarians. As June Dreyer notes, "From their ethnocentric view . . . the Han do not believe that the culture and territorial claims of minority groups are equal to that of the superior Han civilization."[72]

The common understanding of tribute payments is that vassals pay a regular indemnity in exchange for protection or to avoid being invaded by a superior military power. But the Chinese system was not this sort of medieval protection racket; instead, it involved complex economic exchanges that were connected to imperial myths about China's place in the world. These held that the emperor of China ruled over the Middle Kingdom, which was located at the center of the known world (in the central Chinese provinces); he was the "Son of Heaven" (*tianzi*), whose moral authority and divinely ordained power conferred a mandate to rule over the entire earth (referred to as "all under heaven," *tianxia*). According to the *Book of Poetry*, "Under the vast Heaven, there is no land that is not the monarch's."[73] China was the center of world civilization, and indeed the only civilized country. Lands beyond the periphery of China did not possess different cultures; the options were either Chinese culture or no culture at all. Barbarians (*fan*; the standard Chinese term for non-Chinese peoples) could, however, become civilized by adopting Chinese culture. In comparing China with its barbarian neighbors, Yu Yu proclaims:

> In all the world, wherever the light of sun and moon reach, the Chinese occupy the middle ground. There the vital energy (*qi*) that acts upon living things is full and straight. The people have a well-tempered nature and are intelligent; the land has rich and various products; thus it gives rise to sages and wise men, who continually propagate laws and doctrines, remedying the defects specific to the times. . . . China in distant ancient times was in many respects like the barbarians of today. There are those who make their dwellings in nests and caves; there are those who bury their dead without raising a grave-mound; there are those who ball their food together with

their hands. . . . Their lands are marginal, the [*qi*] impeded; no sages
or wise men are produced, and there is no one to reform the old
ways; they are places where imperial instructions and admonitions
are not accepted, and the rites and duties do not reach.[74]

There was no possibility of barbarians possessing anything that could be
needed by the emperor, and so tribute missions brought items for the amusement of him and his court. These might include local handicrafts or exotic
animals, and were generally of little monetary value. In exchange, however,
tributaries received commercially valuable goods from the emperor, such as
silks, porcelains, and precious metals. These could be sold for large profits in
the barbarian lands, and so many people chose to endure the humiliation of
performing the kowtow in front of the emperor and acknowledging his overlordship to gain profit and power in their own regions.[75] Tributaries who refrained from attacking China were also safe from Chinese military incursions
and were generally left alone to manage their internal affairs, provided that
their territories remained stable and so long as they posed no threat to China.

Ming dynasty chronicles report that tribute missions by Tibetan lamas
were so numerous that they clogged the roads into China and placed heavy
burdens on local people who had to supply them. They also caused financial
difficulties for the Ming court, which had to present them with expensive gifts
and provide for them in the Chinese capital. The exchange was so beneficial
to the Tibetans that in some cases, a particular monastery would send missions
one after the other. As a result, the Ming court issued a decree mandating that
a particular Tibetan lama or monastery could send only one tribute mission
every three years. As this story indicates, the tribute missions were not an
onerous burden to the Tibetans, but a source of revenue, and although individual Tibetans came as tributaries during the Ming dynasty, there is no evidence in either Chinese or Tibetan records that any Tibetan ruler did so, nor
that any of them ever acknowledged himself as a vassal of China during the
Ming dynasty.[76]

The Chinese writers we are considering all agree, however, that during the
Ming period Tibet remained a vassal under the direct control of the Chinese
imperial government. Wei Jing[77] asks rhetorically, "Did the Ming and Qing
dynasties continue to exercise the sovereignty over Tibet established by the
Yuan dynasty?" and answers, "Yes. The Ming Dynasty . . . basically inherited
the administrative arrangements of the Yuan Dynasty." According to *Tibet:
Myth vs. Reality*, "It is untrue that ties with the rest of China were severed
under the Ming. . . . This allegation does not conform with the facts." The notion that the ties the Mongols forged with Tibet ended with their overthrow by

the Ming is said to be a "historically false argument" and credited to unnamed forces "in the United States and elsewhere—when the disintegration of multinational China was pursued by the foreign power concerned in its own interest."[78] As evidence for their claims of continued Chinese sovereignty, this and several of the other Chinese works cite a number of official titles that were given by Chinese emperors to Tibetans, a practice that they claim indicates that the emperor of China remained emperor of Tibet, both in theory and in reality. According to Li Tieh-tseng, these "hereditary titles tended to consolidate Chinese power by their psychological effect upon the Tibetan mind."[79]

In response, Tibetan writers cite a number of official titles that were given by the Dalai Lamas and other Tibetan officials to Chinese emperors and Chinese officials. They assert that official meetings often involved an exchange of titles, and the Tibetan sources characterize this practice as a form of diplomatic protocol, with no ramifications for Tibet's status. Shakabpa states that during the Ming dynasty, "the relationship between Tibet and China is clearly indicated by the special treatment and elegant titles bestowed on even minor lamas, and the refusal of invitations by prominent ruling lamas, who would send a disciple as a substitute. It seems obvious that the Ming Emperors viewed Tibet as an independent 'Kingdom of the West.' " According to Shakabpa's analysis, during this period the Chinese government was contending with various Mongol tribes, and because Tibet was politically stable, China was content to have "little contact" with it. He asserts that the real reason behind the cordial attitude toward Tibet and the conferral of titles was that the Ming emperors hoped that the Dalai Lamas would use their religious influence with the Mongols and convince them to stop attacking China.[80] He concludes that "the allegation that the Chinese Emperors of the Ming dynasty . . . inherited claim to Tibet from their Mongol predecessors is not valid historically."[81] *The Mongols and Tibet* makes an even stronger claim:

> The current Chinese allegation . . . that Mongol conquests . . . could in any way give today's People's Republic of China *any* legitimate claims is nothing short of absurd. Equally unfounded is China's claim that the granting of titles and seals is sufficient evidence to prove its historical sovereignty over neighbouring countries and rulers. These allegations are tenable only if Beijing's thorough rewriting of history—in an attempt to legitimize its own aggression and political ambitions—is accepted. But such distortions of history can no longer go unchallenged.[82]

Dawa Norbu contends that during the later Yuan dynasty and the succeeding Ming, Tibet was ruled solely by Tibetans and that the Ming emperors were unable to interfere with its internal affairs. As evidence for this, he cites the fact that no action was taken by the Mongols when Sakya rule was overthrown by the Phakmo Drupas, nor did the Ming court interfere when they were conquered by the Rinpung rulers in 1435. The Rinpung in turn were overthrown by the kings of Tsang, who ruled Tibet from 1566 to 1642. With each change of regime, the Chinese court simply acknowledged the victors by bestowing on them extravagant (and unrequested) titles. Norbu concludes that despite Tibet's internal instability, Chinese rulers were unable to exercise any influence "because Tibet was not under their domain."[83] This is also Richardson's view; he asserts that "there is no substance in the claim of some Chinese writers that Tibet was in unbroken subordination to China from the time of the Yuan dynasty. . . . There is no evidence that [the Phakmo Drupas, the Rinpungs, or the kings of Tsang] made an act of submission, even of the most formal nature, to the Ming emperors."[84]

Wang and Suo, however, believe that during the Ming period China remained in control of Tibetan affairs and that their close relationship brought Chinese culture and economic benefits to Tibet: "As a result the economy flourished as never before and the Tibetans' relationship with other nationalities of the Chinese nation improved."[85] Interestingly, Wang and Suo, the editors of *Tibet: Myth vs. Reality*, Shakabpa, and Dawa Norbu agree on one thing: that misconceptions about the relationships between Mongol and Chinese rulers and Tibetan lamas are the result of misconceptions fostered by foreigners with ulterior motives. The notion that the sinister machinations of unnamed imperialists are the cause of what they consider to be misunderstandings is found in every Chinese source we are considering in this study and in some of the Tibetan ones. According to Ya, for example:

> There existed something special in the modern and contemporary history of Tibet: the subordinate status of the Tibetan local government under the central governments of the motherland. The fact that such a relationship should have become a problem was due to the erroneous attitudes of a handful of Tibetans. Influenced by the imperialists who fomented national discord and by the separatist faction they fostered over a long period of time, these people, with no sense of righteousness, stood for Tibet's separation from the motherland. Their attitude was not only utterly incompatible with the interests of the Chinese nation as a whole, but was also unacceptable to the Tibetan people themselves.[86]

In the Chinese sources, the main villains are unnamed Americans and British (and sometimes Indians) who are seeking to separate Tibet from the motherland so that they can seize it for themselves, but it is generally not very clear exactly what the Tibetan authors are trying to imply in their denunciations of foreigners. Shakabpa, for example, blames foreign imperialists for misconceptions about Tibet. His main villains are the British government of India and China. He implies that they acted in collusion to obscure the truth about Tibet and deceive the world: "It was the policy of the British government of India and the Manchu Court of China to isolate Tibet from the rest of the world, which gave China the means by which to paint a false picture of Tibet's international position and to obstruct Tibet from revealing its political independence."[87] He does not indicate exactly how they did this, nor does he try to explain what the British government's motives might have been or what benefit it may have received from its purported intrigues.

Dawa Norbu also blames misconceptions about Tibet on unnamed foreigners, for example, when he objects to the notion that the relation between the Sakya lamas and their Mongol patrons had a political dimension. He contends that "the Buddhist Emperors of China respected the High Lamas of Tibet, and certainly did not use them as political puppets.... This reading seems disastrously wrong."[88] He also claims that prior to the advent of British colonialism in South Asia, China and Tibet established "a military dependency between an imperial power ... and a non-coercive regime (Buddhist Tibet). The operation of such a relationship assumed relative capacity and willingness on the part of Imperial China to provide military protection to Tibet when and if necessary."[89] In Norbu's view, China had no interest in acquiring Tibetan territory and freely gave its military aid, but their long-standing relationship was undermined and eventually destroyed by British colonialism, which led the Chinese to feel threatened by this expansionist empire. For its part, Tibet decided to close its borders to foreigners in an attempt to keep the British at bay.

Norbu's reading of events during this time is strongly colored by Buddhist assumptions; he views the sponsorship of Tibetan lamas by the Mongols and Ming as nothing more than a sincere act of devotion by Buddhist rulers who supported their spiritual preceptors because of their religious bonds, and who had no ulterior motives whatsoever. Foreigners who imply that there were are either ignorant of the facts or deliberately falsifying the truth.

The Qing Dynasty

Despite having been overthrown by the Ming rulers, the Mongols remained a potent factor in Central Asian politics. Although their military forces were now divided along tribal groupings and controlled by a number of chieftains, the Ming feared that they might once again unite and threaten the Middle Kingdom, and so during their reign they worked to undermine both Mongol power and unity. Although Chinese relations with the Mongols were problematic, Tibetan lamas had close ties with a number of Mongol leaders. A firm bond between Mongols and Tibetans had been forged when Yönden Gyatso (1589–1617), a grandson of Altan Khan, was identified as the fourth Dalai Lama. This event opened the door to missionizing by Tibetan Buddhists, and in the late sixteenth to early seventeenth century, the Western Mongols were converted to the Gelukpa creed. The Eastern Mongols had already been converted in 1578.

In 1638 the leader of the Qoshot Mongols, Gushri Khan (1582–1655), traveled to Tibet and met the fifth Dalai Lama, Ngawang Losang Gyatso (1617–1682). The Dalai Lama bestowed titles on him and some of his subordinates, and the Mongols in turn gave titles to the Dalai Lama and other Tibetan leaders. It is evident from his account of the visit that the Dalai Lama perceived it as an opportunity to acquire a powerful patron and to missionize the Mongols. One outcome of the visit was a decision by Gushri Khan and the Dalai Lama to renew the priest-patron relationship that had been established between Kubilai Khan and Pakpa in the thirteenth century. Gushri Khan probably viewed this arrangement as a way to enhance his prestige among the Mongols. By invoking the glories of the Mongol Yuan dynasty, he hoped to unite the now fragmented Mongols and restore their former power. His alliance with the Dalai Lama gave him a new status as the patron of the most prominent reincarnate Gelukpa lama, and the Dalai Lama in turn now had access to one of the most powerful military forces in Central Asia.

In the following years, Gushri Khan's army fought a series of battles against the Dalai Lama's main rivals, during which all were defeated. In 1642 Ngawang Losang Gyatso was installed as the ruler of Tibet, and Gushri Khan gave himself the title of King of Tibet. Unlike his predecessor Kubilai, however, he decided to move to Tibet, and for the rest of his life spent part of each year there. Our Tibetan writers assert that he was subordinate to the Dalai Lama and seldom interfered in Tibetan affairs, but the Chinese authors who discuss this period claim that he was a vassal of China, and so by extension, Tibet was also subject to China.

During the Ming dynasty, the Mongol tribes remained a potent military force, and a number of Mongol chieftains hoped to once again unite them under a single leadership and reconquer their former territories. This was one of the great fears of the Ming rulers, who worked to foster disunity and to counter the potential threat the Mongols presented. When the Ming dynasty was overthrown by the Manchus in 1644, the new regime immediately began to forge alliances with the Mongols. A part of this process involved courting the Dalai Lama and other Tibetan clerics, who had a high level of influence with the Mongols. Most Mongol Buddhists identified themselves as Gelukpas, and so the Manchus sought to establish themselves as the patrons of the Dalai Lamas.

In 1648 the Manchu emperor Shunchi sent envoys to the fifth Dalai Lama, inviting him to travel to the royal court in Beijing. Tibetan records of the time, particularly the Dalai Lama's autobiography, indicate that he decided to accept because it presented an opportunity for conversion of the Manchus to the Gelukpa branch of Tibetan Buddhism. His autobiography states that when he received the invitation, he remembered a prophecy: that a reincarnate lama who had been born in the Ü province of central Tibet (his own birthplace) would convert "China, Tibet, and Mongolia" to the Gelukpa faith. He believed he was that lama. In traditional Tibetan historiography, the emperors of China were conceived as incarnations of Mañjuśrī, the buddha of wisdom and the complement in Mahāyāna buddhology to Avalokiteśvara, the buddha of compassion. As we have seen, the Dalai Lamas are believed by Tibetan Buddhists to be incarnations of Avalokiteśvara, and in his autobiography the fifth Dalai Lama indicates that he saw the invitation as an opportunity to work with an

FIGURE 2.7. Statue of the "Great Fifth" Dalai Lama, Ngawang Losang Gyatso, in the Potala, Lhasa. Photo by John Powers.

incarnation of Mañjuśrī in spreading the dharma. His account of the journey, and those of other Tibetans, focus on its religious aspects: the emphasis is on holy places he visited, teachings and initiations he gave, and links between his actions and Tibetan mythology. But in the account by Sanggye Gyatso, the Dalai Lama's meeting with the emperor is barely mentioned. From the Tibetan perspective, this was a religious mission, not a visit of state.

In Chinese accounts of the visit, however, the meeting is highlighted and the primary concern is with issues of protocol. They report that the emperor initially proposed to travel beyond the Great Wall to greet the Dalai Lama, and that although some of his retainers (probably Manchus) agreed with this idea, others (probably Chinese) argued that such an action would effectively recognize the Dalai Lama as being of equal stature to the emperor. In the end, he decided not to go, but instead sent the royal prince Shisai and his uncle Jigalang to greet the Dalai Lama. The Dalai Lama's account indicates that he saw their visit as official recognition of his status as the supreme sovereign of the independent country of Tibet. In his words, the imperial greeting implied that "I am the legal King [of Tibet], of whom there was not the like in Tibet."[90]

The emperor also intended to enquire after the Dalai Lama's health when he arrived, which was interpreted by some of his retainers as implying equality of status, and so they counseled against it. The emperor decided to accept this advice, and although the Dalai Lama was greeted with great pomp and ceremony it was carefully choreographed by the Chinese in a way that subtly implied his inferiority to the emperor. The Dalai Lama's account, however, is not concerned with the minutiae of Chinese imperial protocol; he appears to have assumed that he was being welcomed as the ruler of a sovereign state. As Zahiruddin Ahmad argues, "To the Chinese officials, the all-important thing is protocol: whether or not the Emperor should go outside the Great Wall to meet the Dalai Lama; whether or not the Emperor should enquire after the Dalai Lama's health. To the Dalai Lama the visit was simply the establishing of a 'working relationship' between the Emperor and himself for the purpose of converting 'China, Tibet, and Mongolia' to the [Gelukpa] creed."[91] There were also political ramifications for him, of course, and he was clearly aware of the potential benefits of forging close ties with the new rulers of China and converting them. As we have seen, from the time of the Sakyapa hierarchs, Tibetan rulers (or aspiring rulers) routinely sought foreign patronage either to establish or to support their power. The Dalai Lama already had strong support from the Mongols; Manchu patronage would further strengthen his position.

From the Manchu perspective, the Dalai Lama's visit presented an opportunity to confirm the emperor as a supporter of Tibetan Buddhism and as the successor of Kubilai Khan. From this point onward, the Manchu emperors

worked to insert themselves into the priest-patron relationship and created a
state cult that emphasized the notion that the emperor was an incarnation of
the buddha Mahākāla, the wrathful aspect of Avalokiteśvara and the patron
buddha of the Mongols. Early in their reign, the Manchus constructed a massive temple complex at their capital, Mukden, devoted to Mahākāla, and its
symbolism sought to emphasize this association. This became part of the mythological justification of the Manchu dynasty, and was apparently intended to
convince the Mongols to accept the Manchu emperors as the successors to the
early Mongol khans.[92] As Ahmad argues, "Tibet plays only an incidental part
in the history of the Mongol and Manchu Empires."[93] The main players in the
power struggles in Central Asia were the Manchus, the Chinese, and the Mongols; the Tibetans were of consequence only because of their close ties with
the Mongols.

In the early period of their rule, the Manchus faced the problem of being
a foreign dynasty that had usurped the Han Chinese Ming. In common with
previous conquerors, they sought political legitimacy by claiming that the Ming
had become corrupt and had thus lost the "mandate of Heaven." Unless they
had been favored by Heaven, they argued, the Manchus would not have been
able to establish their rule. In the following centuries they became increasingly
sinicized and emperors adopted Chinese names for their reigns, the Manchus
moved the capital to Beijing, and Chinese became the official language of
statecraft. Through these means, they worked to allay the perception among
their Chinese citizens that they were foreign usurpers, and to gain the support
of the ever-dangerous Mongols, they cast themselves as patrons of the Dalai
Lamas and stressed the association of the Manchu emperor and Mahākāla.[94]

According to the Chinese writers considered in this study, however, when
the Manchu Qing dynasty overthrew the Han Chinese Ming, this was merely
another example of one of China's various nationalities temporarily gaining
ascendancy, but they are unanimous in asserting that this was a *Chinese* dynasty, and not an example of a foreign power conquering China.[95] Furthermore,
the new dynasty inherited all the territory that had been controlled by previous
emperors, even those areas that China no longer had the power to actually
administer. According to Li Tieh-tseng, "Up to the end of the Ch'ing [Qing]
dynasty, the Government of China never waived any sovereign rights in Tibet.
Indeed, even on the eve of the revolution, they were arguing with the British
Government over the rights they had exercised and claimed still to exercise,
not only in Tibet, but also in Nepal and Bhutan."[96]

This comment illustrates some of the problems with consulting only Chinese sources, as Li does. First, as we have seen, they assume that the emperor
of China has dominion over the entire world, even those areas that have never

been visited by Chinese. In addition, any time an area came under direct Chinese control, it forever lost any possibility of separating from the motherland, and all of its territories, even ones that it no longer actually controlled, devolved to China and could legitimately be claimed by it. Thus, because Tibet had at several points in its past controlled areas of Nepal, Bhutan, and the Indian state of Jammu and Kashmir, successive Chinese governments felt justified in claiming them as part of their territory, a practice that continues today, even though Tibet had not administered them for centuries prior to the Chinese takeover in the 1950s.

Li, however, appears to be unaware of these difficulties with official Chinese records. At the beginning of both of his books he states that he relied solely on these sources because they are more accurate than Tibetan, Indian, or Nepalese records. He asserts that Tibetan sources are unreliable because several Western scholars who have used them arrived at different dates for certain events and, he adds, "Tibetans lack a sense of history as understood by other peoples. [Their historical works] are histories of a religion rather than the chronicles of a people." He then avers that Indian records cannot be relied on because the *Cambridge History of India* states that they are sometimes inaccurate. Apparently satisfied that he has demonstrated the unreliability of these sources, Li goes on to say that the only viable option for a historian concerned with the "truth" is to ignore everything except for Chinese records: "Chinese records thus become . . . the only foreign sources from which we can draw information having a bearing on the status of Tibet. Western writers on Tibet have, as a rule, preferred Chinese records, the accuracy and authenticity of which are generally recognized." He gives no evidence in support of this assertion, nor does he provide any information regarding who exactly shares his conclusion, apparently because it appears so obvious that it requires no citations to back it up. He also admits that he has never actually looked at either Tibetan, Indian, or Nepalese sources because he does not read any of the relevant languages. But happily he does read Chinese, and because the Chinese records provide the only accurate information regarding Tibetan history, as a Chinese scholar he considers himself uniquely placed to uncover the truth about Tibet's history and clear up the unfortunate "misinformation" surrounding it. Li admits that some readers might be skeptical about his motives and his conclusions because he is Chinese and relies solely on Chinese sources, but he reassures them that he could not possibly be biased, because he received a Ph.D. from Columbia University, "where, presumably, excessive bias would have been discountenanced." Having established his authority and the unique validity of his sources, he asserts that "the facts related in the present and following paragraphs show the extent of the Chinese influence in

Tibet." In common with the other Chinese writers considered in this study, Li indicates that virtually all Tibetan culture and technology were imported from China, and that although some people mistakenly believe that Tibet was independent prior to the 1950s, "the writer believes that there are enough historical facts cited in this study to repudiate these allegations."[97] In *Tibet: Today and Yesterday*, Li makes an even stronger assertion: the claim that Tibet has long been an integral part of China is "historical fact." He adds:

> Nothing is farther from the truth than assertions to the effect that Tibet has always been or was until recently an independent country with sovereign power. A factual answer to these assertions will be found in this book which deals . . . with such matters as how Tibetans regard themselves, whether there is evidence to show that they are able and willing to assume and fulfill international obligations—an essential criterion of statehood—and how Tibet is regarded by all powers concerned.[98]

How he intends to fulfill some of these goals is not clear, because he reiterates that he neither speaks nor reads Tibetan, nor does he cite any evidence that he has actually consulted any Tibetans to determine how they regard themselves. Apparently this is unnecessary, because the truth of the matter is revealed in Chinese records. Li's remarks are interesting in light of the fact that he has a Ph.D. from a major U.S. university and has published his work in a university press, but the story he tells is the same in all of its main aspects as that found in publications by Chinese government bodies. The language is somewhat more restrained and sources are sometimes cited, but he draws the same conclusions as other Chinese authors, and his tone regarding the Tibetan people is equally condescending. He refers to them as "feudal" and "backward," and portrays them as simple and naïvely religious people who "lack a sense of history as understood by other peoples." An underlying theme of his study is the conviction that whatever culture they possess was largely derived from China. To demonstrate the extent of Chinese influence, he cites a number of examples of the impact of Chinese culture on Tibet, the most intriguing of which is the assertion that the present Dalai Lama was born into a Chinese-speaking family (a fact that would no doubt come as a surprise to both him and his family).[99]

Similarly, in *Tibet and the Tibetans*, the other Chinese work considered in this study that was published by a Western academic press, the Tibetan people are referred to as "credulous" and "unsophisticated." According to its analysis, the priest-patron relationship was a fiction of the Tibetan "theocracy" that was "calculated to minimize a somewhat unpleasant fact—Chinese overlordship."[100] This was successful only because the Tibetan populace was too stupid to realize that they were really being ruled by China and that their leaders were in fact dancing to China's tune. Like Li's work, this book is based on Chinese historical sources and is intended to prove that Tibet was ruled continuously by China since the thirteenth century.

Not surprisingly, the assertions of the Chinese writers are comprehensively rejected by the Tibetan side. They view relations between the Qing dynasty and the Tibetan government as being based on shared religious beliefs. The Manchu rulers, who were Tibetan Buddhists, revived the priest-patron relationship, which had lapsed during the Ming dynasty, and became key supporters of the Dalai Lamas, both financially and militarily. According to our Tibetan writers, the Manchus played the role of protectors and benefactors, which allowed the Dalai Lamas and the Tibetan people to concentrate on religious pursuits. China provided protection against outside attack and often lavishly supported Buddhist institutions and lamas. According to Shakabpa, when the Yongzheng

FIGURE 2.8. Golden three-dimensional Kālacakra maṇḍala given to the Dalai Lama by the Qianlong emperor and housed in the Potala, Lhasa. This and other gifts are interpreted by the Chinese as evidence of the overlordship of the Chinese emperors and the Dalai Lamas' vassal status. Photo by John Powers.

emperor took the throne, he "withdrew the [Chinese military] garrison from Lhasa, leaving the administration of the central government entirely in the hands of Tibetan officials, without any military support from the Manchus." Even when Manchu troops entered Tibet and reorganized the government administration in the beginning of the eighteenth century, Shakabpa asserts, "the real power and authority" remained in Tibetan hands. When the Manchu emperor later supplied troops to fend off a Gurkha invasion of Tibet, this was the action of an "ally" rather than a sovereign.[101] Furthermore, in Shakabpa's view, the Manchu representatives (*amban*) who were stationed in Lhasa during the Qing dynasty were merely ambassadors who conveyed messages between the Chinese court and the Tibetan government and possessed no political authority, contrary to the assertions of Chinese sources.

The Chinese writers uniformly view the ambans as exercising official authority on behalf of the emperor of China. They agree that as Manchu power waned, Tibet drifted away from the central government and that China's level of actual control diminished, but this in no way abrogated the long-standing pattern of overlordship. Rather, it reflects the incompetence and corruption of the minority government of the Manchus and the plotting of foreign imperialists. This period looms large in the Chinese national historical narrative as the "Century of Humiliation," during which foreign powers carved up parts of China as their spheres of influence and dictated policy to the central government. For Chinese, the defining period of this foreign interference in China's affairs was the British Opium War of 1840–1842, which followed an attempt by the Chinese government to stop the flow of British opium into China. It saw growing opium use among China's population as a factor that weakened the country and sapped its resources, but the British forbade the government from banning the trade. When the emperor persisted, Britain waged a short but vicious war, and at its conclusion forced the Chinese government to accept its terms and to allow it to continue to import opium. This episode crystallizes for many Chinese the cruel and corrupting nature of foreign interference in China's affairs and is commonly cited by Chinese leaders as a reason for the absolute necessity of maintaining national unity and military power.

Moreover, in the Chinese historical narrative it is not Britain alone that was responsible for China's problems. According to *Tibet: Myth vs. Reality*, "The U.S. imperialists, long covetous of Tibet, ganged up with the British imperialists in a conspiracy to bring about 'Tibet's independence.' "[102] This and other sources blame the "imperialists" for China's problems during this time and assert that the development of the movement for Tibetan independence was initiated by them in order to weaken China and split Tibet from the motherland so that they could control this strategically important area themselves. *The*

Historical Status of Tibet avers that "it was due only to the folly and arrogance of the Manchus in later times, the weakness of their military forces, and the intrigues of foreign powers that Tibet drifted gradually away from its traditional position in the polity of China."[103] According to this view, the Tibetans who foolishly assert that Tibet was an independent country (as well as the often well-meaning but misinformed foreigners who agree with them) are the un-witting dupes of a clever and concerted misinformation campaign by imperi-alist powers, who spread their lies to advance their hidden agendas. Moreover, all the Chinese sources used in this study agree that the overwhelming majority of Tibetans at that time considered themselves to be part of the Chinese moth-erland, and they strongly opposed any imperialist attempts to create divisions within the country.[104] According to *Tibet: Myth vs. Reality*:

> "Tibet's independence," advocated by a handful of reactionaries, for-eign and domestic . . . has always been a dirty trick of imperialist ag-gression against China. Today, a number of people with ulterior mo-tives spread the nonsense that "Tibet is an independent state." Their aim is to draw Tibet away from the motherland, which will never be allowed by the Chinese people, including the people of Tibet. . . . China's sovereignty over Tibet is indisputable. This is history's ver-dict.[105]

The Chinese sources are unanimous in their conclusion that Tibet was a part of China even during the darkest days of the Century of Humiliation and that it remained so after the last Qing emperor was deposed by the Nationalists and a new government was established. Tibetan writers, however, view the beginning of the Nationalist period as a decisive break between Tibet and China. They assert that as long as the Qing remained in power the Tibetan government was content to retain the "fiction" of Chinese overlordship to avoid antagonizing the Chinese government, but when the secular Nationalists came to power there was no longer any possibility of maintaining the former rela-tionship, which was based on shared religious convictions. Thus, in 1913 the thirteenth Dalai Lama officially declared Tibet's independence from China and all Chinese nationals were expelled from the country. According to Shakabpa, one month before this, Tibet and Mongolia signed a treaty (in January 1913) in which "both countries declared themselves free from Manchu rule and sep-arate from China." He views this as particularly significant, because he thinks that it demonstrates that Tibet had the independent authority to enter into treaties with other sovereign powers. He concludes that "Tibet's historical and political development clearly shows that it was a sovereign country, which en-

joyed the right to negotiate treaties and to have direct relations with her neighbors."[106]

Following the declaration of independence, the country's borders were
closed to most foreigners, and Tibet began a period of isolation from the outside world, during which it permitted no outside interference in its internal
affairs, either by the Chinese government or any other foreign powers.[107]

In the Chinese view, however, all power and authority radiates from China,
and the Chinese central government had full control even over religious affairs
in Tibet. Thus, in *Tibet: Yesterday and Today*, Li Tieh-tseng asserts that "in fact,
both the present Dalai Lama and the present Panch'en Lama were installed in
solemn ceremonies officiated by the Chairman of the Commission for Mongolian and Tibetan Affairs of the Chinese Central Government."[108] The Tibetan
writers diminish the significance of the chairman's participation and assert
that he was merely an "observer" who played "no official role" in the ceremonies. In the Chinese view, all affairs in Tibet, even the recognition of Tibetan
reincarnations, are the responsibility of the Chinese government. Thus, several
Chinese sources accept the validity of a proclamation issued near the end of
the Qing dynasty that officially withdrew the title of the thirteenth Dalai Lama.
Thubten Jigme Norbu dismisses the action as a "pathetic gesture that only
served to underline the myth of Chinese authority in Tibet,"[109] but several
Chinese sources accept that from this point until 1913, when the Nationalist
government officially restored his title, he was no longer Dalai Lama (even
though Tibetans continued to regard him as such). The Chinese sources that
discuss this incident unanimously agree that it highlights the continuing authority exercised by China over Tibetan affairs, while Tibetan sources dismiss
it as an empty gesture and point out that it had no effect either on his authority
or on how Tibetans viewed him.

3

Reinventing China

The strongest cause for the feeling of nationality ... is identity of
political antecedents; the possession of a national history, and conse-
quent community of recollections; collective pride and humiliation,
pleasure and regret, connected with the same incidents in the past.
    —John Stuart Mill, *Representative Government*

Barbarians at the Gates

During the early imperial period, China kept foreign nations at
arm's length by means of the tribute system and isolationist policies. Those that were willing to submit to China as vassals and accept the emperor's overlordship (at least verbally) were permitted to
visit the court at prescribed intervals and by routes dictated by Chinese authorities. Foreign countries that sought a special trade relationship on the basis of equality were rebuffed or simply ignored.
An example of such treatment of foreigners is the Qianlong emperor's letter of response to a British trade mission sent by King
George III in 1793, which requested that China agree to formal
trade relationships with Britain. In his reply, the emperor denied the
request on the grounds that barbarians could not possess anything
of value to China and barbarian trade representatives would not be
comfortable living among civilized (Chinese) people. The emperor
further referred to the mission's gifts as tribute and advised his vas-

sal, the king of England, to humbly follow the commands of his sovereign, the emperor of China.

Such attitudes on the part of the Chinese were fostered by long centuries of isolation from the rest of the world and a history of technological and military superiority over their neighbors. During this period of complacency, however, the West leaped ahead technologically, and it was a rude shock when Westerners began to appear on China's shores with warships that were vastly more powerful than Chinese craft, armed with modern weapons. The first Western nations to have extensive contact with China were Portugal and Spain, which sent missions in the seventeenth century. Dutch traders established a base on Formosa in 1624, and the British arrived in 1637. Captain James Weddell sailed into Canton harbor and petitioned for permission to trade. His request was ignored, and so after several days he launched an attack, following which the emperor allowed the East India Company to open a factory in Canton. This remained the sole officially sanctioned treaty port for decades, an arrangement that allowed the Chinese to keep foreigners at a distance and restrict their activities to one area. During this period, foreign traders and government officials were regarded as vassals of the emperor, and local officials made enormous profits by charging extortionate duties and special fees from them. Unsurprisingly, the humiliations they had to endure from haughty Chinese government officials and the huge sums of money they had to pay to do business there led to resentment on the part of the Europeans, who were used to doing business on the basis of equality and relatively open markets.[1]

The Chinese also had their grievances with the foreigners. One reason that was given for restricting them to a single area was that their sailors often engaged in drunken brawling and other sordid behavior. In addition, first the Dutch and later the British began importing opium into China, and addiction to the drug grew quickly, which led the government to ban its sale. Despite this, the British East India Company continued to bring in large quantities of opium, and by 1828 it constituted an estimated 90 percent of China's foreign import trade. Even though the trafficking was possible only because of corrupt Chinese officials who ignored imperial bans in exchange for bribes, the government blamed the foreigners for it and for the problems it caused.

During the early nineteenth century, the East India Company generally tried to operate within the restrictions imposed by the Chinese government, but in 1833 the British Parliament abolished its trade monopoly and opened the China market—without any consultation with China—to all British merchants. In addition, the same act declared that henceforth British citizens who were accused of crimes in China would be tried by British authorities and would not be subject to Chinese law. This was prompted both by an attitude of cultural superiority on the part of the British and a well-founded distaste for the corruption and use of physical force in the Chinese legal system.

Their incommensurable attitudes of cultural superiority led to increasing friction between the Chinese and the British. A letter by a British Christian missionary who worked in China sums up the clash of identities that resulted from the collision of Western and Chinese cultures: "Are we not much superior to them [the Chinese]? Are we not more manly, more intelligent, more skillful, more human, more civilized, nay, are we not more estimable in every way? Yes, according to our way of thinking. No, *emphatically* no, according to theirs. And it would be nearly as difficult for us to alter our opinion on the subject as it is for them to alter theirs."[2]

The Barbarians Invade

The main focus of friction between foreign merchants and the Chinese government was the opium trade, and the flashpoint was a Chinese decision to seize and burn all British opium stores in Canton. Lin Zexu, the viceroy of Hobei and Henan, demanded that the British sign a document consenting to adhere to Chinese law and agree that any foreigners caught smuggling opium could be put to death by Chinese authorities. When the British refused, Lin convinced the central government to issue a decree banning all British ships from Chinese ports. In response, the governor-general of India declared war on China, and a military expedition was sent to protect the lives of British citizens and to demand damages from the Chinese government.

A blockade was imposed on the port of Canton on June 21, 1840, by a fleet of twenty British men-of-war carrying British and Indian troops. The British demanded that the Chinese government participate in negotiations to resolve the situation, but they produced no satisfactory result. In 1841 the new Manchu commissioners Ji Shan and Yili Bu realized that China stood no chance against the superior force, and under duress ceded Hong Kong to the British as their exclusive trade port. In addition, they agreed to the resumption of trade on a basis of equality of nations and to the payment of indemnities. When the British and Chinese governments learned of the conditions of the agreement, however, both decided to repudiate it. The British considered the indemnity to be too small, and the Chinese rejected any payment to the foreigners and the notion of equality with them.

In retaliation, the British invaded and occupied Canton and demanded a huge ransom from the Chinese government. They subsequently seized Shanghai and Nanjing. Realizing that it had no choice, in 1842 China agreed to the Treaty of Nanjing, which officially opened Canton, Amoy, and Shanghai to foreign trade. Thus began a period during which foreign countries negotiated a series of what the Chinese later referred to as "unequal treaties," in which China was forced into agreements on the foreigners' terms. This also opened China to study by foreigners, and increasing numbers of scholars, missionaries, and travelers began to arrive and begin the process of acquiring knowledge about Chinese cultures, customs, literature, and languages. These activities were part of the colonial project, and they were often sponsored by colonial officials who believed that greater knowledge of the Orient would result in greater control and profitability.

The Chinese, however, chose not to reciprocate; they had no interest in gathering information about foreigners for themselves, secure in their centuries-old attitudes of cultural superiority and disdain for barbarians. From the Chinese perspective, it was both bewildering and humiliating that China was increasingly being forced into unequal relationships with foreigners who were able to compel a weak government to bow to their demands, leading to a situation in which their superior military power enabled them to exercise an influence in Chinese affairs that was not justified by either their culture or their methods of governance. For the Han, who were taught from birth that they were destined by their superior culture to instruct and govern other, lesser peoples, this created an intolerable cognitive conflict and led to mounting disgust toward the minority Manchu government.

As a result of the Qing rulers' inability to protect China from these living affronts to Chinese dignity, antiforeign sentiment grew, and some of this was directed toward the Manchus. For their part, the foreigners also displayed ethnocentric attitudes, which served to further antagonize the Chinese. In this situation of mutual misunderstanding and hostility, conflict was inevitable, and in 1856–1857 Britain and China again fought a minor war in Canton. In 1857 a joint Indian-British force seized the city and took its governor prisoner. At first, the imperial government refused to negotiate, but when the foreign armies responded by pushing deeper into China, they capitulated to another "unequal treaty," which for the first time allowed foreigners to travel freely in the interior of China and which legalized the opium trade. The government was also forced to agree to pay a yearly indemnity, which further impoverished the already diminished Manchu regime.

The Barbarians Move In

The cessation of rights to the treaty ports was a source of deep resentment among Chinese, who viewed this as a sign that the government was failing in its sacred duty of safeguarding Chinese territory against foreigners. The ports have become a potent symbol for Chinese of the rapacity of foreigners and their corrupting influence, and these enclaves are commonly characterized as hotbeds of depravity and Chinese degradation at the hands of the interlopers. These notions are widely accepted among contemporary Chinese, but recent studies by Western scholars have called this picture into question. There is no doubt that the establishment of the treaty ports occurred only as a result of the government's weakness, but as Lucian Pye points out, in comparison to interior China, they were comparatively well governed and free from corruption. In the treaty ports, Chinese culture and commerce flourished, and many of the country's best minds moved to them because of their vibrancy and the opportunities they afforded. Despite this, there was also a sense of shame for those Chinese who opted for foreign rule, and interior China was widely viewed as the "real" China, despite its pervasive corruption and stagnation.

> The fundamental and lasting effect of the treaty port system was
> that it provided vivid and all-too-concrete evidence of the weakness
> of Chinese political rule and the apparent merits of foreign rule.
> The huge mass population of interior China were cursed with the
> incompetence, inefficiency and corruption of government by war-
> lords, while in the enclaves there was an environment where China
> could prosper and realize the spirit of modern life. The Chinese who
> went to the enclaves had undeniably voted with their feet in favour
> of foreign rule over Chinese rule. Interior China was thus seen as
> the real China, but it was a flawed and, in modern terms, disgraced
> China. For the Chinese in the enclaves there was an inescapable
> sense of guilt as they became more nationalistically conscious. For
> the Chinese of the interior there was shame and humiliation as they
> became more conscious of modernization.[3]

According to Pye, the treaty ports were places in which Chinese culture successfully interacted with the West and produced a new breed of cosmopolitan Chinese, but even they felt somehow diminished by their contact with foreigners and viewed themselves as less authentically Chinese than their counterparts in the interior. The tension between the coastal enclaves and the more traditional center of the country created a situation in which Chinese who lived in the treaty ports were perceived by other Chinese as less patriotic and as having abandoned their own culture, and many Westernized Chinese also came to accept this characterization of themselves.[4]

It is interesting to note in this context that the virulence of antiforeign sentiment was out of all proportion to the actual impact of foreigners in China or their numbers. Most of them confined their activities to the coastal trade enclaves, and seldom ventured outside of them. The vast majority of Chinese territory was under Chinese control, but the very fact that outsiders had been able to force the government to allow them entry was quite enough to enrage most Chinese. Added to this was the resentment caused by the racist attitudes of many of the interlopers among a people already familiar with their own indigenous racism. During this period, a common theme among Western commentators on China was that there was something fundamentally wrong with John Chinaman, and they detailed the sort of changes that he would have to make to be worthy to regain control over his country. Coupled with this was the assertion that the West's triumph over China was the result of its superior civilization—its culture, technology, morals, religion, and more intelligent populace—compared to the backward and benighted Chinese. Such condescending attitudes further deepened Chinese resentment and provided fuel for the growth of nationalism.

The Natives Grow Restless

In addition to their foreign relations problems, the Manchus also faced a number of internal difficulties. A rapidly increasing population led to resource demands that the government was unable to meet, and a series of rebellions from 1850 to 1870 further sapped the dynasty's military strength. Widespread famines ravaged the countryside during the 1870s, and were particularly acute in 1877–1878. These problems made it increasingly difficult for the beleaguered government to collect taxes, which further diminished its resources.

All of these factors created a weakness that left China vulnerable to the expansionist policies of foreign powers. The Qing dynasty had inherited a vast and essentially unmanageable empire, but to the Qing rulers and the Chinese people in general, every part of this empire constituted a sacred and inalienable part of China. The notion that all territory conquered by past dynasties remained forever a part of the Chinese motherland led to popular resentment against the Manchu rulers when the government was forced to cede Burma to Britain in 1876 and Vietnam and Annam to France in 1897. The most devastating blow was the Sino-Japanese war of 1894–1895, which resulted in Japan's annexation of Formosa and southern Manchuria.[5] Korea was declared independent, but Japan invaded and annexed it to its growing Asian empire in 1910. To resolve its conflicts with Japan, China was forced to pay a huge indemnity, which further diminished its finances and helped Japan to expand its military. The Qing dynasty's difficulties with its own people were exacerbated by the fact that the rule of the minority Manchus was deeply resented by the majority Han, who saw their subjection as humiliating. The Manchus for their part fostered these attitudes by forcing the Han to wear Manchu clothes and shave the front of their heads as a sign of subordination.[6]

Up until this point, European powers had generally assumed that China's vast size was accompanied by military might, but its comprehensive defeat by Japan made them fully aware of its systemic frailty, and several European countries subsequently forced China to sign a series of treaties ceding parts of the country. This led to growing resentment among the populace toward the rapacious foreigners who were seizing parts of China with impunity and toward the foreign ruling dynasty that was unable to protect China from them. This situation sparked more internal rebellions, the most crippling of which was the Boxer Uprising, which began in 1898. It was finally unsuccessful, but in its aftermath the Qing government was fatally weakened.

Trespass and Intrigue on the Roof of the World

Another affront to Chinese sensibilities occurred in the early twentieth century, when Britain sent a message to Qing authorities in Beijing requesting permission to initiate negotiations to establish trade relations in Tibet. This move was prompted by British fears that Russia was gaining influence in the region; it was hoped that by opening trade relations, this influence could be counteracted. In fact, Russia had its own internal problems, and the czarist government had only limited contacts with Tibet, but the British greatly exaggerated their significance. They viewed Tibet as one of a group of buffer states that separated British India from potentially dangerous neighbors, and feared that if Russia (or China) managed to annex Tibet, this would provide a strategic advantage. This maneuvering was part of what was then referred to as the "Great Game," in which Britain, Russia, and China jockeyed for influence in Central Asia. Tibet was a key area of contestation, despite its own desire to remain aloof from all foreign powers and their intrigues.

In 1903 the British viceroy of India, Lord Curzon, sent a message to the governments of China and Tibet requesting that negotiations be held at Khampa Dzong, just inside the Tibetan border with Sikkim, to establish trade relations. You Tai, the Manchu representative (amban) in Lhasa, apparently was willing to attend, but the Tibetans refused to provide transport for him (Shakabpa, Thubten Jigme Norbu, and Richardson conclude that this refusal demonstrates that China had no influence in Tibet at the time).[7] In response to Britain's message, the Lhasa government indicated that it would send only minor officials to Khampa Dzong, but they would have no power to negotiate, and although Chinese authorities ordered the thirteenth Dalai Lama to attend the proposed meeting, he declined to do so. After repeated attempts to get the Chinese government to use its influence to open Tibet to trade, Curzon decided that the core problem was that China had no such influence. In a letter to the secretary of state for India on October 2, he wrote, "They [the Tibetans] are ruled by an ignorant hierarchy of monks, whose continued monopoly on all power and substance in the country depends upon the exclusion of any alien influence. China endows the principal monasteries and thereby keeps a hold on the ruling clique. But she is absolutely without power or authority in Tibet, and she is equally afraid of any outside shock that might expose the hollowness of her alleged suzerainty."[8]

Frustrated by the Tibetans' refusal even to meet with Britain's representatives, Curzon secured approval from London to send a military expedition to Khampa Dzong, led by Colonel Francis Younghusband.[9] It arrived on July 7, 1903, but neither the Tibetans nor the Manchu amban were there. Hoping that they would change their minds, Younghusband decided to remain at Khampa Dzong. Curzon soon became concerned at the immanent loss of face that would result from an unsuccessful attempt to negotiate a treaty, and he ordered Younghusband to advance to Gyantse. After gaining additional troops and porters from Britain's Indian Army, Younghusband marched to Tuna, a town fifty miles inside the Tibetan border. His force by this point consisted of 1,150 soldiers, 10,000 porters and laborers, and thousands of pack animals carrying their supplies. Still hoping that someone would arrive to negotiate, Younghusband remained there until January 1904, when he received orders to advance toward Lhasa. He first warned the Tibetan general in charge of a militia sent to block his advance of his intention and promised that his troops would not fire unless they were attacked by the Tibetans.

The Tibetans had built a wall of stones about five feet high that they hoped would stop the British force, but the foreign soldiers advanced toward them and began to take down the loosely stacked stones. When the soldiers tried to take away the Tibetans' weapons, they fought back, which triggered a fusillade of British artillery and machine guns. The fight was over in ten minutes, but in its aftermath more than six hundred Tibetans lay dead; many more were wounded. The survivors were surprised when the troops that had recently massacred their comrades began treating the injured. The British suffered only twelve casualties.

One of the most tragic aspects of the conflict is that during the early battles the poorly armed and largely untrained Tibetans were given amulets by their lamas, who assured them that they would protect them from harm and turn away British bullets. Firmly believing in the effectiveness of the lamas' magic, the Tibetans fearlessly charged their enemies, secure in the conviction that no harm would come to them. Their faith proved to be misplaced, and they were mowed down in droves. Edmund Candler, a British reporter from the *Daily Mail* who accompanied the expedition, later wrote that after one battle, surviving Tibetans wandered around in a daze, confused by the utter ineffectiveness of their amulets and the lamas' inability to protect them.[10]

Following this engagement, the British were able to advance toward Gyantse, but they met another Tibetan militia along the way, mostly armed with swords and spears and a few ancient matchlock rifles, and another massacre resulted in 180 more Tibetan deaths. Younghusband reached Gyantse in April 1904, but the Tibetan government still refused to send any high-level representatives to meet with him. He decided to take Gyantse Fort, which was held by Tibetan forces; it was captured after an artillery bombardment. The defeated Tibetan commander of the fort, Dapon Tailing, managed to escape

FIGURE 3.1. Gyantse Fort. Photo by John Powers.

and later returned with reinforcements, but during several battles with the British he lost most of his men.

After receiving orders to wait in Gyantse until talks could be initiated, Younghusband sent the bulk of his force back to India. Hoping that the small corps of soldiers was now vulnerable, the Tibetan government launched a surprise attack, which managed to reoccupy Gyantse Fort. Following this, however, the main British force again marched to Gyantse and recaptured it. Younghusband was ordered to advance to Lhasa and force the Tibetans to negotiate. He encountered a Tibetan militia on the way, and their battle left another three hundred Tibetans dead.

Before they arrived, the thirteenth Dalai Lama fled the country to Urga, the capital of Outer Mongolia. Once there, he contacted the Russian government and asked for its aid against the British. This move prompted the Chinese government to issue a decree stripping him of his titles and removing him from the office of Dalai Lama. The amban then had posters put up around Lhasa proclaiming that the Dalai Lama had been deposed and that he (the amban) was now officially in charge of Tibetan affairs, but his proclamations were pulled down by Tibetans and he was ignored by Tibetan officials.[11]

The first official to meet the British when they entered Lhasa was the amban, but he indicated that he had no authority to negotiate, despite his recent declaration of preeminence.[12] The Tibetans Younghusband met told him that only the Dalai Lama could sign such an accord and that nothing could be concluded in his absence. Faced with the immanent possibility that his mission would become a total shambles, Younghusband was able to partially salvage the situation by convincing the acting regent, the abbot of Ganden Monastery, to sign a treaty in which Tibet allowed Britain to establish trade ports in Yadong, Gyantse, and Gartok. A huge indemnity (£562,500) was imposed on Tibet, and the Chumbi Valley was ceded to Britain until it was paid. Tibet recognized the Sikkim-Tibet border, thus agreeing to relinquish its claims to Sikkim, which had been annexed by Britain. The Tibetans also promised that they would have no relations with countries other than Britain.

This compact, which later came to be known as the Anglo-Tibetan Agreement of 1904, further muddied the waters with regard to Tibet's status, because while it was for all intents and purposes a treaty between the government of Britain and the government of Tibet, the Tibetan leader, the Dalai Lama, was not present, and the Chinese amban publicly repudiated it and continued to assert China's claim to overlordship of Tibet. Further, the stipulation that Tibet would exclude all foreign powers except Britain effectively turned the country into a British protectorate. Despite the fact that it had signed what was notionally an agreement between two sovereign powers that excluded China, however, the British government subsequently acknowledged its continuing acceptance of Chinese claims of suzerainty.[13]

Following the signing of the agreement, the British left Lhasa on September 23, 1904 and returned to India. In the aftermath of the invasion, the British government, apparently uncomfortable with the actions of British troops and the fact that Younghusband had greatly exceeded his mandate, unilaterally repudiated many of the gains he had made in Tibet. The acting viceroy, Lord Anthill, cut the indemnity by two-thirds and allowed the Tibetans to pay it in installments; he also promised to end British occupation of the Chumbi Valley within three years, provided that the other provisions of the pact were met by the Tibetans.

In the aftermath of the expedition, Britain and China entered into fresh negotiations from which Tibet was excluded, and in 1906 they signed the Sino-British Convention, which reaffirmed Britain's position that China had legitimate suzerainty over Tibet. One of its articles stipulated: "The Government of Great Britain engages not to annex Tibetan territory or to interfere in the administration of Tibet. The Government of China also undertakes not to admit any other foreign state to interfere with the territory or internal administration of Tibet." Other provisions of the agreement effectively turned the 1904 treaty between Tibet and Britain into an agreement with China; in it, China offered to assume the obligations agreed to by Tibet, including payment of the indemnity.

The expedition caused China to realize the threat foreign imperialism posed for its claims to areas like Tibet and prompted the government to take a more active and aggressive stance in asserting what it considered to be its rights. The Tibetan government no longer paid any heed to the Qing ambans stationed in Lhasa, and China feared that if unchecked Britain would try to annex Tibet to its Indian empire, as it had earlier annexed Bhutan and Sikkim. China considered both of these areas to be part of the territory of Tibet, and thus of China, and the present PRC government still claims them, as well as most of Nepal, all of Ladakh, and much of the northern border area of India, because these areas were at one time under Tibetan control.

The invasion was a huge blow to Chinese pride because it exposed the impotence of the Qing government to intervene and protect a region it claimed as part of its territory. Moreover, the fact that the Dalai Lama had ignored China's orders to remain and negotiate with the British and had instead fled to Mongolia to seek help from Russia was viewed as a further affront. Fortunately for China, Britain had no interest in pushing its newfound advantage and either turning Tibet into a British protectorate or recognizing it as an independent nation. The 1906 convention officially acknowledged China's authority in Tibet even though it was unable to exercise any authority in fact. As Goldstein states, "At a time when China was unable to exercise real power in Tibet, Britain unilaterally reaffirmed Tibet's political subordination to China."[14]

Will the Real Imperialists Please Stand Up?

The Tibetan writers considered in this study all view the powerlessness of China in the face of the British invasion and the conclusion of a treaty between Tibet and Britain as clear indications of Tibet's independence. Dawa Norbu refers to a statement by Curzon that Chinese overlordship was a "constitutional fiction," and he asserts that the events of 1903–1904 "made the Chinese realize that their power in Tibet had disappeared."[15] Thubten Jigme Norbu is even more emphatic in asserting the emptiness of Chinese claims of sovereignty: he contends that Tibet had managed to keep China "at a comfortable arm's length" by allowing it to assert the authority of the ambans, which he refers to as "an effective face-saver" with no real substance. The Tibetans "saw no harm in allowing [China] to pretend to an authority that she could not enforce in fact."[16]

Shakabpa provides the most detailed discussion of the expedition by any of our Tibetan writers. He also emphasizes the impotence of the amban and his lack of authority: "The Tibetans stated there was no need for any Chinese participation in the talks and Ho Kuang-hsi [the amban's representative in Shigatse] returned quietly to Shigatse, citing ill-health as the reason for his departure." He reports that when the British demanded that the amban be present at the negotiations, Tibetan officials replied that "the Ambans had no connection with the commercial affairs of Tibet."[17]

Shakabpa also asserts that many Tibetans were favorably impressed by the fact that the British treated wounded Tibetans and gave presents to their prisoners before freeing them. In his surprisingly positive characterization of the British who invaded his country and killed more than a thousand Tibetans, he states that "Younghusband was known to be sympathetic with the Tibetan soldiers" and "the fact that the British paid well for firewood, grain, and fodder impressed the local inhabitants."[18] This assessment is echoed by other Tibetan writers, and it may be that in retrospect the British invaders now enjoy a more positive image among Tibetans than the Chinese invaders who succeeded them several decades later.

Shakabpa portrays the Manchu amban as completely powerless. He states that when he first met Younghusband, You Tai offered to use his influence to bring about a speedy resolution of the crisis, but Shakabpa dismisses this as "a strange offer in view of the fact that he had been unable to get the Tibetans to provide transport for the trip to Gyantse." He emphasizes the role played by other intermediaries, including a Gurkha representative in Lhasa, a Kashmiri Muslim leader, and ambassadors from the Bhutanese and Nepalese governments, all of whom he implies had greater influence with the Tibetans than the amban. He further contends that Chinese troops were engaging in attacks along the Tibetan border and that the British seemed amenable to the establishment of friendly relations. Despite the fact that they had only recently slaughtered over a thousand Tibetans, in Shakabpa's account it appears that the Tibetans viewed them far more favorably than they did the Chinese, and they decided, "When faced with two enemies, why not make one of them a friend?"[19]

He emphasizes that the agreement between Tibet and Britain was "witnessed" by the Manchu amban, along with the representatives from Bhutan and Nepal, and he avers that the fact that Tibet was able to conclude the agreement on its own, repudiating any Chinese role in the negotiations, makes it "quite clear that the British were dealing with Tibet as a separate and independent state, particularly since the 1904 Convention makes no reference to China or to Chinese authority in Tibet." He also believes that the article forbidding any concessions to other countries by Tibet implied that "China was regarded as a foreign power. . . . The provisions of the 1904 Convention between Great Britain and Tibet completely negate any Chinese claim of sovereignty . . . over Tibet."[20]

According to Shakabpa, the fact that the agreement was reached between Tibet and Britain without the participation of any other country "establishes Tibet as an independent country at that time." He heaps scorn on the amban for his suggestion that the agreement be signed in his residence—which was rejected by both signatories—and he cites a remark by Younghusband, who "asked the Amban how he managed to pass the time of day in Lhasa without any work to do."[21]

While Tibetan accounts stress Chinese powerlessness in the face of foreign incursion, Chinese historians paint a very different picture. Like the Tibetan authors, they characterize the Tibetan resistance to the British troops as a patriotic response, but they believe that this sentiment was directed toward China, not the Dalai Lama's "local government." According to Wang and Suo, when the British troops crossed the border and requested negotiations, "the Tibetan people were . . . enraged by Britain's unreasonable demand. They demanded that the Tibetan authorities request the Qing government to lodge a strong protest with Britain."[22] Their implication is that the Lhasa government would not presume to act unilaterally without first receiving authorization from Beijing.

Wang and Suo do not mention the fact that the Tibetan government refused to provide supplies to the amban for his proposed trip to Gyantse, but Ya does. In his account, however, this was not a sign of their contempt for the amban or their independence from Qing authority; instead, it was prompted by concern that any yielding to British pressure would bring disgrace to the Chinese court. Ya further asserts that they did not really refuse (even though he also quotes a letter by You Tai to his superiors in Beijing that says they did), and he avers that the amban told this to the British only as a clever "pretext" to stall them.[23]

As we have seen, Shakabpa states in several places that the British commander warned the Tibetans in advance of every move he made and attempted to avoid conflict, but Wang and Suo claim that he intended to massacre as many as possible and that while pretending to negotiate, "he had machineguns set up on the sly around the Tibetan troops. Taken unawares, the Tibetans were mowed down in cold blood by heavy fire."[24] They assert that one thousand Tibetans were killed in the exchange, whereas Shakabpa claims six hundred deaths (Richardson admits only three hundred). Wang and Suo report that "the massacre further infuriated the wide mass of the Tibetan people," who viewed it as an imperialist attempt to split their region from the motherland of China, which would never be tolerated by the patriotic Tibetans.

Contrary to Shakabpa's generally positive presentation of British actions, Wang and Suo assert that they "looted, burned and killed." An even more interesting aspect of their account is that they believe that the Tibetans fought effectively and inflicted heavy losses on the British. In contrast with the complete routs described by the British accounts and by Shakabpa, Wang and Suo credit the Tibetan forces with mounting a "massive counterattack" and capturing several strategically important places around Gyantse. Another raiding party was able to launch a surprise attack against Younghusband himself while he slept, and his troops were awakened "too late to offer any effective resistance." Following this defeat (which they appear to have made up themselves, as it does not appear in any account of the expedition by either British or Tibetan observers), "Younghusband with a small retinue escaped southward."[25]

After their victory, the Tibetans (who in Wang and Suo's narrative were both brilliant tacticians and thoroughly familiar with warfare techniques) built strategic fortifications and created "a complete defensive system," which allowed them to "beat back an enemy armed with modern weapons." According to Wang and Suo, the British avoided defeat only by bringing in reinforcements from India armed with artillery and machine guns, but even so they suffered heavy losses at the hands of the Tibetans, who were fighting from strategically advantageous positions. In their description of the siege of Gyantse Fort, they report: "For a long time they were kept at bay by the defenders. . . . At last they demolished the monastery's walls and broke in. However, they came face to face with the militia defenders armed with broadswords. Hand-to-hand fighting ensued. The militiamen battled like lions and in some cases slashed their enemies in half. The British took the monastery but at a cost of more than 200 casualties. They ransacked the monastery and burned down its scripture reading hall."[26]

Despite suffering losses that would have decimated the small force and reduced its numbers by more than one fifth, the British continued to fight losing battles against the courageous Tibetans and their apparently brilliant military commanders. According to Heyu, the thirteenth Dalai Lama "led the monks and laymen in a stubborn resistance. . . . Their heroism will always be cherished in the memory of the Chinese people."[27] During one battle for Gyantse Fort, Wang and Suo write that "wave after wave" of British troops were beaten back by Tibetans, many of whom were armed only with stones. When

FIGURE 3.2. Statue in the "Anti-British Museum" at Gyantse Fort depicting the Tibetan serfs hurling rocks onto the British invaders. Photo by John Powers.

even these were used up, they fought with their hands, and those who remained when the British finally broke through their defenses "leaped over the cliff to avoid being taken prisoner."[28]

Sadly, the valiant efforts of these patriots were undermined by "capitulationists who represented the interests of the big serf-owner class," who convinced the "local government" to negotiate with the British. As a result of a Qing order to cease resistance, the British were able to push forward to Lhasa, and "the Tibetan capital fell on August 3." In contrast to the generally benign picture painted by Shakabpa's and Richardson's assertions that the British treated the Tibetans well, paid generously for whatever they needed, and refrained from looting, Wang and Suo claim that "the British occupation army looted Lhasa. Even ordinary women's silver ornaments were not exempted from the pillage, let alone valuables. Cultural relics . . . were especially prized."[29] Huang Hongzhao paints an even more lurid picture of the depredations of the British: he claims that "they looted every monastery in Tibet and continuously carried bags of booty to India. . . . During the war, at least 4,000 Tibetans were killed. As a result of the war, countless Tibetan families were ruined. Bones of the dead scattered everywhere. Nine houses out of ten were empty. The Tibetans would never forget all these crimes, all these heavy blood debts of the invaders."[30]

While British accounts claim that Younghusband voluntarily left Tibet after concluding the treaty and encountered no resistance on his way back to India, Wang and Suo and Huang tell a story in which he fled in fear of further Tibetan attacks and was constantly harassed by local militias. Wang and Suo claim that one "daring" Tibetan managed to sneak into his camp and murder an officer. In addition to wasting huge sums of money and suffering a decimation of Younghusband's force, in the aftermath of the agreement the British "invasion" proved to be completely unsuccessful because "the treaty had no legal effect since it had not been approved or signed by the Qing central government."[31] Britain had entered Tibet under the pretext of opening trade relations—though it secretly schemed to annex Tibet to its empire—but in the end the actions of Tibetan patriots scuttled its plans and it failed to accomplish either aim. All of the Chinese writers we are considering unanimously agree that the Younghusband expedition was, as Ya puts it, part of a "sinister design to annex Tibet."[32] He agrees with Wang and Suo's assessment that it was only the heroic and patriotic resistance of the Tibetans that convinced the British that they would never be able to hold the country, whose inhabitants had shown such implacable determination to remain part of China.

A core part of the Chinese narrative of this period is the notion that the Younghusband expedition was conceived as the beginning of an invasion by

Britain, the ultimate goal of which was to conquer and annex all of China. This was widely believed by Chinese at the time, and is echoed by contemporary PRC historians. One Chinese official at the time claimed that "Tibet . . . is like the backdoor of a house. If the door is opened wide, robbers will flock into the apartments."[33] Huang believes that "Britain harboured evil intentions to Tibet and glared at it like a tiger eyeing its prey." His analysis of the intentions behind the expedition is typical of contemporary Chinese writers: he asserts that the ultimate objective was to first occupy Tibet, and then continue to Dartsedo and take over Sichuan. After that, British troops would "sail downward through Sichuan Province to Jinmen in Hubei Province, in this way and from these areas [Britain] can occupy all the provinces in the south." Although this notion is found in a number of works by modern Chinese historians, it is highly implausible. There is no indication in contemporaneous British records that such an ambitious colonialist adventure was ever even imagined by British authorities, nor could they have actually accomplished it militarily. This sort of invasion and occupation would have required a force many times larger than what Britain possessed, and maintaining supply and communications lines along such a vast expanse of hostile territory would have been logistically impossible. Nonetheless, Huang echoes a widespread Chinese sentiment when he claims that after taking Sichuan, Britain intended to "occupy the upper reaches of the Yangtze River Valley. And thus Britain could establish its sphere of influence of [sic] Far East, with Yangtze River valley at its centre. Therefore, to invade Tibet was part of Britain's plan of invading China and struggling for hegemony on [sic] Asia." These evil plans were thwarted because of the "furious anti-Britain feeling of the Tibetans," who fought like tigers against the superior invading force, inflicting heavy casualties every step of the way to Lhasa. In common with our other Chinese authors who discuss this period, he appears to assume that the Tibetans would have ultimately triumphed if not for the treacherous and cowardly "capitulationist" actions of the Qing government: "The British troops, though beset with difficulties, were unexpectedly rescued from the desperate situation and finally won the victory. . . . A monstrous absurdity indeed! Judging from this, the failure of the war of resistance of the Tibetans resulted from the Qing Government's capitulatory policy to the enemy and connivance at their aggression."[34]

Serfs Up

Much of the Chinese version of events is clearly a fabrication that attempts to insert Chinese influence into Tibetan affairs and to create a narrative of patriotic Tibetans fighting on behalf of their beloved motherland. Yet, it is important to recognize that these writers apparently believe it to be true, despite the fact that it differs substantially from eyewitness accounts. The Younghusband expedition is a minor incident in the history of British imperialism in South Asia, and for most Tibetans it is not viewed as being particularly significant in comparison to China's military incursions into their country, but for contemporary Chinese it is an important piece of the grand narrative of Western imperialism and Chinese humiliation. An example of its widespread resonance for contemporary Chinese is the popular PRC-produced film *Red River Valley* (*Hong He Gu*), which is set in the Gyantse region and has the British invasion as a central theme.[35]

It begins with images of a Han girl named Xuer who is about to become a human sacrifice but is saved at the last instant by her brother Hung. They run from the pursuing villagers who had gathered for the sacrifice, but while crossing a river on a suspension bridge they are cut off. Xuer severs the ropes of the bridge with a machete and they plunge into the river. In the next scene, she washes up on the banks of a river in Tibet, which is strange because Tibet's rivers flow down into China, and so it is difficult to imagine that following her plunge she would have been carried upstream to Tibet. Nonetheless, in the film she is adopted by an elderly Tibetan woman who speaks Chinese (we know this because when Xuer tells the woman her name she translates it into Tibetan) and subsequently meets Gasang, a handsome Tibetan youth with a propensity for exposing his well-developed torso. Their romance is a central theme of the movie, but the main action centers on the British incursion into western Tibet.

Younghusband himself is not mentioned, and the British officers we see are apparently part of a group under separate command. The British commander is Major Rockland, a chauvinistic and thoroughly dislikable Scot who wants to kill as many Tibetans as possible and seize their country for the Empire. He is accompanied by Mr. Jones, a reporter, who is the only sympathetic British character in the movie (and who condemns every aspect of the invasion). Throughout the film, the British are portrayed as being utterly alien, while the Han characters interact easily with the Tibetans. The film implies that the Tibetans of western Tibet spoke fluent Chinese and thus they communicate directly with the Han, while the British require translators.

The first part of the movie depicts idyllic scenes of Tibetan peasant life, with much horse riding and magnificent scenic backdrops. Tibetans are shown praying in front of Buddhist images, and there is also a great deal of laughing, singing, and dancing, which are common themes in Chinese cinema depictions of minorities. Gasang is portrayed as a noble savage who excels in shooting and riding and who at one point expounds his philosophy to Hung: "You Han people, who set these stupid rules. . . . Look here: our skies are taller here, the meadows are greener; we love who we love, and we love the way we want to." Hung replies, "I envy you, but we are Han." He then informs Gasang that Xuer is also Han, and so she must leave Tibet, apparently because she is being acculturated to its ways. This theme pervades the movie; the Tibetans are depicted as freer than the civilized Han, who are bound by the rules and norms of their superior culture.[36] By contrast, Tibetans appear to have little physical modesty (in one scene, Xuer bathes naked in a river and is unconcerned when Gasang sees her; this indicates that she has adopted Tibetan attitudes) and are portrayed as primitive and wild people leading simple lives full of physical activity with few rules or restraints.[37]

In the opening scenes of part 2, Rockland and Smith arrive in Tibet at the head of a convoy of British troops. Smith rapturously describes the beauty of Tibet's landscape, and Rockland tells him that although the official pretext for the expedition is to enforce trade agreements, the real reason is that "China is an old tree ready to fall; if we don't go in now, someone else will." He then shows Smith a map of China covered with symbols depicting the spheres of influence of various foreign countries, and he states that Tibet is still "virgin territory" that is ripe for annexation by Britain.

Shortly after that the invaders are confronted by a Tibetan force, which has a Han named Daibin as its commander.[38] This is interesting, because the area around Gyantse in western Tibet is as far from China as one can get in Tibet, and at the time of the Younghusband expedition foreigners, including Chinese, had been banned from Tibet for decades, so it is highly unlikely that the people of that area would have ever even seen a Chinese. Moreover, most Tibetans were unaware even that China claimed Tibet as part of its territory, and there is no way that a Han would have been in command of a Tibetan force in western Tibet. Despite these historical inaccuracies, the scenario probably makes sense to most Chinese, who are taught to believe that China has been intimately involved in Tibetan affairs for centuries and that Tibetans have always accepted Chinese leadership.

After craftily seducing Daibin with overtures of friendship, Rockland convinces him to order his men to stand down to avoid bloodshed, but when he does, Rockland secretly orders his soldiers to move their artillery and machine guns into the surrounding hills. During their ensuing conversation, Rockland asserts that the British have come to "free" the Tibetans: "You Tibetans are an independent race; you should be free, of the Chinese, of anyone!"

In response, Daibin tells Rockland that he is in fact a Han, which Rockland had apparently not realized despite the fact that he wears red silk Chinese brocade clothing while the Tibetans wear their native dress. Daibin then points out that Rockland is a Scot who also considers himself to be part of the British empire despite his identity as a member of a minority population. He concludes that the Tibetan fighters gathered behind him regard themselves in the same way: as minority members of the Chinese empire. Although he is unable to counter Daibin's argument, Rockland responds by ordering his men to open fire on the now defenseless Tibetans. During the ensuing massacre, Rockland smirks and looks pleased with the carnage.

Following the battle, Smith walks among the corpses and says, "We killed fifteen hundred Tibetans in fifteen minutes. Only silence on the battlefield; no hail to our victory. The major said nothing would open up the road to Lhasa except bayonets. I feel sick; our boots are stained with blood; a lot of blood. It is a blood red sun that never sets on the British empire."

More scenes of carnage follow; in one, Rockland calmly sips wine while his cavalry troops massacre Tibetans. Smith protests, "This is not a battle; this is slaughter!" Rockland calmly replies, "Civilization is the ocean that drowns the wildness; it is inevitable." Several scenes later, he appears in the home of a Tibetan headman and demands that he provide him with grain and butter for his troops. The headman protests that this would result in starvation for the Tibetan villagers, but Rockland is not dissuaded. He declares that the Tibetan armies have been defeated, but the patriotic headman replies, "The war will not be over as long as there is one Tibetan left!"

Rockland then tells him that the British are bringing civilization and freedom to the Tibetans, but the headman contemptuously dismisses this notion and indicates that Tibetans are part of Chinese civilization. He holds up his hand with fingers outstretched and points to each one, indicating that one represents the Tibetans, and the others the Han, the Mongols, the Manchus, the Uighurs, "and many more." All are part of the Chinese nation, and he concludes, "Our ancestors made one family; our family matters are none of your business!"

Rockland is unmoved by the headman's sincere expression of patriotism and his determination that Tibet remain a part of the motherland, and this scene is followed by more senseless slaughter of Tibetans by British soldiers, accompanied by looting and other atrocities. The arrogant and brutal imperialists finally get their comeuppance, however, during the siege of Gyantse Fort, when many are killed by patriotic Tibetans in hand-to-hand fighting. At one point, Rockland orders that Xuer, who suddenly appears for no particular reason, be held hostage by his soldiers. Again for no apparent reason, Rockland then begins stripping off her clothes, following which infuriated Tibetans charge the British. During a pause in the fighting, the Tibetans begin singing a song of defiance, and Gasang, sitting on the ground near Rockland and Smith, slowly pulls out a cigarette lighter that was previously given to him by Rockland. As he lights it, Rockland becomes aware that fuel is leaking from several casks; just as the recognition dawns, Gasang smiles and tosses the lighter into the fuel, igniting a huge explosion that destroys the fort and most of the British force.

Despite being in the epicenter of the blast, Rockland and Smith somehow manage to survive, and they begin a dejected retreat toward India. They are led by the boy who has been narrating the film, who deliberately leads them into a quagmire, where artillery and soldiers sink into the mud and are drowned. At the end, only Smith is left of the entire British force, and in the next scene he is standing in a large plain with yaks stampeding all around him. He sadly reflects on the British military adventure: "Why should we destroy their civilization with ours? Why change their world with ours? One thing is for certain: these people will never give in and never disappear, and the immense land behind them is the Orient we shall never conquer." The film closes with the words: "This is a film based on the historic facts that happened in Tibet in 1903. The book *Bayonets to Lhasa* by Peter Fleming also recorded the historical facts. This film also took three English officials' letters from the book as references."

Despite these assertions, the film is riddled with historical inaccuracies and improbabilities, only a few of which have been mentioned here. As I have noted, however, the story it tells is widely accepted by Chinese. In fact, I have been struck by the attitude of a number of Chinese I know who have seen *Red River Valley*, who all view it not as heavy-handed PRC propaganda, but as a historically accurate depiction of real (or at least representative) people involved in actual events. The film's version of the battles in Gyantse is also reflected in displays in the reconstructed Gyantse Fort, which has been turned into a propaganda museum by the Chinese government. Much of the fort contains life-size figures in scenes illustrating the brutality of old Tibet, and there is a room with a sign announcing that it is an "Anti-British Museum" that chronicles the valiant battles of the Tibetan serfs who fought against the British invaders. Posters on the walls tell the story of how the patriotic Tibetans, inflamed by nationalistic fervor, fought with hand weapons against the imperialists who sought to separate them from their beloved motherland. Those who had no weapons hurled rocks from the walls of the fort, and a large statue in the middle of the room shows the angry Tibetans holding large stones above their heads and yelling at the invaders. When I visited the fort in 1999, I smiled at the historical inaccuracies and outright fabrications contained in the government's account of the Younghusband expedition and the battle of Gyantse

Fort, but I was struck by the fact that Chinese visitors were clearly impressed by the bravery of those Tibetan patriots who fought to remain part of China and defended its territory against foreign encroachment. One panel in particular, which stated that although the corrupt and inept Manchus allowed imperialists to carve off parts of China the Tibetans remained loyal and retained a fierce desire to maintain their ancient links with it, caused several Chinese to nod and smile in appreciation. I saw no indication that any had doubts regarding the veracity of the narrative, and it was clear that this was a story that most had heard before and accepted as true. What appeared to a Western visitor as PRC propaganda was history to them, and most were clearly moved by what they read.

Contemporary cultural studies assume as a core tenet that everyone is profoundly conditioned by his or her society and its myths and values. This is no less true of Westerners than it is of Chinese, and Western histories often contain a powerful element of myth that reflects the assumptions and shared narratives of the cultures that produce them. As we have seen, the nationalist assumptions of our Chinese writers profoundly shape their perceptions and interpretations of Tibetan history. They perceive the events of the British expedition into Tibet as part of a larger narrative of imperialism and the victimization of China by Western powers. Several heap contempt on the dithering, impotent Manchus and their failure to protect a region that they consider to be an integral part of China, but they are even more incensed by the effrontery of the British in taking advantage of China's weakness and greatly embellish the facts of the invasion by creating tales of British atrocities and secret intrigues to annex Tibet.

Richardson's account of these events is also powerfully colored by his cultural background. He discusses the Younghusband expedition at length, and though he regrets the loss of Tibetan life at the hands of British troops, he adopts a defensive tone in response to Chinese characterizations. He rejects the notion that the expedition was an "atrocity" and contends that this idea was created by Chinese, who "have a transparent motive in their eagerness to conceal what they themselves have done and are doing in Tibet; and the subject is treated with the customary Communist frenzy and exaggeration."[39]

Even though the British were unable to uncover any evidence of Russian influence when they entered Tibet, Richardson believes that it is "clear beyond all doubt that the Russians were intriguing in the capital of a country bordering on India in which they had no good reason to take an interest." Although it turned out that their fears were groundless, he contends that the British government had "good reasons" to be suspicious and dismisses critics of the expedition for relying on hindsight and failing to realize that at the time British concerns appeared to be well justified.[40]

He also rejects the notion that the expedition was ultimately a waste of time and resources and implies that it generated goodwill among segments of the Tibetan populace. He vehemently objects to the notion that British troops engaged in slaughter of defenseless Tibetans and says that Younghusband demonstrated the "utmost reluctance to begin hostilities and tried to win his object by patient, resolute pressure."[41] His troops only defended themselves against attacks by Tibetans; he never considers the possibility that a military force armed with field artillery and machine guns advancing into Tibetan territory might legitimately be viewed as an attack in itself. Interestingly, Richardson attributes the heavy casualties suffered by the Tibetans to their "antiquated armament and inexperienced leadership," but he seems to have overlooked another possible explanation: that they were attacked by British soldiers wielding weapons designed to kill large numbers of people. He concludes that because the British treated wounded prisoners and later departed the country after achieving their objectives, they made a positive and "lasting impression" on the Tibetans, who were won over by "the frank, honourable, and sensitive character of Younghusband and the gay friendliness and command of the Tibetan language"[42] of his assistant, Frederick O'Connor.

Richardson dismisses as "completely unfounded" claims that the British engaged in looting, but further on, he appears to admit that some looting might have occurred in monasteries that offered opposition to the British. He asserts that no "peaceful" monasteries were looted, but apparently those that resisted the British were fair game. In Richardson's account, the behavior of British troops was "exemplary," and though he regrets that force was employed by Britain in Tibet, he appears to believe that it was necessary, measured, and appropriate to the situation. He even goes so far as to assert that it was "inevitable" and concludes that "there is no cause in it for shame."[43] He never considers how these events might have been viewed by the Tibetans who were killed or wounded, the impact of the invasion on families and friends, or the fact that in the final analysis, the British attacked Tibet because its inhabitants wished to be left alone and the imperial mind-set found this stance intolerable.

As a direct result of the Younghusband expedition, Richardson became the British trade representative in Gyantse. Because he was a long-serving colonial administrator, it is hardly surprising that his perspective is colored by his background. Although his account has a generally scholarly and academic tone, throughout the book he vigorously defends British actions against Chinese accusations, and he demonstrates a thorough dislike for Chinese officials, whom he characterizes as congenital liars. In his view, China is an aggressive, imperialist nation that senselessly invaded a sovereign and peaceful country in violation of international law; he fails to comprehend that from the Chinese perspective, they had a legitimate right to Tibet and a long-established legal claim to overlordship. Even though Chinese troops had entered Tibet numerous times at the behest of Tibetan governments prior to the 1950s, he sees no contradiction in denying China a right to send in its military while arguing that Britain's military incursion was legitimate.

The Republican Revolution

While these events were going on in Tibet, a combination of internal unrest, economic malaise, and external pressure further diminished the remnants of the Qing empire. Its end finally came in 1911, following a revolt sparked by the government's decision to nationalize the country's railroads. A number of revolutionary groups combined to force it to agree to the formation of a republic, which was to be led by Yuan Shigai (1859–1916), who had formerly commanded China's southern armies. Yuan's revolutionary movement was transformed into the Guomindang political party, and in 1913 it easily won the majority of seats in the new Parliament. Yuan became president of the new republic. His increasingly autocratic rule led to widespread opposition, however, and several governors declared their independence from the central government. After his death, the country suffered increasing fragmentation, and in its aftermath many areas of China came under the control of local warlords. Although the central government continued to claim all of the Qing dynasty's previous territories, the reality was that it held dominion over only a small part of China. Areas such as Tibet and Mongolia, which had never been directly administered by the central authorities, continued to distance themselves from China and pursued their own independent agendas, no longer even bothering to maintain contact with the purported government.

During World War I, China enlisted on the side of the Allied forces, but was bitterly disappointed at the war's conclusion, when the Western powers failed to help it out of its difficulties and instead confirmed Japan's ownership of southern Manchuria and other conquered Chinese territories. On May 4, 1919, students at Beijing University began a protest march against the agreements that had been reached at Versailles at the conclusion of the war. The government attempted to suppress the march; one student was killed and thirty-two arrested and sentenced to death. This led to even larger protests and increasing radicalization among, first, the intellectuals of the country, and later, other segments of the society. The May Fourth Movement, as it came to be known, became a watershed in modern Chinese history and a potent symbol of popular unrest.

The Nationalist Government

As more of the populace became disenchanted with the government, a small group formed the first Chinese communist organization in 1920. Sun Yat-sen, the Guomindang leader, decided to admit communists into his party, a move that led to increasing radicalization. Sun's death in 1925 created a power vacuum, following which the military commander Chiang Kai-shek began a series of military operations and a purging of communist elements from the Guomindang. In 1927 he succeeded in forming a new Nationalist government headquartered in Nanjing, and he became commander-in-chief of the army and chairman of the Central Executive Committee of the Guomindang. During his tenure, Chiang attempted to foster nationalism, which was mixed with traditional Chinese xenophobia and modern distrust of outsiders that had arisen from the role played by foreigners in weakening the country. He looked to the traditions of the past for models of good governance, and much of his vision was based on Confucian ideals and the practices of the imperial period. At the same time, his government was heavily dependent on the foreign powers that supported it, a fact that he bitterly resented. His public speeches were most vehemently anti-Western during the periods when his regime's very survival depended on U.S. support. And although Chinese elites were willing to forgive the government's brutality toward its own citizens, many felt that its inability to exclude foreigners seriously undermined its legitimacy.

A central concern for Chiang was the formation of a strong state, one that would have the power to regain China's lost territories, restore unity, abolish the unequal treaties, and end the humiliations inflicted on China by foreigners. The mainstay of this program was the creation of a strong army, but Chiang's efforts also included attempts to foster a sense of pride in China's glorious past and nationalist solidarity. The focus on military might has become one of the main features of modern Chinese national identity, and it is widely believed by Chinese that only a strong state can protect them from the depredations of foreigners and the threat of social disruption.

Waking the Dragon

According to John Fitzgerald, Chiang and many of China's intellectuals were convinced that China was asleep and needed to be awakened.[44] They believed that they formed an elite, newly conscious vanguard and that their duty was to rouse the rest of the country. They perceived an immanent challenge from outside forces that threatened the very fabric of the country and its continued survival, and their writings and speeches often forecast the eventual dismemberment of China if the country failed to awaken from its slumber. Once awakened and properly mobilized, they believed, China's masses would become an unstoppable force that could be used to end the humiliation of foreign incursion, reverse military defeats, and overcome the stagnation and corruption that contributed to the country's weakness. The desired outcome was the creation of a China that could stand proud and strong as an independent state. As Liang Qichao expressed this idea, "To what do we awaken when we attain self-awakening? . . . First, we awaken [to the fact] that all who are not Chinese lack the right to control Chinese affairs. Secondly, we awaken [to the fact] that all Chinese have the right to control Chinese affairs."[45]

This process would require that the already awakened elite must take charge of instructing the masses in exactly how to become fully Chinese by indoctrinating them with nationalist propaganda. Their task was to lead the people of China to acceptance of what the elite wanted them to believe in order to forge a unitary consciousness among the populace. Through this process the masses would learn to accept the leading role of the government and its authority to dictate proper attitudes and beliefs:

> National consciousness was located in the leadership of the Nationalist party under a tutelary (xunzheng) state, which was legitimated by its role in teaching people how to be Chinese citizens. . . . The respective nations of the Nationalists and the Communists were to be counted self-conscious not when all nationals had awakened under their instruction, but when all obstacles to political instruction had been removed—that is, when the pedagogical state could say whatever it liked, wherever it chose, without fear of contradiction. At this point the myth of national or class consciousness would cease to be mythical, for community consciousness extended as far as the reach of the state, into the heart of society and to the outermost borders of the land.[46]

Chiang and his government had inherited a country that was plagued by internal dissension and corruption, its resources further depleted by the perceived need to maintain and defend a vast and diverse empire. In the ideological climate of the time, it was easy to find reasons to blame foreigners for China's problems, whereas the comprehensive reforms the country really needed were far more difficult to envision. Moreover, antiforeign rhetoric proved to be a popular unifying theme among the populace, and Chiang made use of xenophobic sentiments. The notion that China was an ancient and culturally superior nation ruthlessly violated by foreign, particularly Western, powers became a mainstay of the works of both government bodies and literati during this period, and issues of racial and political impotence continue to be discussed in China today. One general area of consensus among Chinese is the belief that the world is an essentially amoral field of contention between states and that the strong expand and prosper while the weak are victimized. The lesson Chinese draw from this is that China must either become strong and feared by other countries or it will be divided up by them and exploited.

Tibetan Lamas in China

At the same time as the government disseminated its official rhetoric of the unity of China's nationalities in school curricula and official pronouncements, many Chinese Buddhists began to consider Tibetan Buddhism to be a part of their religious inheritance.[47] This was largely due to the unprecedented popularity of two Tibetan lamas residing in China, the ninth Panchen Lama, Losang Tubten Chökyi Nyima (1883–1937), and Norhla Hutukhtu Trinle Gyatso (Chinese: Nona houfo, 1865–1936). Both had fled Tibet as a result of the thirteenth Dalai Lama's efforts to expand his control over formerly autonomous religious estates. In the early twentieth century, the Dalai Lama invoked an eighteenth-century precedent which required the Panchen Lama's estate to provide one quarter of the military's operating expenses. This move was designed both to secure much needed cash for his vision of an expanded army and to reduce the power of the Panchen Lama, who ruled over what was effectively an autonomous region centered in Shigatse. In an attempt to force his compliance, the Lhasa government imprisoned monastic officials from the Panchen Lama's monastery of Tashihlünpo, following which he appealed to British officials in India for aid. When they refused to help him, he fled to China, where the Nationalist government welcomed him, hoping that it might use him to exert some influence in Tibet. He apparently hoped that the Chinese government might give him military aid to establish a separate state under his control, but although it agreed to provide money for his living expenses, it was unwilling to become involved in a military adventure in Tibet.

For his part, the Dalai Lama was working to consolidate his own power and that of a centralized Tibetan state. The Norhla Hutukhtu ran afoul of him when he was found to be collaborating with Chinese forces in the Kham region of eastern Tibet. He was the religious and secular leader of a small area near Chamdo who hoped to establish a separate state under his own control. When the Lhasa government managed to extend its control over this area in 1919, he was arrested and brought to central Tibet. In 1923 he was transferred to a jail in southern Tibet, but managed to escape. He fled to Nepal and then made his way to China.

When they first arrived in China, the Panchen Lama and Norhla Hutukhtu were welcomed by Mongolian and Manchu communities that practiced Tibetan Buddhism, but beginning in the 1930s, they began to attract ethnic Chinese followers. During the late Republican period, they traveled all over China, performing tantric rituals for increasingly large audiences. Their popularity attracted the attention of both local and national leaders, who saw their presence in China as an opportunity to regain some of the influence in Tibet that had been lost with the overthrow of the Qing dynasty. The most influential supporter of this idea was Dai Jitao, Sun Yat-sen's secretary, who in 1933 proclaimed that Buddhism was the central unifying principle for China's peoples, particularly Han, Tibetans, Mongols, and Manchus. He hoped to promote a vision of Buddhism that merged Tibetan and Chinese traditions, and he proclaimed that this policy would be the cornerstone of both Sino-Tibetan interactions and China's relations with other Asian countries. In 1934 he wrote a letter to the thirteenth Dalai Lama urging him to agree to amalgamate Tibet with China on the grounds that in order for Buddhism to prosper, it was necessary that China be unified. Gray Tuttle argues that this rhetoric, combined with the increasing popularity of Tibetan lamas in China, helped Chinese to imagine Tibet as a part of China, but I think that their influence was mainly limited to Buddhist groups and probably had little impact on the wider Chinese population or on government officials.[48] China had claimed Tibet as part of its territory for centuries, and even when Chiang Kai-shek's government was on the verge of being overthrown by the Communists, he still proclaimed a vision of a strong and unified China that included all the territories of the Qing dynasty.

The Communist Revolution

Unfortunately for Chiang, while he aspired for China to be one of the strong states, internal and external factors rendered the government congenitally impotent. Between 1911 and 1949 there were literally hundreds of civil wars in China, and the conflict with Japan that began in 1931 further diminished China's military capacity. There were major famines in 1920–1921 and 1928. In 1931 and 1935 there were severe floods along the Yangtze; in 1938 the river's dikes were breached in an attempt to slow down the invading Japanese, and its banks were not controlled again for ten years. Any government would have experienced difficulties with these disasters, but the already enfeebled Nationalists simply had no answers. The final blow was the emergence of a well-organized revolutionary movement led by communists who had fled to the mountains of Kiangsi province after their earlier persecution by the Nationalists. There they had gained increasing support among the peasantry, mainly due to their proposals for land redistribution and their reputation for honesty and fair dealing.

Even more important, communist forces took a leading role in opposing Japanese expansion in north China. While Chiang dithered and avoided confrontation with the invaders, the communists offered to join with their Nationalist enemies in a common front. The atrocities of Japan's military adventures in China—most famously, the "Rape of Nanjing" in December 1937—led to growing outrage among Chinese, who yearned for a government that could put a stop to foreign encroachment, make China strong again, and restore stability.

Following the Japanese attack on Pearl Harbor in 1941 and the subsequent entry of the United States into World War II, the Chinese government obtained powerful foreign allies in its battle with Japan. After its defeat in 1945, Japan was forced to withdraw from its Chinese possessions, but the Nationalist government was unable to capitalize on this. Chiang began a campaign against the communists, but he and his commanders committed a series of tactical blunders. Despite this, the United States increased its aid to the Guomindang, hoping that it might keep China free from communism, but in the end its actions served only to further deepen negative Chinese attitudes toward outsiders and their intervention in the country's affairs. The communists won a series of battles against Nationalist forces, and by 1949 were in control of most of the country. In a last desperate move, Chiang sought intervention by Western powers, offering to allow them to establish military bases in China and the restoration of the unequal treaties, but none responded.

Nationalism and Cultural Chauvinism

On April 20, 1949, the People's Liberation Army crossed the Yangtze River, and the remaining Nationalists fled to Taiwan, where they established a provisional government that still claimed to be the legitimate rulers of China. On October 1, the inauguration of the People's Republic of China was officially proclaimed.

In his speech commemorating the event, Mao Zedong declared, "Our nation will no longer be an insulted nation; we have stood up."[49] This theme became central to the self-definition of the new government, which sought to restore China's past glory by making it militarily and economically strong. Mao and the communists dreamed of a China that could stand up to the foreign imperialists and restore their country to a position of international respect.

An important aspect of their agenda was the reclamation of those territories that had been part of (or at least claimed by) earlier dynasties but had become separated. Because they inherited traditional Chinese notions of cultural superiority, they assumed that all of their former possessions longed to return to the motherland and that their present state of estrangement must have been due to the actions of imperialists whose deceitful tactics enticed minority populations to temporarily forget their long-standing ties with China.

The fact that assimilation of a minority population by a majority might seem more desirable to those doing the assimilating than those being assimilated does not appear to have occurred either to China's leaders or to most Han, for whom it is incomprehensible that a people might consciously choose to remain apart from their superior culture. Even for those who acknowledge this possibility, many believe that such attitudes are based on ignorance and that it is the duty of the Han "big elder brothers" (lao da ge) to incorporate the minorities—forcibly, if necessary—so that as a result of contact and instruction they will gradually renounce their backward (luohou) ways and be lifted up to the level of their instructors. Ultimately, the assimilation will benefit the minority, which, when it becomes sufficiently advanced, will come to recognize this fact and express its gratitude.

In the case of Tibetans, the Han felt particularly justified in insisting on (re)integrating them into the motherland because it was commonly assumed that they were part of the Chinese race. Moreover, it was widely believed that as a result of its temporary estrangement from the interior of the country and the ineptitude and brutality of local rule, Tibet had slipped into an abyss of barbarism from which it could be rescued only by the Han.

Traditional China adhered to the notion that in all social situations there is a hierarchy, with one person or group in the superior position. As Michael Walzer[50] has noted, hierarchies are never "innocent"; they always imply a devaluation of one group by the other, and when a minority is classified as inferior it is unlikely that the majority will willingly leave them alone to manage their own affairs. The majority will always assume that they can do a better job and that the minority are incapable of governing themselves without their help. According to William Jenner, "History as it is written in China makes it very hard even to consider the possibility that significant numbers of the subjects of Chinese regimes refused to think of themselves as Chinese or to accept the legitimacy of any Chinese rule over them and their territory."[51]

During the Nationalist period, both Sun and Chiang proclaimed that all of China's nationalities constituted one people and ordered the minorities to alter their views and acknowledge this fact. Part of their program involved policies of ethnic amalgamation, in which distinctive aspects of minority culture would be subsumed under Han models.[52] Those elements of minority customs that were considered to make beneficial contributions to the society as a whole (for instance, martial spirit, loyalty, singing and dancing) could be retained, but anything the Han deemed backward or worthless would be discarded in the interests of the common good and racial solidarity.[53] The yardstick by which worthiness was to be measured was, of course, Han culture and attitudes. The goal was to merge all the various races into one homogeneous civilization, which was felt to be a necessary component of the restoration of unity and strength.

The notion of the unity of races was exemplified in the five colors of the Republican flag, which represented the five main races (*wu zu*) of the Republic: red for the Han, yellow for the Manchurians, blue for the Mongolians, white for the Tibetans, and black for the Muslims. According to Chiang, "The fact that [China] comprises five stocks is due not to diversity in race or blood but to dissimilarity in creed and geographical environment. In a word, the distinction between the five stocks is territorial as well as religious, but not ethnological. This is something that our people must thoroughly comprehend."[54]

Contemporary Chinese often refer to the analogy of the five fingers of a hand, which the Tibetan headman used in *Red River Valley* to illustrate the unity of China's peoples. Just as the hand will not function effectively if one of the fingers is missing, so China would be crippled if one of its races were to separate itself from the others. During the Republican period, Chinese children were taught that Tibet and other minority areas were integral parts of China and that it would be a national tragedy if they were to be separated from it. This notion continues to be an element of communist propaganda, and most Chinese (including overseas Chinese who have been exposed to competing information) accept it as an article of faith.

The notion that all of China's populations constitute one race was a cornerstone of Sun Yat-sen's policies, and in *The International Development of China* he proposed further colonization of Tibet, Mongolia, Manchuria, and Xinjiang to assist the peoples of those areas to realize their common racial identity. Sun asserted that their Chinese identity continued even if a particular minority became estranged from the motherland, and so when Mongolia declared its independence and formed the Mongolian People's Republic in 1912, Sun proclaimed that the Mongolians were still Chinese and would remain so, even if they had temporarily forgotten that fact. According to Fitzgerald, "When Sun insisted that the Chinese people were racially distinct from all other 'races' of the world, he drew the boundaries of the race along the borders of the Chinese state and would allow no comparable ethnic distinctions to be drawn within China itself. The gene-pool of the race, in other words, happened to coincide with the borders of the state."[55]

The Nationalists' plans to reincorporate China's minority races were unsuccessful because they lacked the military capability necessary to force them to submit. The fact that armed force was needed to reunite the Chinese race was not seen as a sign that the minorities might have separate identities; that they might not wish to be integrated was never a concern. The Nationalists indicated on a number of occasions that they were prepared to use force if necessary to accomplish their ends, but because their armies were otherwise occupied, Chiang decided to invite the Tibetans to return to the motherland. In 1927 he asked a Tibetan monk who was visiting China to take back a letter to the Dalai Lama, in which he offered China's full support if he would agree that Tibet would "rejoin" the motherland. The Dalai Lama refused the offer, but welcomed the possibility of better relations. In Wang and Suo's version, however, the Dalai Lama agreed to the proposal and "voiced his allegiance"; they assert that his submission "marked the end of the abnormal relationship between Tibet and the motherland that had persisted for almost two decades."[56] They do not attempt to explain the fact that Chinese were still banned from entering Tibet and that the Dalai Lama continued to assert his country's independence.

When the Communists came to power, they inherited the Nationalists' ideas of the unity of the minorities and the Han and the imperative to actualize the dream of a strong and unified state that included Tibetans, Mongolians, Manchus, Uighurs, and other groups—brought about by force if necessary.

But unlike the Nationalists, they had the military capability to make this long-standing dream a reality.

Education and Nationalism in Communist China

Following their victory over the Nationalists, the Communists set about solidifying their power, and then began to transform Chinese society in accordance with their conception of Marxism. The first problem the Communist Party faced was that although it had widespread support among the peasantry, the country's intellectuals (that is, people who had graduated from a school) had become largely disaffected during the later period of Qing rule. They generally despised the Qing rulers, but they were slow to embrace the Communists, and few shared their ideology. To combat this problem, the Communists initiated a massive public reeducation campaign to indoctrinate the populace in Marxist theory. This became a core focus of the school curriculum, and a system of local reeducation campaigns was created throughout the country.

During the decades following the Communist Revolution, most of the population was forcibly organized into work units, which became the main institutions for disseminating Party policies and indoctrination. The methods they used reflect Benedict Anderson's notion that in recently decolonized states the process of nation building involves "both a genuine, popular nationalist enthusiasm, and a systematic, even Machiavellian, instilling of nationalist ideology through the mass media, the educational system, [and] administrative regulations."[57] The Communists effectively used mass organizations and the media to spread the Party's message into every village and neighborhood, and because China was a one-party state, no competing sources of information or opinion were allowed. To provide focal symbols, the Communists began developing the standard apparatus of modern state nationalism, including a national flag, a national anthem, the pervasive use of red as a symbol of communism, the creation and dissemination of images of revolutionary heroes, and, most important, the figure of Mao Zedong, the "Great Helmsman," who became the sacrosanct father-figure of the new nation and the Party.

In the shambles of the fall of the Nationalist government, many Chinese who were not convinced of the new ideology were still willing to give the Communists a chance because at first they appeared to be a party that was able to get things done. Whereas the preceding regimes had been paralyzed by incompetence, corruption, and impotence, the Communists enjoyed a reputation for honesty, frugality, and methodical efficiency. They espoused a coher-

FIGURE 3.3. Slogan painted on a wall at Sera Je Monastery near Lhasa, exhorting the monks to love their country and to contribute to moving the Cultural Revolution forward, in order to bring progress to everyone. Such Cultural Revolution–era slogans are seldom seen in China but are still common in Tibet. Photo by John Powers.

ent message, and apparently most of them sincerely believed it. Moreover, when Communist troops moved into the cities, they appeared to be different from the Nationalists they had driven out: they were strictly disciplined, and unlike their predecessors, they did not loot or rape after their victories. The fact that they were often as brutal in their methods of indoctrination as their predecessors had been was not generally viewed as a mark against them, because most Chinese had been conditioned to tacitly accept the idea that a strong government will force recalcitrant elements of the society to follow its directives.

> By the beginning of 1954 the Communist Party could claim to have started building a new China and to be the first government since the irruption of the West in the middle of the nineteenth century to have made a start towards achieving the dream of making China a country that was rich and powerful. . . . In the cities the relentless and unending process of indoctrination through political study meetings had taught the people the language of the new order. The Party had replaced chaos with order, war with peace, weakness with strength, impoverishment with a modest turn towards prosperity, confusion with certainty, aimlessness with purpose. In almost all re-

spects the Communists were performing far better than any predecessor. A national identity and value system was being remade.[58]

The efficiency and ruthlessness with which the Communists began reor-
ganizing Chinese society impressed many of their erstwhile critics, and when
Chinese forces beat Western armies during the Korean War most Chinese were
overjoyed that they finally had a government that could stand up to the "big
noses" and reverse the military humiliations China had recently suffered at
their hands. Moreover, the army's success in forcibly annexing bordering territories to the newly expanding Chinese empire was warmly welcomed by the
populace. In just a few years, the People's Liberation Army was able to establish
sovereignty over most of the territories that had either declared their independence or been annexed by Japan during the later Qing, including Mongolia,
Tibet, and Manchuria. This ability to achieve broadly popular national aims
helped in the process of gaining control over Chinese minds and indoctrinating
them with the new ideology.

It is ironic in retrospect that a revolutionary party that appeared poised to
fundamentally change China, and perhaps the world, run by revolutionaries
with radical new ideas who enjoyed impressive early success in their endeavors,
also created tragedies like the Great Leap Forward and the Cultural Revolution,
which destroyed much of China's traditional cultural inheritance and crippled
the economy. Following these disasters, the Party leadership became increasingly stagnant, and now China's octogenarian elite has become a deeply con-
servative regime that has run out of new ideas on how to manage the country
and has perforce moved toward a free market economy, while still attempting
to retain both the rhetoric and the apparatus of control of a Marxist state.

With the virtual collapse of communism as a viable ideology in the 1980s
and 1990s, the Party has turned to nationalism as an alternative tool for keeping the masses in line. But, as Lucian Pye has noted, it is an unusually "con-
tentless" sort of nationalism, narrowly identified with Chinese patriotism and
adherence to current Party policies, rather than shared ideals and values.[59]
Instead, contemporary Chinese nationalism makes appeals to patriotism and
fear of the chaos that would occur if the power of the Party were diminished.

The process of creating and developing nationalist sentiments was aided
by the fact that most Chinese already had a clearly defined idea of the nation
and its borders, a shared language and system of writing, and an ancient culture whose values and myths formed their cultural inheritance. According to
Gellner, "Nationalism is not the awakening of nations to self-consciousness; it
invents nations where they do not exist."[60] But this does not appear to be the
case with China. Most Chinese were already deeply conscious of themselves

as Chinese and had a corresponding animosity toward foreigners. There was no need to "invent" China, in Anderson's terms, because the idea of China was already a potent image for most Chinese. This image was in part a product of the experience of the degeneration of the late Qing, and it was further enhanced and augmented by the Nationalist government in the early twentieth century, but its antecedents can be traced back at least to the early Qin dynasty, and probably before that. Present-day Chinese nationalism mingles collective memories of past humiliations, a perceived need for a strong state, ethnic Han identity, and a culturalist pride that is linked to perceptions of China's ancient and glorious civilizational legacy and its present growing status within the community of nations.[61]

According to Pye, "The Chinese have been generally spared the crisis of identity common to most other transitional systems," and this is largely due to the fact that "they have little doubt about their identities as Chinese . . . the more they have been exposed to the outside world, the more self-consciously Chinese they have become."[62] James Townsend contends that the most passionate loyalty for the majority of Chinese is not to the PRC state but to the Han Chinese nation, and this ethnic identification is "more spontaneous, volatile and potent than the state nationalism that it often challenges."[63] Because of its power and persuasiveness for most Han, it is difficult for them to understand that large numbers of minorities have failed to develop the same sentiment and continue to agitate for cultural and political autonomy.

When the Communists began their program to build Chinese nationalism, they had a solid base from which to operate and a populace that already shared a nationalist (or at least protonationalist) vision. As Stuart Schram argues, "Neither in the realm of organization nor in that of ideology and culture would Mao and his successors have striven so hard to promote uniformity if the unitary nature of state and society had not been accepted . . . in the Chinese tradition, for the past two thousand years, as both natural and right."[64]

When the Communists formulated their vision of a nationalist ideology, it was strongly linked with the notion that they were a revolutionary party at the vanguard of immanent changes that would reshape the world. But in retrospect, they were more traditionally Chinese than revolutionary, and their image of the new China shared much in common with that of the Nationalists. There was, of course, a long history in China of patriotism characterized by a shared sense of racial distinctiveness, cultural chauvinism, xenophobia, and allegiance to imperial institutions and ruling dynasties, but for the vast majority of rural Chinese peasants, their worldview was primarily dominated by local perspectives and concerns. As Gellner has noted, one of the central features of modern nationalism is "the striving to make culture and polity congruent,"[65] and one of the Communists' main aims was to lead the masses to understand their shared identity as Chinese and the national mission they faced in restoring the nation's lost greatness. This could only be accomplished, they believed, by an ideologically unified state led by a single Party whose power and authority were unquestioned.

One of the problems the Communists faced in their program to instill a nationalist consciousness among the Chinese people was the fact that within China's borders there were a number of minority peoples who did not identify themselves as Chinese and whose own emerging nationalist consciousness emphasized their differences from the Han and resistance to assimilation. In combating this, the Communists adopted the Nationalists' notion that all minorities constituted part of the Chinese race, and they embarked on a program of cultural assimilation through which, it was hoped, the differences between the races would wither and disappear, leaving in the end a coherent, monolithic, and unified culture that, naturally, was based on the Han model.

One obstacle they faced was identifying unifying symbols of shared struggle and solidarity. Chinese from the interior provinces were easily moved by tales of foreign imperialists and their sinister deeds, of revolutionary heroes who had fought against the Qing and the Nationalists and established the new People's Republic, and of the heroic struggles of the Long March and other solidarity-building myths, but these had no resonance for minority peoples like the Tibetans, Uighurs, or Mongolians, who had not experienced the humiliation of foreign expansionism or taken part in the Chinese revolution. When Chinese propagandists attempted to invoke symbols of the Chinese struggle, they had little effect on the minorities, who viewed them as stories about foreigners who, after defeating their imperialist enemies, began a program of imperialist expansion of their own. Far from feeling part of the heroic struggle to establish the People's Republic, the minority nationalities generally perceived themselves as its victims.

The Chinese perspective is fundamentally different. Chinese students are taught that these minorities lived in brutal and barbaric conditions prior to their liberation and reincorporation into the motherland, and they commonly point to the fact that China has poured vast amounts of money into minority areas like Tibet and built roads, hospitals, schools, and airports. Most Chinese conclude that Tibetans should be grateful for their largesse and consider their continuing intransigence to be both unreasonable and unwarranted. Coupled with this is a common notion that minorities are incapable of managing their own affairs, and so they waste much of what China has given them. Such paternalistic attitudes, of course, serve only to further alienate the minorities.

The PRC strategy to overcome minority resistance to Chinese rule involves a combination of force and propaganda. When traveling in Tibet, one is immediately struck by the pervasiveness of Chinese military force. In the airport outside of Lhasa during a recent visit, I saw at least one hundred uniformed soldiers. The bus into town passed several military bases, and buses and trucks filled with soldiers are a common sight on the streets of Tibetan cities. During a walk around the Barkhor (the most popular pilgrimage circuit in Tibet), I counted twenty-three uniformed soldiers armed with rifles and another twenty Chinese not in uniform who appeared to be undercover security personnel. Monasteries that in the past have been involved in anti-Chinese agitation often have military bases next to them; at Tashilhünpo, one monk told me that there were twenty-one Chinese security personnel living in the monastery and maintaining a constant watch on the monks.

Tibetans who witness the Chinese military presence in their midst realize that their small population has no chance in either a direct confrontation against the Chinese or even limited guerrilla actions. But the Chinese government is not content simply to subjugate them militarily; it also wants to win their hearts and minds, and to this end it has embarked on a program of economic development and propaganda. The propaganda asserts the need for national unity and stresses themes that have positive associations for Chinese from the central provinces, such as antiforeign sentiment, hearkening back to China's glorious past, and stories of revolutionary heroes. But despite concerted efforts to convince Tibetans that China's history is also Tibet's history, most Tibetans still perceive the Chinese as foreign invaders. Revolutionary stories have little resonance for them because Tibetans were simply not involved in China's revolutions, nor did the cataclysmic changes of twentieth-century China affect them until Chinese troops entered their country, toppled the only government the people had ever known, and caused their spiritual leader, the fourteenth Dalai Lama, to flee into exile. In light of these factors, it is hardly surprising that the declaration in the PRC Constitution that the country is "a unitary multinational state [*tongyi duominzu guojia*] created in common by its various nationalities" is more convincing for Han Chinese than the minorities they officially claim as compatriots.

4

Family Reunion or Shotgun Wedding?

Every Communist must understand this truth: Political power grows out of the barrel of a gun.
—Mao Zedong, *Problems of War and Strategy*

The Motherland Drops in for a Visit

On November 24, 1949, Radio Beijing announced that the Panchen Lama (who was twelve years old at the time) had pleaded with Mao to "liberate" Tibet from "foreign imperialists." The January 1, 1950, broadcast promised that this would be one of the People's Liberation Army's tasks for the coming year. Alarmed by this announcement, the Tibetan government sent messages to Beijing indicating that Tibet did not need to be liberated and that there were no imperialists in the country. This was true: at the time, only five foreigners were living in Tibet, and none had any influence with the government. But China's leaders may well have believed that Tibet had come under the influence of imperialists and viewed this as a plausible reason for its self-imposed isolation and estrangement from China. Wang and Suo express this sentiment when they describe the situation in Tibet at the time:

> When the People's Republic was founded, most of the Tibetan areas in the country were not yet liberated. The people in Tibet

... were longing for the arrival of the P.L.A. to help bring an end to their sufferings, drive the imperialist forces out of their region and frustrate the schemes of the imperialists and separatists to sever Tibet from China. . . . Subsequently, the patriotic people of Tibetan nationality . . . voiced their desire for the central government's prompt dispatch of troops to liberate Tibet. They pinpointed the region as an integral part of Chinese territory and warned the imperialists to end all their aggressive designs on it.[1]

As we have seen, it is generally assumed by Han Chinese that minority people naturally want to associate with them in order to absorb their superior culture and thus be uplifted, and the Communists also fervently believed in the superiority of their ideology and the benefits it would bring to all who adopted it. This confidence in their Marxist doctrines was mixed with traditional Han chauvinism, and it was easy for them to believe that the Tibetans would not have chosen independence if they had not been coerced to do so by foreigners with ulterior motives. None of China's leaders had been to Tibet, and Tibetan exiles who lived there at that time commonly assert that China simply was not a part of their consciousness because the country had isolated itself from foreigners. There were contacts with merchants, traders, and pilgrims, but the Tibetan government followed a policy of excluding most outsiders, particularly Westerners. Most Tibetans had never even met a Chinese prior to 1950.[2] In such a situation of mutual ignorance and incommensurable ideologies, misunderstanding and misreadings were inevitable.

In October 1950, advance troops of the PLA began launching incursions into eastern Tibet. Because China had had little contact with Tibet for decades—and because its leaders believed that foreign imperialists had been secretly arming and training the Tibetans—they wanted to ascertain the strength of their opponents before launching a full-scale assault. Even Mao acknowledged the fact that China had no presence in a speech to his generals prior to the first incursions: "Tibet and Xinjiang are different: In Xinjiang in the old society there were 200,000–300,000 Chinese, but in Tibet there was not even a single Chinese. So our troops are in a place where there were no Chinese in the past."[3]

In the initial engagements between Tibetan militias and Chinese troops in eastern Tibet, the PLA discovered that its opponents were armed mainly with hand weapons and that they fought poorly. Their leadership was inept, and the Chinese won every battle easily. According to Chinese sources, the Tibetans viewed the Chinese soldiers as their liberators, and Wang and Suo report that "when the victorious P.L.A. troops marched through Tibetan communities, people lined the streets to give them a warm welcome or entertain them in every possible way."[4] According to our Tibetan writers, Tibetans lined the streets and hurled invectives at them, threw stones, dirt, and manure at them, and cursed them in hopes of driving the alien invaders from their land.

On November 17, 1950, in response to the crisis, the Tibetan Assembly (Kashag) decided to enthrone the fourteenth Dalai Lama, Tenzin Gyatso (1935–), and invest him with full temporal authority, even though he was only fifteen years old. Following this, the Tibetan government sent letters to the United Nations and the United States protesting the Chinese incursions, but Tibet's long period of isolation had left it with few friends in the international community, and there was a general reluctance to risk China's wrath by objecting to what it characterized as an "internal matter." Tibet's appeal to the UN was rejected because it was not a member state. Moreover, because Tibet had never bothered to publicly contradict China's claims of sovereignty, most other countries accepted them.

The Seventeen-Point Agreement for the Peaceful Liberation of Tibet

Despite its early victories, China was wary of prompting a major Tibetan counterattack, which Mao feared might encourage other nations to intervene in the conflict, and so he decided that a negotiated agreement with Tibet would be useful in allaying international concerns. With twenty thousand Chinese troops massed at its eastern border, Tibet was ordered to send representatives to Beijing to negotiate a treaty for its "peaceful liberation." The result was a document generally referred to as the "Seventeen-Point Agreement," which is one of the most hotly contested aspects of this period of Tibetan history. As its name implies, it contained seventeen provisions, and although China officially regarded Tibet as a temporarily wayward province, it had the form of an international treaty. Moreover, no other region annexed by China was invited to agree to such a pact prior to its incorporation into the PRC.

The final draft contained a number of contradictory articles: some provisions pledged that nothing would change in Tibet; others indicated that everything would change. The Tibetan delegates took solace in promises that their religion and traditional way of life would not be affected, but the agreement also stipulated that changes would be made by China when "the people demanded them." And because the Communist Party is by definition the people's party and represents their will and interests, it could determine when the people wished for "reforms" to be carried out, and there would be no need to actually consult the people since the Party's wishes are congruent with theirs.

Article 1 of the Agreement states: "The Tibetan people shall unite and drive out imperialist forces from Tibet: The Tibetan people shall return to the big family of the Motherland—the People's Republic of China." The document further stipulates that Tibet acknowledges Chinese sovereignty, but in exchange, Articles 3, 4, 7, and 11 promise that the country's traditional political and economic systems will be maintained until the Tibetan people themselves call for "reforms." The office of the Dalai Lama would also be maintained, and Tibet's religion and culture were to be left intact.

After being presented with a draft version by the Chinese representatives, the Tibetan delegation was told that they could discuss any of its provisions. Several of them later reported, however, that whenever they attempted to do so the Chinese threatened them with an invasion of their country if they failed to comply. P. T. Takla asserts, "The Chinese were polite when the Tibetans were not saying anything; when the Tibetans tried to say anything, the Chinese got very angry."[5] According to the Dalai Lama:

> As soon as the first meeting began, the chief Chinese representative produced a draft agreement containing ten articles ready-made. This was discussed for several days. Our delegation argued that Tibet was an independent state, and produced all the evidence to support their argument, but the Chinese would not accept it. Ultimately, the Chinese drafted a revised agreement, with seventeen articles. This was presented as an ultimatum. Our delegates were not allowed to make any alterations or suggestions. They were insulted and abused and threatened with personal violence, and with further military action against the people of Tibet, and they were not allowed to refer to me or my government for further instructions.[6]

When presented with this document, the Tibetan delegation protested that they had no plenipotentiary powers to sign on behalf of the Tibetan government, but the Chinese ordered them to do so anyway, using seals that had been manufactured for them. After the signing, the PRC issued an announcement on May 26 indicating that the Tibetan "local government" had approved the agreement, even though it had not yet even seen it or been allowed to communicate with the delegation. China announced that the delegates had been granted full powers to negotiate and that it was a binding compact. The event was depicted as an important step in China's glorious fight against imperialism:

In the last one hundred years and more, imperialism penetrated into China and at the same time also into Tibet. As early as the latter half of the 18th century, British imperialists began to penetrate into this part of our country; and after the Second World War, American imperialism also barged in. Following the victorious development of the great revolution of the Chinese people and the people's liberation war, the imperialists and their lackeys became still more frantic like mad dogs, and hastily manufactured the so-called "Tibetan independence" and various "anti-communist" plots in an attempt to make the Tibetan people to be completely cut off from their motherland, to lose their independence and freedom completely and become their complete slaves.[7]

The announcement was a gamble on the part of the Chinese because the agreement had not yet actually been ratified by the Tibetan government. In the following days, more proclamations came from Beijing, one made by Mao Zedong, that the Tibetan authorities had accepted the agreement; if they decided to repudiate it, this would have been a loss of face for China's leaders and could have damaged their international credibility.

The Dalai Lama has repeatedly stated that the delegates who were sent to Beijing to negotiate were never given authority to sign an agreement with China, but faced with immanent invasion and threats of personal violence, they agreed to affix the Chinese seals to the document; some indicated that they reasoned that the Lhasa government could later repudiate it if it chose. When the Dalai Lama first heard of the signing and the provisions of the agreement, he was reportedly deeply shocked,[8] but subsequently the Tibetan Assembly decided to ratify it, apparently figuring that although many of its provisions were repugnant to them, it was the best deal they were likely to get with the Chinese.

According to Shakabpa, when the delegates arrived they soon realized that the Chinese had no intention of negotiating, and instead presented them with an already prepared document that had a number of provisions to which the Tibetans objected. They were told that no alteration of the text would be permitted. They asked to be allowed to communicate with their government in Lhasa, but this request was refused, and in Shakabpa's account they were finally forced to sign under duress: "Once in Chinese hands, the Tibetan Delegation had no alternative but to fall prey to Chinese pressure and to serve as an instrument for the construction of the so-called 'Agreement on Measures for the Peaceful Liberation of Tibet.' " He states that the manufacture of seals by the Chinese exhibited "contempt and disregard for the generally accepted rules of international law" and that the delegates were "forced" to sign.[9] Dawa Norbu is even more emphatic: he claims that "the Chinese Communists made the Tibetan delegation sign the Agreement at gun-point."[10]

Wang and Suo, however, repeatedly stress the forbearance of the Chinese government, which they say patiently worked to persuade the recalcitrant Tibetans of the inevitability of the reincorporation of their region into the motherland. Despite a number of outrages perpetrated by the Tibetan government, Chinese patience never wavered, and they rankle at the suggestion that force or coercion was used to persuade the Tibetan delegates in Beijing: "In the course of the negotiation . . . central government leaders repeatedly met with the Tibetan representatives and explained away what misgivings they might have had. The negotiation proceeded very smoothly and it took only a little over a month for both sides to reach agreement." They proudly describe the document as "epoch-making" and characterize it as a voluntary compact between Tibetans and the Chinese government that ushered in momentous and positive changes for Tibet. It brought the Tibetans and Chinese closer together than ever before and enabled the Tibetans to cast off their chains with the help of the PLA: "It serves as a new basis for unity among all nationalities, particularly between Han and Tibetan nationalities."[11] After it was signed, the Tibetan people eagerly awaited the immanent arrival of the PLA, knowing that it would liberate them from their misery and bring cultural and economic progress to their benighted land.

The agreement looms large in the Chinese narratives. For them, it clearly is a legally binding compact that was reached through peaceful negotiations and was welcomed by the Tibetan people. While our Tibetan writers either ignore it or dismiss it as a farce, the agreement is quoted in full in *100 Questions about Tibet, Tibet: Myth vs. Reality, Highlights of Tibetan History, Tibet and the Tibetans,* and *The Biographies of the Dalai Lamas,* and every article is described in detail in *The Historical Status of Tibet.*[12] Li Tieh-Tseng believes that it "settled the issue of the status of Tibet" and that since its conclusion, "there can be no more question of boundary dispute between Tibet and its neighboring Chinese provinces." In common with the other Chinese writers, he asserts that "the Chinese Communists seem to have acted very carefully in Tibet. This writer has . . . not heard any averse [sic] comment from a non-partisan compatriot on the agreed measures for the peaceful liberation of Tibet."[13]

Grunfeld largely agrees with the Chinese view. In his presentation, the Tibetan delegation negotiated with China and was not forced to sign. He mentions that they were able to send and receive messages from the Lhasa government, but he ignores the fact that they were able to do so for only a few days and that when the Chinese became concerned about the content of their messages they no longer allowed any outside communication. In Grunfeld's view, "There was no outright coercion," though he admits that the Tibetans were "negotiating from an extremely weak position." He indicates that the pact definitively settled the status of Tibet, and he appears to have no qualms about the conditions under which it was negotiated or its legality. He admits that some Tibetans were "cautious" when PLA troops began arriving in Tibet after the agreement was signed, but he also indicates that many welcomed the Han soldiers and embraced this "opportunity to make some positive changes."[14]

Unlike the Tibetan writers who claim that the Tibetans were browbeaten and threatened, Goldstein asserts that the Chinese were "very polite," although during one part of the negotiations they threatened to invade Tibet if the Tibetans rejected one of the agreement's provisions.[15] He admits that the Tibetan delegates signed the agreement only "reluctantly," but he also thinks that it conclusively settled the question of Tibet's status with respect to China: "Tibet, for the first time in its 1,300 years of recorded history, had now in a formal written agreement acknowledged Chinese sovereignty." Unlike the Tibetan writers we are considering, he does not appear to have any qualms about its legality, and he states that it "gave Mao the political settlement he felt was critical to legitimize unambiguously Tibet's status as a part of China."[16] He stresses that the agreement was an example of Mao's "policy of moderation" with regard to Tibet and that he wanted to "create cordial relations between Han . . . and Tibetans." Like our Chinese writers, Goldstein also asserts that the PLA troops were respectful of Tibetan culture, paid for everything they required from the Tibetans, and generally created goodwill by their exemplary behavior.

Several of our Tibetan writers ignore the Seventeen-Point Agreement, probably because they consider it invalid or because it presents difficulties for their narratives of Tibetan independence. Those who do discuss the agreement characterize the Chinese as duplicitous bullies who forced a helpless Tibetan delegation with no plenipotentiary powers to sign an outrageous document they view as illegal because it was concluded under duress. The Chinese side, however, proudly points to it as an indication of the legality of China's claims to sovereignty over Tibet and its magnanimity in negotiating a settlement. *100 Questions about Tibet* asks, "Q: What was the Dalai Lama's attitude towards this agreement? A: The Dalai Lama supported the Agreement. . . . In his telegram to Mao Zedong . . . he said that the local government of Tibet and the Tibetan people, monks and laymen alike, would unanimously support the agreement."[17]

The Chinese writers all claim that the PLA soldiers showed respect for Tibetan culture and religion, helped the people in their work, and paid for everything they required. Through these actions, they "won the hearts of the Tibetans" and allayed any minimal concerns they might have had at the arrival of their estranged big brothers, who were now returning to free them from slavery and educate them in the communist doctrines that would liberate their minds from outmoded ideas. As Wang Feng expressed the Chinese attitude: "It is absolutely impossible for the various minorities to build socialism without the leadership of the Communist Party. For reasons of historical development, the minorities in China are not advanced politically, economically or culturally."[18] To uplift them from their backwardness, patient education and social revolution were required. From the Chinese perspective, this was purely a family matter; the Han had at last returned to this benighted minority area to assume their rightful place as teachers, and their only concern was to raise the Tibetans up to their level.

The Motherland Decides to Move In

Following the Tibetan government's ratification of the agreement, China began sending troops into Tibet. The first advance units entered Lhasa on September 9, 1950, and immediately established a military command for the region. At this point, there were no motorable roads connecting China and Tibet, so PLA supply lines were stretched to the limit. To bring food and equipment to the forward divisions, the Chinese had to rely on air drops, but because of the difficult terrain many of the packages fell into inaccessible ravines or were otherwise lost. By the time many of the troops reached Lhasa after their difficult journey from eastern Tibet, they were subsisting on the most meager rations, but according to all reports they scrupulously avoided taking anything from the Tibetans and paid for whatever they received. This is grudgingly admitted by our Tibetan writers, but they characterize this early attitude as a cynical ploy by invaders whose position was tenuous and who hoped to lull the Tibetan populace into a false sense of security with their superficially benign actions. According to several writers, most Tibetans were not fooled by their demeanor and suspected that the Chinese were planning to destroy their culture and religion.

As more troops arrived in Tibet, they requisitioned more and more supplies, pack animals, and food, which resulted in ever-rising prices. The Chinese set the rate of payment at less than the going rate, and continued to maintain this rate even after the inflationary pressures created by their incursion caused prices to skyrocket. It became increasingly difficult for Tibetans to afford basic necessities, and although the Chinese continued to avoid engaging in behavior that might give offence to Tibetans, the changing economic conditions began to create growing resentment. Added to this was the gap between Chinese expectations and what they actually encountered among the Tibetans: they had been taught by their superiors that they would be welcomed as liberators by a grateful populace, but instead, many Tibetans shouted at them to go back to China and others simply stared at them suspiciously as they marched past. Some aristocrats and lamas, hoping that by ingratiating themselves with the Chinese they might be able to maintain their positions of privilege, were friendly toward them. But the masses with whom they expected to share a bond of comradeship generally wanted nothing to do with people whom they regarded as alien invaders. Anticipating a warm welcome, the Chinese government at first encouraged PLA troops to cultivate personal relationships with Tibetans, but by 1952 there was so much animosity toward the new arrivals that the troops were ordered to avoid contact.

Frictions within the Family

During this period, the Dalai Lama and his government attempted to cooperate with the Chinese officials, who originally proposed to set up a parallel administration that would work with the old government in administering the country. To consolidate their position, the Chinese began building roads to link Tibet with China, which would allow them to move supplies and personnel more efficiently. Most of the labor for such infrastructure projects was supplied by Tibetans, who, by all accounts, were paid well for their work. As their power increased and their position strengthened, however, the Chinese administration sought to further marginalize the Dalai Lama and his government to purely nominal positions, and actual power resided in Chinese hands. At the same time, Chinese troops in eastern Tibet (under separate administration from the central provinces, which had been designated the "Tibet Autonomous Region" by the PRC government) were making radical changes in the society, forcing the people to move toward communization. This was linked to an effort to suppress religion, and a number of monasteries were destroyed. This unsurprisingly led to the formation of a resistance movement, which was brutally suppressed. As refugees poured into central Tibet with tales of destruction of religious sites, attacks against religious leaders, and violent reprisals against ordinary Tibetans who supported (or were suspected of supporting) the resistance, people in Lhasa, who had been largely allowed to continue their traditional way of life, became increasingly radicalized.

As the Dalai Lama describes this period, "Among the Tibetans, I saw mounting bitterness and hatred of Chinese; and among the Chinese, I saw the mounting ruthlessness and resolution which is born of fear and lack of understanding."[19] In this situation of mutual misunderstanding and incommensurable ideologies and expectations, conflict was inevitable, and when the PRC began forcing Tibetans in the central provinces to become collectivized in 1958, relations further deteriorated. A well-organized rebel movement called Four Rivers, Six Ranges (Chushi Kangdruk; Chu bzhi gang drug) had already been operating in eastern Tibet for several years, fighting a guerrilla campaign against PLA troops. They managed to inflict some casualties and had won minor battles, but the Chinese had better weapons and training, and the rebels had no way of countering Chinese aircraft. During this period, Chinese propaganda continually stressed the PLA's overwhelming technological superiority and its huge numbers. Although most Tibetans realized that they were at an impossible disadvantage in any conflict with China, resistance to Chinese rule continued to grow, along with an incipient national consciousness.

The March 1959 Revolt

The conflict that the Dalai Lama had worked to avoid finally broke out in March 1959. The flashpoint was an invitation from the Chinese commander in Lhasa for the Dalai Lama to attend a theatrical performance on March 10. According to some reports, the invitation stipulated that he must come alone, without his bodyguards; in the emotionally charged atmosphere of the time it was widely rumored that the Chinese intended to kidnap him. Sorting out the details of these events is extremely difficult because reports from actors and observers contain numerous inconsistencies and differences. Various parties have recast them in accordance with their presuppositions and biases, or have retrospectively rewritten them to make them fit into a particular historical narrative.

If the facts of the matter are unclear today, the situation was even more confused in Lhasa at the time: wild rumors were circulating among both the Tibetan populace and the Chinese, leading to a sharpening of differences and heightening of mutual distrust. To prevent the Dalai Lama's attendance at the performance, a crowd of Tibetans gathered outside the Norbulingka (summer residence of the Dalai Lamas) on March 10. In response, the Dalai Lama announced that he would not go to the performance, and further requested the crowd to disperse to avoid confrontation with the Chinese. Despite the reverence the Tibetans had for him, they ignored his plea, and instead formed a guard around the Norbulingka, and an ad hoc group that called itself the People's Assembly (Mimang Tsongdu; Mi dmangs tshogs 'du) declared Tibet's independence.[20] In the following days, most of the officials of the Tibetan government also echoed this sentiment, and the three major Gelukpa monasteries outside Lhasa—Drepung, Sera, and Ganden—all issued decrees in support of independence.

As tensions grew, the PLA moved troops into positions around the Norbulingka and on March 17 fired two mortar shells into the compound. When they heard the explosions, the Dalai Lama and his advisors decided that he must escape. That evening, disguised as a soldier, he slipped out of the Norbulingka and, together with a small entourage of family members and advisors, rode on horseback to the Kyichu River, where they were met by members of Chushi Kangdruk, who ferried them across the river and led them toward the Indian border. The Chinese remained unaware of his escape for several days; when they learned of it, troops were sent to intercept the party, but they managed to cross the border before the Chinese arrived. Mao later claimed that he had known of the escape and personally allowed it to happen, but this seems unlikely as patrols were dispatched to intercept the group.

Once in India, the Dalai Lama issued a proclamation repudiating the Seventeen-Point Agreement and asserting Tibet's independence from China. Meanwhile, back in Lhasa, the Chinese continued shelling the Norbulingka, believing that the Dalai Lama was still there, and the Tibetans outside reacted with a revolt that is now characterized by Tibetans as a "national uprising" against Chinese rule. Chinese accounts of these events indicate that they had become increasingly frustrated by what they regarded as Tibetan intransigence, and their reaction to the revolt was predictable: they responded with force, and scores of Tibetans were killed. They then announced that the Tibetan government had been dissolved, and the Chinese administration took full control.

After quelling the rebellion, they faced an increasingly restive populace, and they abandoned their previous policy of gradually introducing changes and opted to subdue the Tibetans with an overwhelming show of their military power. As conditions worsened in Tibet, an estimated eighty thousand refugees poured across the Indian border to join the Dalai Lama in exile. The Indian government offered to provide the hill station of Dharamsala in Himachal Pradesh as a headquarters for the Tibetans, and later large tracts of land in southern India were allocated to them. Although Jawaharlal Nehru, the Indian prime minister, stipulated that the Dalai Lama not be allowed to engage in political activities, he soon set up a government-in-exile headquartered in Dharamsala, and this remains the central leadership of the Tibetan exile community in South Asia.

Whose Heaven? Whose Hell?

In the Chinese historical narrative, the weakness and corruption of the late Qing rulers, combined with the maneuvers of foreign imperialists and a "handful of Tibetan reactionaries," formed the basis of the misguided notion of Tibetan independence. This narrative justifies the armed incursion into Tibet that began in 1950 and culminated with the dissolving of the Tibetan government in 1959. In addition to these reasons, Chinese sources also assert a moral authority based on the shared notion that, prior to the Chinese takeover, Tibet was a "feudal serfdom" and a "hell on earth." The authors of our Chinese sources wax rhetorical about this period, using negative superlatives in an attempt to provide some inkling of the overwhelming awfulness of Tibet under "local Tibetan rule."

One conclusion that they commonly draw from their descriptions is that it is absurd to imagine that a people who created and maintained such a terrible system could ever be capable of managing its own affairs. Without the benevolent and enlightened hand of their "Han big brothers," the backward and congenitally brutal Tibetans would inevitably sink back into the hellish system that prevailed before the "peaceful liberation." According to *Great Changes in Tibet*:

> Before liberation Tibet was a hell on earth, where the labouring people suffered for centuries under the darkest and most reactionary feudal serfdom. The three manorial lords . . . owning all the land and other means of production, ruthlessly exploited and oppressed the labouring masses. Tibetan serfs and slaves were deprived of freedom of the person and lived worse than animals. . . . On top of this, a century of aggression and enslavement in Tibet by imperialist forces plunged the Tibetan people into an abyss of misery. In 1951 Tibet was liberated, and imperialist aggressive forces were driven out. This marked a great turning point in the historic development in Tibet. Since then the Tibetan people have lived with China's other nationalities in the family of the great motherland on the basis of equality, unity, fraternity and mutual help. The Tibetan people are revolutionary and patriotic.[21]

As we have seen, although Chinese characterizations of the barbarity of old Tibet may not be supported by evidence, they are nonetheless fervently believed. Like other aspects of Chinese nationalist narratives, they have a long pedigree and are generally accepted without question. A history of Tibet written by He Ning in 1792, for example, reports, "The customs of the [Tibetans] are completely abject and despicable. The people all appear unwashed and uncombed. Their figure resembles a dog or a sheep. Both monks and laity are equally greedy. [Tibet] is a place where the old is being preserved and nothing changes."[22] An updated version of this notion can be seen in the film *Serfs* (*Nongnu*; Tibetan: *Zhing bran*), which was produced by the PLA's Military Movie Studio (Bayi Dianying Zhipian Chang) in 1963.[23] Tibet is represented as a savage, medieval country in which the overwhelming majority of the population are serfs. They are cruelly mistreated by the feudal lords, who constantly work to break their spirit through humiliation and denigration and who also break their bodies with physical violence and ceaseless manual labor. The movie opens with a message informing the audience that

> this is an indictment of the sad history of the serfs and of the old feudal system. It will tell people what it was really like for the millions of serfs. The Tibetan nationality is one of the brother nationalities of the Chinese minorities. The working people of this nationality in the past used to wear heavy chains on their feet and were living terrible lives, but no one knew. In 1951 after the peaceful liberation of Tibet, the central government had been patiently educating the counterrevolutionaries in Tibet; however, in attempting to maintain their feudal serf system they did not change at all, but actually became worse. Then in March 1959 they decided to rebel against the country, against the people, and to destroy the unity of the nationalities. After the PLA subdued the rebels most Tibetan people wanted to enter a new period of democratic reforms.

The movie depicts a society that is eating itself alive; the serfs all hobble slowly and painfully, even when not carrying burdens, and at several points viewers are informed that the population was in decline prior to the arrival of the PLA. The manorial lords are too wrapped up in their brutality to realize that they are killing off their workers and reducing their potential productivity. The serfs are all filthy and wear rags, and their faces reflect the brutality of the pathetic lives they lead. As Edward Said has noted, this is a standard theme in Western cinema depictions of the Oriental Other, which commonly make use of the notion that societies ruled by brutal, avaricious, and arbitrary Oriental despots become corrupt and indolent.[24] The populace is dishonest and servile due to having their spirits crushed by their rulers, and as a result the culture is stagnant until revived by vigorous invaders.

The star of the movie is a young Tibetan named Jampa (Chinese: Qiangba), whose father dies from torture in the opening scenes, following which Jampa is subjected to various indignities and physical abuse. At one point he bites off his own tongue in protest at the treatment he has received, and for most of the movie he is mute, symbolizing the notion that the serfs in old Tibet were not able to express their bitterness at the conditions in which they lived.

After depicting the horrors of old Tibet, the film then introduces the PLA, whose arrival is greeted by general excitement and enthusiasm by the serfs. After a few more scenes establishing the repulsiveness of the lamas and aristocrats—including a lengthy part in which they receive arms and ammunition from foreign imperialists following a secret cable to India and then hide them in a buddha statue—the heroic soldiers defeat the ruling classes and free the serfs. After they become communist cadres, the former serfs begin to bathe regularly and walk quickly and confidently. Everyone who has met the PLA is deeply impressed and speaks rapturously about their honesty and helpfulness. After his liberation, Jampa miraculously regains the ability to speak, and he extols the glory of Chairman Mao. The movie ends with a final song: "No matter how high, there is a roof; no matter how long there is a source; no matter how terrible Tibetans' sufferings have been, they have an end, and now things have changed from bitter to sweet."

The script writer, Huang Zongjiang, indicates in *Serfs: From Script to Screen* that he had only limited knowledge about Tibet and its history. He traveled to the region three times before and during the filming, and only for a few months at a time. He had no previous background in Tibetan history, and his information was derived entirely from Party documents.[25] He states that his plan in writing the script was to focus on three main points: "1. It should expose the darkness, cruelty, and savagery of the serf society; 2. using the viewpoint of class struggle, it should clearly show who was fighting to undermine the system and who was insanely trying to perpetuate the system; and 3. it should show the function of the Party in the Tibet Revolution and the great role played by the Tibetan people, who began to build socialism after the democratic reforms."[26]

Huang states that some people criticized the script for being overly graphic in its portrayal of the brutalities of the old system, but he felt that this was a necessary focus of the film:

> I rejected the suggestion, because I wanted to expose the cruelty and savagery of the lords. Some people said that it was not necessary to have plot themes like stepping on a slave to mount a horse or riding a slave like a horse. I felt that since the lords did these things, why shouldn't I put them in the play? Using these details I can tell people what the so-called "wonderful" system was really like. Some good-

hearted people said that it was ridiculous to have scenes like the one
in which [serfs] are taxed for having a single eyelid and for two eye-
lids. But in the old system there were actually even more "ridiculous" things than this. The Tibetan actors did not feel that these
things were ridiculous at all. Don't forget that in old Tibetan society
it was common for the lord to use the slaves' bones to make eating
vessels. How can we pretend that this did not happen? These [mo-
tifs] were retained because they were helpful for the main theme [of
the movie]. . . . Where there are classes, there is class struggle.
Where there are slaves, there are revolts. Suffering for a long time
under the old system, the Tibetan people longed to be free. This is
unavoidable. They must eventually stand up. Nothing can stop
them. The lords, the imperialists, and the foreign counter-
revolutionaries wanted to stop the struggle. But we cannot just pretend that it did not happen. In one word, *Serfs* was intended to be an
epic tale of class struggle.[27]

This film was widely distributed in China, and millions of people absorbed
images of Tibet from this and other products of the PRC propaganda apparatus.
While it is easy for non-Chinese to see through the film's overblown rhetoric
and exaggerated stereotypes of Tibetan brutality, the film has a great deal in
common with Hollywood Westerns of the 1950s, in which Indians were depicted as cruel savages who senselessly attacked virtuous settlers and cowboys.
For most American filmgoers of this period, there was little doubt that these
were accurate portrayals, and it was only when competing discourses began to
appear that they became widely problematized.[28] As Said has noted, one important product of Orientalist discourse is a limiting of what can be thought
about the Oriental. Chinese depictions of Tibetans in film and literature share
significant aspects of what Said has termed "Orientalism." As with Western
depictions of the Oriental Other, the production of knowledge about and images of Tibet in China are part of the process of "making statements about it,
settling it, authorizing views of it, describing it, teaching it, ruling over it."[29]
Chinese who produce historical studies about Tibet or make movies with Tibetan themes are able to do so because of the unequal power relations resulting
from their military annexation of the region and imposition of direct control
over it.

Like Western Orientalists, Chinese scholars study and depict Tibetans as
part of the process of control and domination, and their productions share a
repository of terminology, images, and accepted "facts" out of which they develop a representation of the Tibetan, who is alternately conceived as exotic,

foreign, savage, deceitful, recalcitrant, backward, indolent, or passive. These images constitute what Foucault termed a "regime of truth," the accepted common sense shared by people in that society, within which the party line appears obvious and incontestable.[30] As with *Red River Valley*, Chinese people with whom I have spoken about the film do not view *Serfs* as propaganda, but as an accurate reflection of the society of old Tibet. The sufferings of the unfortunate serfs made them sad or angry, and their liberation by the PLA was a source of pride. Although it appears to a foreign viewer as a badly acted and poorly produced film with turgid dialogue, for Chinese it is a sad tale of oppression with a happy ending brought about by the patriotic soldiers of the PLA.

Similarly, there is no dispute among the Chinese sources considered in this study regarding the nature of old Tibet: it was a cruel and medieval society in which torture and economic exploitation were rampant, in which the vast majority of the people were ruthlessly suppressed by a small elite of lamas and aristocrats. Descriptions of the tortures inflicted on the unfortunate "serfs" and "slaves" are often lurid and reveal a great deal about Chinese conceptions of "barbarians." They describe torture chambers in which limbs were lopped off, eyes gouged out, and people were disemboweled, and a common theme of these accounts is that the tortures were enacted both to keep the masses in subjection and for the casual amusement of the lamas and aristocrats. Most of these images, as far as I am aware, have no support in contemporaneous Tibetan records, but the lack of documentary evidence is apparently unimportant. These appear to be not so much descriptions of historical circumstances as graphic productions of Chinese racial fantasies of the barbarian Other. Thus, given the belief that the Tibetans were backward savages living in a feudal society prior to their full (re)incorporation into the Chinese motherland and the region's transformation by China, whatever sort of depraved and vicious behavior one could imagine was likely to have been the case, and so it is not necessary to provide documentary evidence.

I have not seen any Chinese descriptions of the purported tortures of old Tibet that cite sources for their assertions. Some sound highly implausible, such as the claim made in several of the Chinese accounts used in this study that there were two "scorpion dungeons" in Lhasa, one located beneath the Barkhor and the other beneath the Potala. According to *Tibet: Myth vs. Reality*, "Before the democratic reform, many serfs were thrown into these dungeons and stung to death by the venomous creatures which sucked the blood of the corpses."[31] This is, of course, unusual behavior for scorpions, and it is also implausible that the Barkhor area itself was a torture pit, as several Chinese writers claim. They assert that the area of what has traditionally been the most popular pilgrimage circuit in Tibet (and remains so today) was used by "exe-

FIGURE 4.1. Khampa man circumambulating the Barkhor. Photo by John Powers.

cutioners" who continually tortured helpless Tibetans by flaying them alive, roping them to red-hot metal carts and parading them through the streets as they screamed in agony, and where body parts of those who had been killed were put on public display. If this area had indeed been the scene of such abominations, it is difficult to explain why it continues to draw large numbers of pilgrims, who can be seen praying fervently every day.

Party Lines

My reservations regarding the accuracy of Chinese descriptions of old Tibet does not imply that I believe, as many exile Tibetans do, that it was an idyllic, religious land of peace and general contentment, but it is also highly unlikely that it bore much resemblance to the Chinese version of Tibetan history. Nor do I believe, as is sometimes suggested, that "the truth" lies somewhere in the middle between these two extreme views. I never visited old Tibet, but I expect that the actual state of affairs there was far more complex than either of these two rather simplistic visions indicates, that situations and perceptions varied from person to person and region to region, and that there were different conditions in various periods of Tibetan history. Using contemporaneous accounts, one could construct virtually any narrative concerning any given society. For example, while most Americans generally perceive their country as a reasonably pleasant place in which to live, a selective perusal of newspaper articles would allow a commentator to create a documented picture of a culture rife with random violence, lone gunmen massacring people for no good reason, rampant drug use, crime, official corruption, and social decay. Similarly, it appears that most of the accounts of old Tibet considered in this study begin with a particular conclusion and then select sources to corroborate it. I believe that it is important to exercise caution with respect to *every* source that purports to describe the situation in Tibet, either before or after the Chinese takeover. As we have seen, this is an emotionally charged issue for Tibetans and Chinese, as well as many Western writers, and the respective narratives of our authors reflect highly consistent party lines that apparently allow no significant deviation.

These are strictly enforced by the two communities. China is a one-party state in which the government controls the media. History is a tool of political control, and the Party regularly rewrites the past in accordance with changing imperatives and policies. Because it holds the dominant position in the marketplace of ideas, it is able to dictate what version of events the public will hear, and because it controls the educational system and the mass media, it has the power to make its version of events function as true.

It is often supposed by supporters of the Tibetan cause that the Tibetan exile community enjoys full freedom of thought and expression, but as anyone who has spent time in refugee settlements knows, the sources of information there are also circumscribed. As a refugee community, the Tibetans have from the beginning of their residence in India stressed the need for solidarity and for the articulation of a consistent message to the outside world, and the party line is strictly enforced. The unanimity of the Tibetan sources we are considering is partly a reflection of pressure for people to conform their beliefs to the norms of the group, but it is also clear that most Tibetan refugees passionately believe their community's party line, which is largely articulated by officials in the Tibetan government-in-exile and a small elite of intellectuals, most of whom live in Dharamsala.

My own observations of Tibetan refugees have convinced me that most sincerely believe the party line, but there are also powerful mechanisms to bring doubters into line. Those who deviate risk being ostracized. Dawa Norbu reports that when he publicly criticized some of the Dalai Lama's policies he was accused by fellow Tibetans of being "a Christian convert, a Communist, an atheist, in iconoclast, and whatnot!" His questioning of the supreme symbol for Tibetan refugees was viewed as "blasphemy," and he states that he began receiving death threats. He believes that if the Dalai Lama had not personally intervened and ordered Tibetans not to harm him, the controversy might have "cost my life."[32] Similarly, Jamyang Norbu, an outspoken critic of the government-in-exile and its policies, asserts that an "ugly climate of fear and suspicion" exists in Dharamsala, maintained by "threats and intimidation" directed toward people like himself who dare to question the Dalai Lama or the administration.[33]

It is understandable that a refugee community that perceives itself as being under siege would respond by emphasizing group solidarity and that it might decide that it is necessary to limit people's freedom of expression in order to coordinate its message. But we should also not assume that Western scholars or eyewitnesses who are not bound by these restraints have revealed the "truth." As we have seen, Western scholars who write about this period of Tibetan history tend to exhibit clear biases, despite their professed goal of reporting the facts and striving for objectivity. Eyewitnesses who traveled to Tibet prior to the Chinese invasion also brought their cultural biases with them: Christian missionaries risked many dangers and traveled great distances because they were convinced that the Tibetan people were heathens who lived in pagan darkness and needed to be converted by them. British colonial administrators generally implicitly believed in the superiority of their culture and their right to annex other people's territories to their empire. Western travelers to Tibet went there expecting to encounter exotic people and a wondrous land; some found what they were seeking, but their accounts often reflect a strong element of projection and wishful thinking. Others were disappointed that their often vague expectations were not realized, and their narratives reflect anger and disillusionment. All of these writers brought their biases and cultural presuppositions with them to Tibet, and these inevitably colored what they saw and how they reported it.

Similarly, the Tibetan and Chinese writers we have been studying share in the collective imaginings of their respective societies, and these shape the events they report, how they interpret them, and the motivations they ascribe to historical actors. As we have seen throughout this study, Tibetan and Chinese accounts tend to be highly consistent in their respective narratives and reflect the respective biases of the two groups, but one should not assume that the records of British colonial officials and Western missionaries who visited old Tibet—or contemporary Western academics whose conclusions about this period are generally interpretations of these sources—do not reflect their own interests and prejudices.

Writing history is an interpretive practice, not a neutral, objective science. All historians begin their studies with biases, attitudes, and assumptions, and these necessarily color how they research and what they find, as well as how they conceptualize the traces of the past with which they work. History is not the mere repetition of chronological data; it always involves selection and interpretation, and this process is both the most important and most fictive aspect of history writing. Often, the data are disjointed, conflicting, or vague, but out of the jumble of the past historians work to produce narratives of cause and effect. One of the most difficult aspects of this process involves reconstructing the psychology of historical figures—figuring out why they acted as they did. This requires an imaginative leap that necessarily goes beyond what the data report.

A War of Words

In both the Tibetan and the Chinese accounts, the Chinese military incursion and subsequent takeover of Tibet are core elements. The Chinese sources uniformly refer to this as a "peaceful liberation," but Tibetan sources variously describe it as a "disaster," an "unbelievably tragic attack" that resulted in "persecution of monks, their murder, torture, and degradation," a "tragedy," and a "monumental loss to human civilization" that led to "intense human suffering."[34] According to a resistance fighter who opposed the Chinese:

> It was a beautiful land, and the lives we led there, though simple
> and hard, were happy. Then the Chinese came. At first with soft
> words and bright silver and later with guns and death. They took
> away my fields, my animals and my home. They looted, desecrated
> and burnt the temples and monasteries I worshipped in. Like ver-
> min, they slew my friends, relatives, lamas, and all the people dear
> to my heart. [Tibetans today] live in despair night and day, in a coun-
> try that has become an endless nightmare. Everything has been

taken away from them: Their faith, their dignity, their manhood and their freedom . . . except, perhaps, the freedom to starve, to slave and to die. Yes, I remember it all. Pain and bitterness have etched every moment and event forever into my mind.[35]

Similar descriptions are found in the other Tibetan sources that describe the Chinese takeover. Images of violence and brutality abound, linked with depictions of the Chinese as duplicitous and utterly alien. *In Haste from Tibet*, for example, recounts one family's escape from Tibet into exile; much of the account reflects the pervasive fear they had of the foreign invaders and the need to avoid any contact with them. Similarly, Dawa Norbu relates that one of his neighbors warned his family that the Chinese ("our dreaded enemies") "are the enemies of our faith, and have already destroyed the monks and monasteries in China and Mongolia. They are bloodthirsty monsters; they eat human beings and any animal they can lay their hands on. They are devils incarnate."[36] Several sources also indicate that Chinese assertions that they had come to drive out foreign imperialists made no sense to Tibetans, for they had never encountered a foreigner (a category that includes Chinese in the Tibetan narratives). Shakabpa rhetorically asks, "Liberation from whom and what? Ours was a happy country with a solvent government and a contented people till the Chinese invasion of 1950."[37]

The Chinese accounts paint a rather different picture. According to *100 Questions about Tibet*, for example, "Since the peaceful liberation of Tibet, the Chinese government has strictly upheld the policy of equality and unity of all nationalities, the policy of freedom for religious belief, and the policy of uniting with personages of the upper classes to develop the patriotic united front, respecting national customs and habits and gradually introducing regional autonomy."[38]

Table 3 lists key words used by the two groups to describe their perspectives on the military incursion and Chinese takeover.

Western Authors' Perspectives

As we have seen with other aspects of Tibetan history, Grunfeld's reading of events echoes the conclusions of our Chinese writers. He refers to the Chinese takeover as a "reassertion of rule" over a region in which "radical reform was long overdue." What Tibetans refer to as brutal indoctrination and propaganda he terms "political consciousness raising," and he emphasizes the notion that China followed a policy of "moderation" and only gradually introduced "re-

TABLE 3. China's Entry into Tibet and Subsequent Takeover

Chinese Sources	Tibetan Sources
peaceful liberation	genocide (T11, 316)
democratic reform (C1, 41)	mechanized slaughter (T9, 244)
great historical mission (C3, 26)	unbelievably tragic attack (T8, 336)
no serious complaints (C5, vii)	horror (T8, 337)
emancipation (C3, i)	colonial oppression (T6, 138)
happy life (C11, 99)	constant terror (T11, 324)
social stability (C11, 99)	rule with force (T6, 291)
rapid progress (C3, i)	disaster (T8, 337)
leap forward (C3, i)	tragedy (T6, xii)
joyful historical event (C10, 7.1)	legacy of desecration (T8, 343)
buoyant and hopeful (C13, 11)	hatred and opposition (T11, 317)
treated as equals (C7, 170)	persecution (T8, 336)
never harassed (C7, 170)	murder, torture, and degradation (T8, 336)
misgivings dispelled (C2, 170)	intricate web of deception (T7, 83)
meticulous maintenance (C3, 11)	looted, desecrated (T7, 9)
People's Liberation Army	occupying forces (T3, v)
development (C2, 7)	marginal benefits (T8, 337)
educate	indoctrinate
historical facts	outright lies (T7, 103)
won hearts	lulled, wooed, and deceived (T6, 112)
comrades	alien overlords (T6, 153)
social productive forces (C3, i)	vermin (T7, 9)
Han big brothers	dreaded enemies (T6, xiii)
new arrivals (C13, 44)	bloodthirsty monsters (T6, 96)
brothers and sisters	oppressors (T6, 97)
facts	lies
lies	facts
patriots (C14)	traitors
traitors	patriots

forms." The conduct of the Han soldiers was "exemplary" in contrast to that of Tibetan officials, which "left much to be desired." While he admits that some Han were guilty of chauvinism, he also asserts that they "practiced egalitarianism." He concludes that in their presentations of these events, "the emerging evidence tends to substantiate China's view of events . . . when events were depicted for public consumption, China appears to have fabricated the least." As an example of a "plausible" Chinese account, he cites the following passage:

> These traitors have used their legal status . . . to muster reactionary
> forces from among the upper strata, collaborated with the external

enemy and actually directed some of the most reactionary major serf owners in Sikang and Tibet to organize armed rebel forces . . . and betray the motherland. Their rebellion was engineered by the imperialists, the Chiang Kai-shek bands and foreign reactionaries. Many of their arms were brought in from abroad. The base of the rebellion to the south of the Tsangpo River received air-dropped supplies from the Chiang Kai-shek bands on a number of occasions, and radio stations were set up there by agents sent by the imperialists [the United States] and the Chiang Kai-shek clique to further their intrigues.[39]

It is difficult to imagine exactly what he finds persuasive about this statement or why he cites it as an example of accurate reporting in contrast to Tibetan accounts and reports by the international media, which he accuses of "doctrinaire anti-communism." First, the rebels would have had good reason to perceive themselves as patriots rather than traitors. Prior to the Chinese incursion, most Tibetans had never even seen a Chinese, and those who were even aware that China claimed their country would have dismissed this as an absurd fiction. Furthermore, the notion that the rebellion was "engineered" by Chiang Kai-shek and the Nationalists is ridiculous; following their defeat by the Communists, they retreated in disarray to Taiwan, where their situation was highly precarious. They survived only because of U.S. protection and lived under constant threat of attack from the mainland. It is extremely unlikely in such circumstances that they would have deployed some of their limited military resources to a remote region like Tibet to support a guerrilla movement that was bound to fall before the superior forces of the PLA. Even if they had been foolish enough to do so—and if they had the means somehow to move military equipment over the vast distances separating them from Tibet—it is extremely unlikely that the Tibetans they encountered would have welcomed them, or even differentiated them from other Chinese. It is also unclear how they would have communicated with their Tibetan pawns, as few Tibetans spoke Chinese.

Goldstein is much more willing than Grunfeld to admit that the Chinese takeover created problems in Tibet, but he appears to believe that Mao's intentions were essentially benevolent. He claims that Mao "sought to create cordial relations between Han . . . and Tibetans, and allay Tibetan anxieties so that Tibet's elite would agree to a societal transformation." He pursued these goals through a "policy of moderation." Mao and other communist leaders are portrayed as being endlessly patient with the "feudal" and recalcitrant Tibetans in their efforts to introduce "democratic reforms." Despite this, the Dalai Lama allowed hard-line nationalist Tibetans to create a "confrontational and adversarial atmosphere."[40]

It is surprising that Goldstein does not appear to realize that what he characterizes as unreasonable resistance on the part of the Tibetans would have appeared completely justified to them. They lived in a country that had worked to keep outsiders outside but had been overrun by soldiers who spoke a foreign language, spouting arcane terminology that made no sense to them, who proposed to fundamentally change their society, the only one they had ever known. Added to this was pervasive Han chauvinism, which led the newcomers to denigrate Tibetan culture and religion, the core elements of Tibetan identities.

Goldstein's proposal to solve the Tibetan problem is even more surprising: he thinks that the best solution would involve the Dalai Lama's throwing himself completely at China's mercy, returning to Tibet (even though the PRC has indicated on numerous occasions that if he did so he would be required to live in Beijing and would only occasionally visit Tibet when allowed to do so by the authorities), working to promote harmonious relations between Tibetans and non-Tibetans, and using his influence to convince his people to accept the inevitability of their country's remaining a part of China. Goldstein does not appear to understand what a wild gamble this would be, as there is little in China's past or present record in Tibet that could warrant such confidence on the Dalai Lama's part. The Dalai Lama believes that over 1.2 million Tibetans were killed by the Chinese during their invasion and the Cultural Revolution era, that huge numbers of Tibetans have been imprisoned and tortured, and that thousands of monasteries were looted, ransacked, and destroyed. Following a mortar attack on his residence, he was forced to flee into exile fearing for his life. Since then, the Chinese have worked to eradicate Tibetan culture and are sponsoring a massive influx of Chinese immigrants to the region, which has reduced Tibetans to a minority. In addition, Chinese leaders and their propaganda apparatus regularly vilify him and characterize the period of his rule as a time of brutality and despotism. In such circumstances, he would be a fool to make the sort of gamble Goldstein recommends.

In contrast to Goldstein's and Grunfeld's depictions of the Chinese as honest and endlessly patient, Richardson portrays them as sneaky, deceitful, and vicious. In his account, the Chinese are thoroughgoing imperialists who are completely unreasonable and bent on brutal conquest of their defenseless neighbor. His presentation of this period seeks to demonstrate that Tibet was fully under Tibetan control until the Chinese "invasion." He emphasizes that his eyewitness status provides a unique authenticity to his presentation, and he claims that he observed the fact that Tibetans viewed the Chinese as foreigners and felt no sense of connection with them. Throughout his book he asserts that the Tibetans felt only "hatred" toward their oppressors. In an attempt to explain why the Chinese had such an "overpowering desire to possess Tibet" he looks to China's history as the background for PRC "acts of aggression":

> There was no hostile move by the Tibetans to account for it. The only answer that appears essentially satisfactory goes deeply into Chinese character and the Chinese past. The Chinese have . . . a profound regard for history. But history, for them, was not simply a scientific study. It had the features of a cult . . . with the ritual object of presenting the past, favourably emended and touched up, as a model for current political action. It had to conform also to the mystical view of China as the Centre of the World, the Universal Empire in which every other country had a natural urge to become a part. The conflict of that concept of history with the violent intrusion of the outside world in the latter part of the nineteenth century led to the obdurate irredentism with which the Republican and Nationalist Governments of China persisted, against all the facts, in claiming that Tibet had always been part of the Chinese fold and was longing to return to it.[41]

Richardson represents the Chinese people as being so traumatized by their collective experience of subordination and domination by foreigners that they could only envision a national recovery that involved dominating others: "The Communists, like their predecessors, continued to be influenced by the traditions of their ancestors. They inherited the same peculiar historical perspective embittered in the more recent past by resentment at the humiliation and exploitation inflicted by the West; and they were the first Chinese to have the power to convert their atavistic theories into fact. They saw their opportunity, calculated that no one was likely to oppose them, and acted." Richardson's account of this period seeks to deny the Chinese any shred of justification for their "military occupation," and he deploys a barrage of negative characterizations of their actions in Tibet. He contends that China's "savage punishment and repression" and "atrocities" led to "bitter resentment" on the part of Tibetans.[42]

While most of the writers we are considering in this study focus on the political and human rights issues involved in the Chinese takeover, Thurman's primary interest is the impact that it had on religion in Tibet. He characterizes Chinese policies as a "systematic effort to exterminate Tibetan religious belief and cultural identity" that has been connected with "abuse of land, wildlife, and natural resources." He also provides a religiously based explanation for why events happened as they did: he contends that the "most compelling" theory regarding Chinese motivations and actions is that the buddha Vajrapāṇi decided to incarnate himself as Mao Zedong because he knew that the Chinese were preparing an invasion of Tibet. By manifesting as China's leader he wished to "prevent other, ordinarily human, materialists from reaping the consequences of such terrible acts, to challenge the Tibetan Buddhists to let go of the trappings of their religion and philosophy and force themselves to achieve the ability to embody . . . their teachings of detachment, compassion, and wisdom," and to facilitate the worldwide spread of Tibetan Buddhism by compelling lamas to move into other countries.[43] Thus he hoped to better prepare the world for the coming apocalypse foretold in the *Kālacakra-tantra*, in which the forces of the hidden Buddhist kingdom of Shambhala will be attacked by enemies of the dharma; both sides will fight a momentous battle, which will culminate in Shambhala's victory and the establishment of Buddhism throughout the world. Leaving aside the mythological presuppositions behind Thurman's theory, the "materialists" Mao/Vajrapāṇi worked to save engaged in wholesale destruction of Buddhist institutions and virtually eradicated religion in Tibet, so it would appear that his efforts were a complete failure.

Imagining the Revolt

Following the suppression of the March 1959 revolt, the Chinese increased their control, and all of our Tibetan sources agree that the vast majority of Tibetans opposed them. The few Tibetans who sided with the Chinese are described as malcontents, beggars, criminals, and other disaffected elements of the society, along with aristocrats who hoped that through collaboration they would be able to maintain their traditional status. Chinese accounts all assert that the PLA was eagerly welcomed by the Tibetan "serfs," who realized that they had come to liberate them and make them "masters of the land."

Because of these contentions, Chinese writers struggle to explain why thousands of Tibetans took to the streets of Lhasa in protest against Chinese rule. The rebellion was put down with massive force, and Tibetan exile sources claim that thousands of Tibetans were killed during the riots and their aftermath. In Tibetan accounts, this is presented as a spontaneous and popular "national uprising," supported by people from all strata of society. They stress the general hatred of the population for the foreign invaders: "Nearly all Tibetans hated the Chinese, and . . . we secretly made rude jokes and comments about them."[44]

TABLE 4. The Chinese Invasion and Its Aftermath

Goldstein, Epstein, Grunfeld	Richardson, Smith, Thurman
alien Chinese value system (W3, 85)	deeply conscious of separateness (W7, 240)
demand reform (W1, 13)	resenting foreign intrusion (W7, 240)
highly localized (W4, 138)	deep dislike of the Chinese (W7, 248)
arrival (W4, 164)	Chinese conquest (W7, xiii)
restraint (W4, 167)	colonization (W7, 352)
reassertion of rule (W4, 116)	foreign domination (W7, 397)
sending in troops (W4, 123)	invasion and occupation (W5, preface)
entered the region (W1, 11)	alien conquerors (W7, 366)
policy of patience (W1, 13)	colonial dictatorship (W5, 248)
democratic reforms (W3, 53)	Communist occupation (W5, 183)
honest (W4, 115)	coercion and deceit (W7, 386)
political consciousness raising (W4, 115)	constant indoctrination (W5, 245)
noninterference (W1, 13)	extensive surveillance (W5, 245)
common participation (W1, 24)	a few favoured puppets (W5, 245)
great and basic process of change (W1, 7)	tragic events (W5, preface)
utmost respect (W1, 13)	mounting ruthlessness (W7, 381)
policy of moderation (W4, 123)	forcible repression, persecution (W6, 92)
revolutionary counterviolence (W1, 12)	brutality (W7, 402)
exhilarating and instructive (W1, 15)	intimidate (W7, 402)
profoundly emancipatory (W1, 7)	suicides, despair, and hatred (W7, 402)
gradual reform (W4, 123)	repressive measures (W7, 409)
benevolence (W4, 167)	massacred (W7, 443)
loss of life (W3, 59)	mass public executions (W6, 13)
peaceful democratic reform (W1, 12)	atrocities (W7, 506)
joyful and invigorating (W1, 15)	raped (W5, 202)
food shortages (W3, 59)	starvation (W5, 238)
respect for local customs (W4, 127)	violated human rights (W5, 242)
moderation (W3, 52)	merciless repression (W7, 538)
errors of the past (W4, 217)	executions, attacks, deaths (W5, 201)
paid for everything (W4, 127)	barbaric vandalism (W5, 246)
exemplary (W4, 127)	savage (W5, 202)
liberating Chinese revolution (W1, 8)	turned all Tibetans into serfs (W7, 660)
economic progress	depressed economic condition (W5, 249)
democratic revolution (W1, 11)	military dictatorship (W5, 211)
patience (W4, 136)	tyranny (W5, 239)
damage (W3, 59)	genocide (W5, 241)
by no means popular (W4, 115)	Tibetan popular opposition (W7, 373)
discontent (W4, 133)	furious resistance (W5, 201)
rebels (W4, 135)	national uprising (W7, 447)
outside forces (W4, 125)	Tibetan discontent (W6, 19)
Tibetan separatists in self-exile (W1, 15)	Tibetan exiles
chiefs, wealthy traders (W4, 125)	common people (W5, 194)

In Chinese presentations, however, the riots are portrayed as the actions of a few disaffected elite "reactionaries" who feared the loss of their power and influence. In *Tibet: Myth vs. Reality*, for example, the rioters are described as "rebellious bandits" instigated by "a number of wealthy serf-owners."[45] Several sources assert that the riots were not spontaneous at all, but were in fact instigated by the "Dalai clique" and "foreign imperialists" working in secret collusion. Moreover, all the Chinese works agree that the Tibetan people actively helped and supported the PLA, and that many even fought in solidarity beside them. According to *Tibet Leaps Forward*, "Against the wishes of the people of Tibet, the reactionary clique of the upper strata in the region, with the Dalai as their chieftain . . . aided and abetted by the Indian expansionists, mustered a gang of traitors to stage an armed rebellion against the motherland on March 1959. The People's Liberation Army, supported by the clergy and people of various circles, swiftly quelled this counter-revolutionary rebellion."[46]

Despite his purported role in planning the uprising, the Dalai Lama, according to several Chinese government-produced works, did not leave Tibet of his own free will, but instead was "kidnapped" by resistance fighters, who forcibly brought him to India.[47] This odd-sounding assertion is apparently intended to counter the fact that over a hundred thousand Tibetans have fled Tibet since 1959. According to this explanation, after the Dalai Lama arrived in India under duress, some foolish Tibetans thought that he had escaped voluntarily, and so they followed him into "self-exile," not realizing that Tibet was being changed for the better by the Chinese. Tragically, once there, they continued to receive misinformation from reactionaries, and so they persisted in the misguided belief that their country had been negatively affected by the Chinese and thus missed their opportunity to live in the new "socialist paradise on the Roof of the World" after centuries of brutal oppression under the old regime.

The list of key words in Table 5 used to describe the riots illustrates the differences between Chinese and Tibetan perceptions of the event.

Grunfeld's Reading of the 1959 Revolt

Grunfeld's presentation of the revolt emphasizes that it was "by no means a popular uprising of the serfs and herdspeople," but was instigated by "chiefs of the clans and wealthy traders" who were aided and abetted by foreigners. He characterizes the Tibetans who massed outside the Norbulingka as a "mob" whose actions exhausted the heroic forbearance of the Chinese, leaving them with no choice but to respond with force.[48] He also indicates that the PLA was

TABLE 5. The March 1959 Riots in Lhasa

Chinese Sources	Tibetan Sources
betray the motherland (C1, 46)	fight for freedom
rebellious bandits (C1, 46)	the Tibetan people (T11, 318)
a number of wealthy serf-owners (C1, 46)	the masses
rebel army (C7, 168)	Voluntary National Defence Army
small group of secessionists (C7, 190)	tens of thousands of Tibetans (T9, 1)
reactionary clique (C3)	local people (T11, 312)
gang of traitors (C3, 1)	patriotic
separatist faction (C12, vi)	widespread (T9, 5)
counterrevolutionary rebellion (C3, 1)	spontaneous revolt (T6, 153)
sinister manoeuvres (C1, 46)	massive demonstrations (T9, 1)
instigated by the Dalai Lama's clique (C7, 190)	popular
separatist activities (C11, 96)	undaunted struggle (T6, 52)
strongly condemned (C11, 95)	supported
patriots	traitors
splittists	patriots
splitting the motherland	independence

under strict orders not to fire on the Norbulingka, and so he concludes that the Tibetan rebels themselves must have attacked their spiritual leader. He contends that they hoped to foment rebellion by making it look like the PLA shelled the compound, but it is improbable that the Tibetans, for whom the Dalai Lama is the supreme symbol of their religion, would have risked killing him for this reason, because the Tibetan populace was already in full revolt against Chinese rule. It is also unlikely that the rebels had field artillery or that they could have transported it to Lhasa, which was under Chinese military occupation.

Grunfeld's Dalai Lama, in contrast to Tibetan portrayals, is an inept liar, and Grunfeld cites several examples of his duplicity and fabrication. He also appears to be a man of limited intellect, because his bumbling and ineptitude are obvious to Grunfeld, who concludes that he "was a victim of circumstances" who was trained from birth to implicitly do whatever his handlers ordered and who was unable to overcome this conditioning. Grunfeld contends that he is still under their control and unable to think for himself. As a result, he foolishly believed that the Norbulingka had been attacked by the PLA soldiers, which Grunfeld believes is impossible despite the fact that they had deployed artillery around the perimeter, rather than the rebels, who somehow managed to acquire field artillery and smuggle large weapons past Chinese soldiers and the tens of thousands of people around the Norbulingka and fire them without anyone noticing. Taken as a whole, Grunfeld's version is ridiculous; it shares all the shortcomings of Chinese propaganda, while adding errors that are all his own.

The Cultural Revolution and Its Aftermath

Following the suppression of the revolt, the Chinese authorities abandoned their policy of making gradual changes in Tibet and began to fundamentally transform the society. As we have seen, this reaction was partly due to Chinese disillusionment at their reception by the Tibetans, but it also reflected a debate within the Communist Party. The moderates who had advocated a gradualist policy were now discredited, and hardliners came to the fore. They asserted that the Tibetans had been coddled for too long and that the revolt was a sign of ingratitude and backwardness that could be corrected only by more vigorous policies of social transformation coupled with large doses of punishment. They believed that the recalcitrant Tibetans could be beaten into love of the motherland, but as Chinese repression increased, Tibetan resistance and resentment grew.

Both repression and Tibetan antipathy reached a high point during the Cultural Revolution of 1966–1976, during which Mao attempted to greatly shorten the period required for full communization of the country by destroying all vestiges of the old society. It was led by those who had been fully awakened by communism, who thus became the "vanguard of the proletariat." It was hoped that the cultural vacuum created by smashing the old order would enable people to radically alter their thinking, embracing communism and quickly eliminating the old class divisions.

This initiative led to disaster for China and Tibet, however: an estimated 30 million Chinese died as a result of famines that were exacerbated by government bungling and ineptitude. At the same time, fanatical Red Guards traveled the country working to smash symbols of the old society, such as religious institutions, and those who represented old ideas and customs were subjected to public humiliation and, often, death. In minority areas like Tibet, Han cadres denounced indigenous culture as an impediment to socialism and economic development, while Han culture was said to be "progressive." Tibetans were forced to join collectives, and their property was confiscated by the government.

These policies led to widespread revolts. They were put down with excessive force, which further antagonized the Tibetans and fueled nationalist sentiment. The Chinese, however, failed to recognize that from the Tibetan perspective, they were acting like imperialists, because they believed that socialist assimilation of a minority population is benevolent, unlike military takeovers by foreign imperialists. As Zhou Enlai expressed this idea, "Assimilation is a reactionary thing if it means one nation destroying another by force. It is a progressive act if it means natural merger of nations advancing toward prosperity. Assimilation as such has the significance of promoting progress."[49]

As part of the assimilation process, Tibetans were pressured to cut their hair in Chinese styles, and Tibetan street names were replaced with "progressive" Chinese ones. They were told to abandon traditional Tibetan dress in favor of Chinese fashions and were also encouraged to speak Chinese, which was said to be "modern," instead of Tibetan, which was "backward." At the same time, Tibet's old order became the target of government propaganda. In an attempt to deflect attention from the dreadful state of the country resulting from the excesses of the Cultural Revolution, the government promoted an image of old Tibet as "hell on earth." An example of this program was an exhibition of 106 clay statues in the Potala entitled "Wrath of the Serfs" that depicted various purported horrors of the old society, such as monks burying children alive in the foundation of a new monastery. They were divided into four sections: "Feudal Estate Owners' Manors: Miserable Infernos on Earth," "Lamaseries: Dark Man-Eating Dens," "Local Reactionary Government of Tibet: Apparatus of Reactionary Rule," and "Serfs Rise in Struggle and Yearn for Liberation." For years, groups of foreign tourists were required to view them, but because they tended to provoke snickering or disbelief rather than sympathy and support for Chinese rule, they have been dropped from the tourist itinerary in recent years.[50]

While the Cultural Revolution and its architect enjoyed wide support in China, in Tibet Chinese attacks against the religion and people of Tibet deepened the general sense of resentment felt by most Tibetans. At the same time, improved infrastructure allowed people in different parts of the country to communicate with each other, thus helping them to develop a shared sense of persecution and national solidarity. It also deepened the rift between them and the Chinese because the latter saw their rejection of "reforms" as a rejection of both their communist ideology and their culture, which of course it was.

While the Cultural Revolution was a disaster in China, in Tibet it was exacerbated by the chauvinistic attitudes of the Han cadres who arrived there to usher in the new order. They focused their energies on eradicating Buddhism, which was the core element of Tibetans' cultural identity, and the religious leaders who had chosen to remain were physically assaulted and denigrated in public "struggle sessions" (thamzing) in which they were forced to confess their "reactionary" thoughts. In an attempt to break down the traditional bonds linking members of Tibetan society, children were forced to physically and verbally abuse their parents, and laypeople were set against monks and nuns.[51] Prior to this period, Tibet had thousands of monasteries and other religious structures, but by the end of the Cultural Revolution there were fewer than ten intact monasteries. In addition, a large number of Tibetans died during this period, but it is impossible to get a clear idea of how many because the issue is highly politicized. According to the Tibetan government-in-exile, over 1.2 million Tibetans died as a result of the Chinese invasion and the horrors of the Cultural Revolution. These figures were obtained through oral interviews with people who escaped into exile but, as has been pointed out by several commentators, given the number of reported casualties in relation to the exile population, each informant would have had to report an average of ten deaths.[52] In a traditional agrarian society like Tibet, people would know their neighbors better than in contemporary Western countries, but these figures still stretch the limits of credibility. On the other side, the PRC now admits that some "mistakes were made" during the Cultural Revolution, but angrily denounces the Tibetan exile government's figures as fabrications created for propaganda purposes. Unfortunately, the polarized debates over numbers obscure the fact that large numbers of Tibetans (as well as Chinese) died unnatural deaths as a result of the Cultural Revolution, and responsibility for these ultimately lies with the Chinese government.

When the Cultural Revolution finally came to an end, China had been devastated by a decade of famine and continuous internal revolution designed to transform the consciousness of the people. The destruction was particularly severe in minority areas like Tibet, where the entire culture was perceived as backward and feudal. During a visit to Tibet in the early 1980s, Communist Party General Secretary Hu Yaobang was reportedly deeply shocked by the deplorable conditions in which Tibetans were living, and he ordered that the more repressive measures imposed on them be lifted and that economic aid be provided to the region. This resulted in a brief period of relative liberalization, during which Tibetans became increasingly restive, and in 1987 they again rose up in revolt. As before, their protests were put down with massive force, and the hardliners in Beijing again gained the upper hand in dictating Tibet policy.

The repression continues today, and the signs of Chinese military presence are everywhere in Tibet. At the same time, the PRC government is trying to win over the Tibetans by investing huge amounts of money in infrastructure and economic development, hoping that as the region becomes wealthier, Tibetans will come to feel greater solidarity with China as they reap the rewards of development. When I was in Tibet in 1999, however, it was clear that although the economy is booming, Han settlers are the main beneficiaries. Every shop I visited, every restaurant, and every business was owned by Han Chinese who had moved to Tibet to cash in on the government's sponsorship of entrepreneurial activities, while Tibetans have been shoved toward the margins of the economy. Fifteen years ago one seldom saw beggars, apart from those who had been physically maimed or were mentally deficient, but today foreign tourists are confronted with them in all larger towns. At the same time, an estimated three thousand Tibetans escape into exile every year, crossing some of the world's highest passes in treacherous conditions for an uncertain life in India or Nepal, risking death or imprisonment. Despite the upbeat assessments coming from Beijing regarding Tibet's current situation, it is clear that many people are voting with their feet, which would not happen if Tibetans were really experiencing economic progress. Many of the escapees are monks and nuns who report that they fled because freedom of religion is nonexistent in Tibet, a conclusion that has been echoed by human rights groups.[53]

Reinventing Tibet

For Tibetan exiles today, the March 10, 1959 uprising has come to function as a potent symbol of the dawning of a national consciousness, and it is commonly presented as the spark that ignited a nascent awareness of Tibetanness among their people. It is commemorated by Tibetan exiles all over the world every year. In Tibetan exile communities, most of the population gathers and recounts the events of March 10 and their aftermath. It is an occasion for fostering group solidarity and dedication to the struggle. The Dalai Lama and other Tibetan leaders make speeches, which are disseminated on the Internet. The themes of invasion, violation, and nationalism feature strongly in their pronouncements, along with Buddhist motifs. In his 1968 speech, for example, the Dalai Lama referred to it as "that fateful day which united the whole country in defiance of the Chinese and re-declared our sense of nationhood in no uncertain terms to the outside world, and that struggle to assert ourselves as a people still continues today both inside and outside of Tibet."[54]

According to Margaret Nowak, March 10 has become for the refugees "the *illud tempus*, or archetype, that sustains a recurrent but deeply meaningful new secular ritual."[55] It is also an occasion for Tibetans to interact with non-Tibetan supporters of their cause. In most major cities around the world in which there is a Tibetan community or Tibet support group, demonstrations are staged on March 10 every year. They commonly target Chinese embassies or other Chinese interests and often march to significant public places in an attempt to draw media attention. Symbols such as the Tibetan flag and pictures of the

FIGURE 4.2. March 10 protest by Tibet supporters outside the U.S. Capitol, Washington, D.C., 1986. Photo by John Powers.

Dalai Lama, both banned in China, feature prominently, along with the Tibetan national anthem. The stated goals are to draw the world's attention to the plight of Tibet, increase international support for the cause, and confront China's leaders with the message that the "Tibet issue" will not go away.

In addition to the collective memory of March 10, the Tibetans already possessed a repertoire of shared cultural markers, a number of which have been touched upon in this study, that contribute to their sense of communal identity. For example, Songtsen Gampo and the early Tibetan empire have been invoked as symbols for reconstruction at various times of crisis by Tibetan leaders, and in recent decades popular movements have coalesced around millenarian leaders claiming to be reincarnations of Songtsen Gampo or Gesar, the legendary Tibetan king whose mighty deeds are recounted in various versions of Tibet's great epic. In addition, Tibetans have a shared language and culture, despite regional differences. Tibetan Buddhism has a long history of sectarianism and also differs from region to region, but following the 1959 revolts and the new phenomenon of Tibetans from various regions and affiliations living together in close proximity, Tibetans have become increasingly aware of how much they share culturally, linguistically, and religiously. Moreover, the government-in-exile has stressed unity and has worked toward cultivating a cohesive conception of pan-Tibetanness, which has been remarkably effective. From these common cultural motifs, many of which were habits, customs, and practices that were taken for granted prior to 1959, while others have been invented since then, the exiles have selected certain aspects and fashioned them into a coherent cultural package that is modified as necessary for indigenous consumption and for export. The Department of Information and International Relations of the government-in-exile is the primary locus for this activity. As Heather Stoddard has noted, many of the images it produces appear in English-language publications before they are repackaged in Tibetan-language sources, which indicates that the external deployment of new paradigms is a central concern.[56]

Their shared Buddhist heritage has become the most important unifying factor in Tibetan nationalist conceptions. As the White Paper expresses this idea, "Buddhism has not been a mere system of belief to the Tibetans; it encompasses the entirety of our culture and civilization and constitutes the very essence of our lives. Of all the bonds that defined Tibetans as a people and as a nation, religion was undoubtedly the strongest. Tibetan national identity became indistinguishable from its religion."[57]

An important element of the exiles' presentation of their religion is the notion that in Tibet, all of the various strands of Buddhism were imported; the Tibetans selected the best elements of all of them and incorporated them into what is now the most highly evolved Buddhist tradition. Connected with this is the sense that Tibetan Buddhists have a mission to spread their faith to others and that they possess a spiritual repository that can be of immense value to the rest of the world. As Samdhong Rinpoche expresses this notion, "Our struggle is not primarily an ethnic or political struggle. Rather, all people born in the spiritual land of Tibet have a universal responsibility to all beings, and the fulfillment of that responsibility is a duty that we all incur simply by the fact of our births."[58] This claim is commonly associated with the notion that the outside world should intervene on behalf of Tibet in order to preserve this unique culture. If the Chinese communists succeed in eradicating it, the world will lose one of its greatest cultural resources, one that has the potential to rescue the modern world from the abyss of materialism, militarism, and environmental degradation that threatens humanity.

In Tibetan refugee publications and in the speeches of exile leaders, Buddhism has come to be identified with progressive political ideas like democracy, human rights, and concern for the environment, and it is also part of the ideology of opposition to Chinese rule. Beginning in March 1959, monks and nuns have played leading roles in anti-Chinese protests, and they commonly conceive their actions as having a religious sanction that is based on the Mahāyāna ideal of sacrificing one's own interests for the benefit of others. According to Ronald Schwartz, who witnessed some of the revolts in the late 1980s:

> Tibetan nationalism is very much a modern phenomenon; the thinking of the young monks today has been politicized in a way that would not have been possible in pre-1959 Tibet. . . . The monks see themselves as acting for the general interests of society in a specifically political sense, allied with ordinary Tibetans against foreign invaders. . . . Chinese rule . . . has threatened Tibetan religion through forcible repression and persecution, not by enticing Tibetans to abandon traditional culture for an attractive modern alternative. Tibetans have not been persuaded by the Chinese communist claim to represent modernity—a claim always accompanied by the use of force. Today, in fact, Western political ideas—democracy, human rights—are perceived as compatible with Tibetan nationalism.[59]

As we saw in the previous chapter, modern Chinese nationalism arose in the context of foreign encroachment into domains that the Chinese had traditionally viewed as their exclusive preserve, coupled with the cultural tensions that came with enforced contact with competing ethnocentrisms and ideologies. For Tibetans, however, nationalism is a much more recent phenomenon, whose primary impetus is the incursion of China into Tibet and the subsequent uprising that led to Chinese military suppression and the flight of large numbers of Tibetans into exile. China has always had factions that backed certain foreign interests, but in Tibet the situation was different. Chinese institutions never exerted any significant influence in Tibet, nor was there a class advocating the importation of Chinese culture or religion or representing Chinese interests in Tibet. Prior to 1950, most Tibetans had no experience with Chinese or contact with them, and although some of Tibet's neighbors may have contributed to internal conflicts there has been little interest in Tibet in importing foreign culture since the "second dissemination" ended with the eradication of Buddhism in India.

This is one of the difficulties faced by PRC authorities in attempting to convince Tibetans that Chinese nationalism is their nationalism and that they form a part of the ethnic and cultural mosaic of China. Celebrations of the victories of the PLA and invocations of the memories of revolutionary heroes, military parades, patriotic songs, and so on have generally had little effect on Tibetans, who appropriate them as stories and symbols of a foreign power that invaded their country and is attempting to eradicate their culture and religion. As Hobsbawm[60] has noted, these are the tools of modern nationalism, which seeks to generate feelings of solidarity through the manufacture of such shared symbols, but for Tibetans revolutionary stories and heroes are reflections of *Chinese* history, and not of their own. Their history, by contrast, is pervaded with Buddhist motifs and defined by the struggle against China, and past events have retrospectively been reconstructed as part of this developing narrative.

Tibetans' most important cultural markers relate to religion, and because China's leaders are not Buddhists, they cannot use them as part of their campaign. Indeed, many of their attempts to do so—for example, claiming that sole legal authority to recognize reincarnations rests with non-Buddhist officials of the Communist Party—have the reverse effect, resulting in absurd situations in which reincarnations are enthroned by officials who do not believe in reincarnation. Contrary to Chinese intentions, these clumsy attempts to appropriate Tibetan Buddhist symbols generally lead to increasing disaffection and cognitive distance on the part of Tibetans. The fact that they have generally been viewed as intrusive foreigners rather than comrades or "big elder brothers" has been a constant source of frustration for the Chinese.

Moreover, in attempting to create patriotic feelings among Tibetans, Chinese authorities often attack their religion, particularly the Dalai Lama, who continues to be revered both inside Tibet and among the exiles. These actions are intended to undermine Tibetan notions of separateness and lead them to embrace their (subordinate) role in the mosaic of Chinese minorities; instead, such actions heighten Tibetans' sense of difference and create offense by negative characterizations of their faith and its supreme symbol.

In this situation, Tibetan attempts to reclaim their heritage and sense of distinctive identity place a strong emphasis on history. As we have seen, the production of a coherent historical narrative that constructs a Tibet that was independent prior to 1959 is viewed as an essential part of the struggle against Chinese rule. Several of our Tibetan authors indicate that they hope their works will convince readers of the veracity of Tibetan claims and undermine China's position. Ronald Schwartz states that "a younger generation of Tibetans equates its recovery of Tibetan history, despite Chinese efforts at its repression, with the eventual success of the cause." He refers to several underground leaflets produced and distributed by Tibetans in Tibet that focus on history, and he quotes one as proclaiming, "Recounting even a brief history will make the communist Chinese invaders feel ashamed."[61]

This attitude is echoed by many Tibetan exiles, who commonly believe that the historical record unambiguously supports the cause of Tibetan independence and undermines Chinese claims to their country. Thus, the production of history is connected with the cause of independence and is seen by many as the most potent weapon they possess in their struggle. In this situation, those elements of the past that are inconvenient need to be explained away, generally by inventing psychological motivations for historical actors that recast them as devout Buddhists working to promote the dharma or Tibetan patriots intent on maintaining the country's independence.

Within Tibet, histories that support independence circulate among intellectuals, along with handwritten accounts of Tibetan history that select those elements of Tibetan or Chinese historical records that support the conclusions they desire. These texts also analyze Chinese publications on Tibetan history for inaccuracies and inconsistencies. The most popular work for dissident Tibetan intellectuals is Shakabpa's *Tibet: A Political History*, which is widely disseminated despite being banned by the government of the Tibet Autonomous Region. Possession of a copy can result in imprisonment, but Schwartz indicates that it is "perhaps the most treasured reference work in the country and circulates underground among Tibetan intellectuals in government offices, the university, and monasteries."[62]

For Tibetans who have remained in Tibet, there is a collective sense that their land has been overrun by a foreign presence; this is exacerbated by Han chauvinism, which undermines Chinese government attempts to foster a sense of shared identity. Many Tibetans have reported that they first developed nationalist feelings as students in Chinese schools, where they were regularly exposed to Chinese notions of cultural superiority. Dawa Norbu states that he and other young Tibetans first became "nationally conscious" in this situation: "When we arrived in China, we united to face the challenges. Sect, province and social class were all irrelevant. The important point was that we were all Tibetans."[63] The Chinese government is largely responsible for the alienation many Tibetans feel, which is exacerbated by government-produced information used in schools. This often contains messages that are condescending or insulting toward Tibetans and their history.[64] In their classes they are taught to loathe their past, and their culture and religion come under constant attack in Chinese propaganda. Some Tibetans respond to these assaults by losing their sense of Tibetan identity, but many others become intensely aware of the cultural differences separating them from the Chinese.

In the exile communities, the land of Tibet functions as an important symbol for nationalist consciousness. There is a strong sense in exile publications and public discourses that diaspora Tibetans are not where they belong, but now that the reality of exile has lasted for almost fifty years for many of them, the real land of Tibet fades farther into memory, while at the same time it is being fundamentally transfigured by the Chinese. For the younger generations, many of whom have never even seen Tibet, a shared imagining of their land has been developed that perforce stands in for the real thing. As the period of exile lengthens, many Tibetans become aware that they may never return, which creates a powerful shared longing for their lost country and contributes to loyalty and group solidarity.

But the Tibet of Tibetan diaspora imaginings is an idealized vision, in which the problems in the old society, while publicly acknowledged, are submerged in the shared conception of a deeply religious land of pervasive peace and tranquility, ruled by wise lamas. This virtual Tibet contains elements of shared memories of those who left following the 1959 uprising, but these are highly selective and are constantly being negotiated and altered within the exile community. This process is similar to Malkki's observations in her research among Hutu refugees that "identity is always mobile and processual, partly self-construction, partly categorization by others, partly a condition, a status, a label, a weapon, a shield, a fund of memories, et cetera. It is a creolized aggregate composed through bricolage."[65] But while the nationalist identity of diaspora Tibetans is a shifting construct that incorporates traditional shared symbols and newly concocted images, for people within the community the fissures and ruptures are generally not apparent, and they tend to perceive it as having a timeless and essential quality that reflects their core culture and shared ideals.

Diaspora Tibetans have become increasingly effective in exporting this vision, which is negotiated with Western political and cultural discourses, while the machinery behind this production remains largely in Tibetan hands. Robert Barnett observes, "Rather than merely responding to Western discourses . . . exile Tibetan policymakers were already . . . encouraging this trend as part of an intended and considered strategy. In doing so, they were continuing a tradition of Tibetan self-representation, using images that were developed in Lhasa long before the Chinese invasion and that they have continued to shape and reconstruct in response to changes in their conditions and objectives."[66]

Toni Huber has convincingly argued, however, that these discourses are globally disseminated, but also limited; they have little or no resonance among Tibetans in Tibet. While the Tibetan exiles who produce them claim to be doing so for their benefit, the Chinese government effectively blocks their dissemination, and so they circulate mainly within the exile community and among Tibet supporters overseas. Huber also contends that they have little impact among the masses of refugees and are mainly produced and consumed by the educated elite centered in Dharamsala, who have "skillfully adapted a repertoire of modern representational styles and strategies during the course of their enforced and prolonged contact with the modern world."[67]

While Western commentators tend to stress the influence of Western concepts in their texts, another significant aspect of Tibetan nationalist productions is the incorporation of Chinese communist terminology, which is commonly used to accuse the PRC of engaging in the sort of activities that they attribute to Western imperialists. Thus, Tibetan exile publications often refer to "imperialist Red China" (*btsan rgyal rgya dmar*) and label its policies in Tibet as "fascist" (*hu shi si'i lam lugs*). Posters and leaflets produced by dissidents commonly characterize the Chinese as "reactionaries" (*log spyod pa*).

According to Barnett, both Tibetan exile publications and writings by sympathetic Westerners stress the notion that Tibet was a unique and special place of profound spirituality that has been violated by the Chinese invasion. As Barnett argues, however, these representations are superfluous to the central Tibetan claim that their land has been illegally annexed by China. By asserting that their unique spiritual culture and the sanctity of their leaders entitles them to assistance and sympathy from the rest of the world, Tibetans obscure the facts of their situation. As Barnett points out, when Allied forces liberated Kuwait from the Iraqi invasion in 1990 there was no perceived need on the part of Western leaders to construct its ruler as a man of exemplary virtue, nor did they justify their actions by claiming to be saving Kuwait's unique and valuable culture. Rather, the Iraqi incursion was denounced as a violation of international law and of the human rights of the Kuwaitis.

In the discourses of Tibetan exiles and many of their Western supporters, Tibetans are portrayed as helpless victims, and images of rape and trespass are common. In Barnett's view, these images may elicit sympathy from outsiders, but they tend to disempower Tibetans by constructing them as innocents in need of outside help, incapable of defending themselves. As Robert Thurman expresses this idea, "Tibetans have become the baby seals of the human rights movement."[68]

Conclusion

Another Fine Myth

Getting history wrong is part of being a nation.

—Ernest Renan

Imagined Hegemonies

In his book *Prisoners of Shangri-la*, Donald Lopez contends that
when Tibetans went into exile they encountered an image of Tibet
that had been formed in the Western imagination from sources like
James Hilton's novel *Lost Horizon* and its idyllic valley of Shangri-
la.[1] According to Lopez, this virtual Tibet was so well established
and powerful that the Tibetans immediately became imprisoned by
its images and were forced to adapt themselves to it. Thus, they
were ensnared by the constructions of outsiders and could not break
free.[2]

When I first read Lopez's book I wondered if he had ever visited
a Tibetan refugee settlement. During a number of visits to settlements in India and Nepal, I have seen little evidence of the sort of
pervasive influence Lopez imagines. In fact, aside from a small educated elite concentrated in Dharamsala, I was struck by how little
Western images of Tibet had affected Tibetans. Most appear to be
completely unaware of Western myths about Tibet, and far from being deeply affected by them, they are generally indifferent. After
reading Lopez's book and during a subsequent research trip to

South Asia, I asked a number of Tibetans what "Shangri-la" meant to them; the most common response was that it is "a Western name for Tibet." When I pressed Tibetan exiles about the associations it had for them, they generally looked puzzled and indicated that it was just Tibet. None had read Hilton's novel or seen Frank Capra's 1935 film *Lost Horizon*, which was based on it. This sort of attitude is aptly summed up by Tsering Shakya, who remarks, "Penetration by western constructs, whether cultural or political, remains at the margins of Tibetan subjectivity. . . . The majority of Tibetans living either in exile or in Tibet are not conscious of the western discourse on Tibet, and they continue to practice their faith as they did in the past. . . . Lopez's emphasis on the western construct as shaping the contemporary Tibetan alterity is not reflected on the ground."[3]

Tsering Shakya's comments accord with my own observations, and highlight a common error on the part of Westerners. We tend to believe that our culture is so powerful, so compelling, that if we formulate constructions of the Other, the Other must be altered by them, and thus the West inexorably moves across the globe, transforming all it encounters in its image. This belief is an easy one to accept, first, because every culture tends to imagine itself as being the center of the world, and second, because the images of Western imaginings are reproduced all over the globe. But as Pico Iyer perceptively noted in *Video Night in Kathmandu*, when other cultures adopt these images they generally rework them and incorporate them into a well-established cultural network that is not significantly altered by this adoption.[4] In fact, they tend to become nativized and are recast in ways that resonate with those who have appropriated them and their audiences. Iyer gives the example of how the Rambo motif has been used in Indian cinema and adapted to the norms and values of Hindi Bollywood films. A number of Bollywood productions with Ramboesque characters have been produced, which are pervaded by Indian values and imagery; in one I saw during my first visit to India in 1988, a woman goes into the jungle armed with automatic weapons to protect her children, and various Hindu deities come to her aid. Her figure is recognizably derived from Rambo, but it is so overlaid with Indian cultural trappings and resonances that its American origins are barely discernible.

A similar process can be seen among Tibetans who are producing works for indigenous consumption or for non-Tibetans. While most Tibetans are largely unaware of Western images of them and appear to be unaffected by these constructions, the educated elite who produce books, articles, pamphlets, and other texts have shown an impressive ability to selectively adopt foreign-made images and technologies and skillfully adapt them to their needs and to indigenous perceptions. An interesting example of this is the film production of the life of Padmasambhava directed by Penor Rinpoche, the supreme head of the Nyingma order of Tibetan Buddhism.[5] He became interested in cinema as a result of his association with action movie star Steven Segal, whom he officially recognized as a reincarnate lama (*tülku*). The film recounts the legend of the life and activities of Padmasambhava, and is an interesting example of cultural adaptation. The acting, cinematography, costumes, and special effects are taken from the Indian Bollywood textbook and are very amateurish and contrived. All the roles are played by Tibetans who are not professional actors, and the dialogue is in Tibetan; the intended audience is obviously Tibetan. The movie is a dramatization of the Nyingma order's core foundation myth, produced by its main authority. Its length and pacing are reminiscent of Tibetan public festivals, which from a Western perspective are slow-moving, even ponderous, but which are hugely popular among Tibetans.

Another example of current Tibetan efforts to directly affect the production of Tibetan images is *The Cup*, directed by Khyentse Rinpoche, a senior reincarnate lama who resides in Bhutan. It focuses on the efforts of a group of young soccer-mad monks attempting to see a World Cup match. In a number of interviews, Khyentse Rinpoche has stressed the idea that he decided to produce and direct the movie because he wanted the world to see images of Tibet produced by Tibetans.

In addition to feature films, Tibetans are increasingly producing documentaries about Tibet, as well as novels and other products of popular culture. Some are intended only for Tibetan audiences, but increasingly, Tibetans are endeavoring to create narratives for the global market. Productions of Tibetan myths for export reflect the exiles' ability to address representations of Tibet by outsiders, appropriate elements they find useful, and create counternarratives that challenge Western imaginings. Toni Huber notes, "The 'myth of Tibet' was historically a Western enterprise. However, new Tibetan exile identity claims represent, at least in part, appropriation of Western discourse by the objectified Tibetan 'Other' and its creative reflection back to the West. Exile identity claims are often so appealing to, and uncritically accepted by, many Westerners precisely because of such feedback."[6]

Exporting the Nation

A similar concern can be seen among the authors of the Tibetan works considered in this study, a number of whom state that they wanted to explicate a Tibetan perspective on Tibetan history for the benefit of non-Tibetans. As we have seen, they also intend for their works to have particular effects, such as convincing their readers that Tibet was an independent country prior to the Chinese takeover and that Chinese rule is illegal under international law. They are part of a highly successful effort by this small community to tell its story to the international community. In comparison to other displaced peoples, they have done a remarkable job of this, and are producing ever more sophisticated texts and garnering international support for their cause, both through direct activism and the production of images that are disseminated throughout the world.

Tibetan authors have seized on motifs with positive resonance for Westerners, such as pro-environment messages, human rights, democracy, gender equality, and spirituality, and have incorporated these into an evolving production of Tibetan identity that is largely created for the benefit of outsiders. The Tibet of their imagination is one that was a deeply Buddhist nation in which people naturally respected their environment, women were the equals of men, human rights were enshrined in their religious ideals and social practices, and the nation lived in peace and harmony. At the same time, a cottage industry has emerged among Western commentators who seek to "demythologize" Tibet and show how these self-serving images are merely fictions produced for foreign consumption. But despite this, the idealized Tibet remains strong in the Western imagination, and it is increasingly a combination of both Western texts and Tibetan image making.

Histories and Strategies

The historical narratives of the two groups of authors we have examined are a crucial part of current notions of identity and alterity among both Chinese and Tibetans. I have found that the Chinese version is not only dominant within the PRC, but also is almost universally accepted by Chinese in Hong Kong, Taiwan, and overseas Chinese communities (as well as by a number of Western academic sinologists). Because of space limitations, this study has presented only the most significant aspects of the general narrative, but I have also been struck by the fact that the various sources I have examined demonstrate change and adaptation within its re-presentation over time. As the needs and paradigms of the two communities change, so do their constructions of the historical narrative of Tibet. Moreover, they also adapt to new challenges from the other side, as well as to the productions of knowledge regarding Tibet by Western academics and the entertainment industry.

The changes one sees in works produced during the past fifty years reflect significant shifts in the consciousness of Tibetan and Chinese writers, which are accompanied by amnesias and blind spots on both sides. Their respective historical narratives coincide with these amnesias and their current under-standings of themselves and their communities. Both parties use history as a weapon in their ideological battle, but at the same time they also have to con-tend with aspects of the Tibetan or Chinese past that either problematize or undermine the coherence of their respective narratives and the messages they want their intended audiences to appropriate.

History is not static; it changes in accordance with shifting perceptions and changing needs. China wants to create a narrative that provides it with a right to be in Tibet, according to which its presentation of history proves con-tinuous political control over it and ongoing cultural ties. This construct as-sumes ancient borders that, though loosely defined and subject to pragmatic negotiation, are nonetheless depicted as inviolable. China's current position of overlord is also morally justified by its vision of pre-1950 Tibet as a cruel and medieval serfdom and its subsequent leap forward into modernization and economic prosperity.

Tibetan exiles, however, want to deny China the right to be in Tibet. Their shared history is one in which China played a merely peripheral role prior to 1950 and in which Tibet enjoyed full independence for centuries before the invasion. As Tsering Shakya states, "They [Tibetans] find meaning and identity in glorification of the past, when the land of snows was the exclusive terrain of the Tibetan people."[7] For both sides the development of a particular para-digm precedes history and determines both how it will be constructed and how it will be used. The present historical imaginings of both Tibetans and Chinese emerged in conjunction with their respective self-definitions. Both sides appeal to primordiality as a basis for their conclusions. In the Chinese case, the nation is conceived as a unified entity with a history dating back five thousand years, in which various peoples, including Tibetans, have long been organically in-cluded. The Tibetan paradigm presents a people who have controlled their own destiny for millennia; they are culturally, religiously, ethnically, and linguisti-cally separate from China, which has violated their territory in an illegal act of annexation. While the Chinese argue for an inclusive narrative in which Ti-betans are integrally included, Tibetans make exclusivist identity claims in which Chinese are kept at the periphery, mainly as an antagonistic element. Both sides appeal to a preexistent and sacrosanct principle, for example, the right of the Tibetans to self-determination and universal human rights, and the claim that China is a unified country that has included Tibet for centuries.

In China history is a tool of political control, which is used against both Tibetans and China's foreign critics. For China, the only valid history is an inclusive one that conceives China as a harmonious conglomeration of different races joined together as equal parts of the Chinese motherland. For Tibetan exiles, the writing of history is an attempt to reclaim something that has been taken from them: their homeland and the sense of identity that was connected with it.

A number of published interviews with Tibetan refugees indicate that prior to the Chinese invasion, most Tibetans tended to see themselves primarily as residents of a particular area or as members of a certain clan, rather than as "Tibetans." This changed with the Chinese military takeover of the Tibetan plateau and the subsequent experience of exile and diaspora; contemporary Tibetan identity has developed with a sense of difference from China and conflict with it. This sense of distinctiveness as a "people" creates a consciousness of solidarity among the Tibetan exiles, many of whom prior to their escape from Tibet had little contact or sense of shared identity with people in distant parts of the Tibetan plateau. In Benedict Anderson's terms, the Chinese incursion into Tibet, their shared sufferings under Chinese rule, and the experience of being forced to live together in exile have allowed them to "imagine" themselves as Tibetans, rather than as Khampas, Amdowas, Golokpas, and so on and have also made it possible to think of people from distant regions of the Tibetan plateau as compatriots.[8]

As Walker Connor has noted, a nation is "a body of people who feel that they are a nation" and are "characterized by a myth of common descent."[9] The main problem faced by Chinese ideologues seeking to foster a sense of patriotism among Tibetans is their general reluctance to imagine themselves as part of the Chinese nation, coupled with their assertion of a history that begins with indigenous origin myths and emphasizes cultural differences and historical conflicts between Tibet and China. Chinese narratives attempt to undermine the sense of difference that Tibetans derive from their shared historical paradigm, and in constructing the Chinese alternative emphasize China's role in shaping both Tibet's past and present, along with the positive benefits of past historical contacts and present economic and political integration with the PRC. When apparent evidence of independence appears in the historical records, it must be either ignored or explained away. Any evidence of contact or influence is highlighted (and often exaggerated). In some cases, historical events are created to make the Tibetan past conform to the desired model.

The production of historical narratives for indigenous consumption or export is part of the process of naturalization of the shared imaginings of the Tibetan exile community and the Chinese people, respectively, which contributes to a sense of solidarity and group identity. Such narratives constitute an important aspect of what Foucault called "technologies of the self," the ideological apparatus produced by societies that conditions the attitudes and assumptions required for their perpetuation. These are necessarily political and serve to strengthen the dominant ideology while simultaneously suppressing oppositional paradigms. Thus, the production of historical knowledge creates a gloss of obviousness that obscures inconsistencies, ruptures, and contradictions and naturalizes the limits of ideology. It provides readers with coherent narratives that encode a largely hidden repertoire of cultural assumptions and present a particular version of events as the only plausible one.

Packaging Historical "Truths"

The Tibetan term for history is *de lta bu byung bar brjod pa*, a translation of the Sanskrit *itihasa*, "what is said to have occurred in that way." The term encompasses both historical and mythological sources, as well as chronicles and hagiographies. There is no clear distinction between factual accounts of events and mythological narratives and beliefs about the past that have been passed down from generation to generation.

The production of contemporary Tibetan history is closely connected with the question of how things came to be as they are, who the Tibetans are as a people, and the nature of their claim to the land of Tibet. Similar notions operate in the production of knowledge regarding Tibetan history in China. Tibetans want to stress their separateness from China, their shared religious paradigms, and their national solidarity, while Chinese accounts describe a long history of Chinese control over and administration of Tibet, coupled with close cultural ties that have immeasurably benefited the Tibetans. In modern China, history changes frequently in response to the changing needs of the central government and new policies in its information apparatus. For many peoples (including the Tibetans), an important part of their shared sense of identity is derived from commonly circulating religious narratives, but since the PRC has officially denounced religion and worked toward its eradication, this is not a valid option for government sources seeking to construct shared cultural paradigms. For a government officially committed to dialectical materialism, however, history is a natural tool of control, and the manipulation of history is easier for a regime that controls the media and other information organs than for one that has to negotiate its story with a free press. In China, history is regularly resurrected and rewritten in accordance with the needs of the moment, and previous versions are destroyed. In contemporary China, the production of history is a central tool for fostering nationalism, a process that is also aided by identifying foreign enemies that are attempting to deny China the validity of whatever version of its history is being promoted at a given time.

This, I believe, is part of the difficulty facing China in the history war described in this study. It is the major player in the production of information within its own borders. The Communist Party is accustomed to being able simply to mandate which version of events is to be officially accepted; once this has been determined, the government has the power to directly influence public opinion through its propaganda apparatus and even physically coerce the population to verbally endorse its version of events. The same is not true, however, in the countries in which China has attempted to circulate the texts discussed in this study, for the rhetoric that works in China is commonly viewed as propaganda in other cultural settings. What a Chinese reader might perceive as a forceful statement of the truth, the intended audience of these works will often dismiss out of hand because of their tone.

In contrast, the Tibetan exile community has become increasingly sophisticated and adaptive in its use of the international media and in the production and dissemination of its version of Tibetan history. The history war it wages with China is as unequal in the Tibetans' favor as the military one that was fought in the 1950s, which China won easily. But despite my opinion that much of the rhetoric of the Chinese sources undermines the persuasiveness of their arguments and the fact that a number of factual errors have been pointed out, I do not accept the implicit belief held by both factions that if one side's story could be proved wrong, the other must be correct. Rather, I think that both sides incorrectly conceive Tibet and China prior to the modern period in terms derived from the modern nation-state, but this paradigm is clearly not appropriate for Tibet or China prior to the Chinese takeover. Unlike the modern nation-state, in the past the borders between the two countries were unclear and often shifted. Borders were far more porous than those of modern nation-states, and vast areas of the frontier were unpatrolled. The use of travel documents such as passports was rudimentary in comparison to contemporary practices, and people in border regions often viewed themselves as being independent of either the Tibetan central government or the Chinese state. The situation was one in which two governments exercised primary authority within their respective central provinces, and their power diminished as one moved toward the periphery. They were neighbors, and so the two peripheries overlapped, and there was ongoing military, political, and cultural contact between them.

From the Chinese point of view, prior to the development of modern transportation technology the vast distances between the central areas of China and the Tibetan plateau made direct administration impossible, and so as long as Tibet remained stable and posed no threat to China, the government was content to leave it alone to manage its own affairs. For the Tibetans, the institution of the Dalai Lamas, which led to periodic times of weakness and political infighting between the death of one Dalai Lama and the maturity and investiture of his successor, coupled with the inward-looking nature of Tibetan society, led to a situation in which Tibet needed military support from its neighbors. As long as China provided that support and refrained from directly annexing Tibet, the government was content to allow China to officially proclaim its overlordship. As the works studied in this essay amply demonstrate, however, such an ambiguous conclusion is unacceptable to both sets of contemporary writers, who are convinced that "history" can prove their points and defeat their enemies.

One striking aspect of the competing narratives is their incommensurability. There is no real debate between proponents of the Chinese paradigm and those who accept the Tibetan exile version of Tibetan history. In the sources we have examined (particularly those by Chinese authors), there is little attempt to convince readers through reasoned arguments or consideration of all aspects of historical records; rather, choice of sources is highly selective, and readers are generally presented with a particular conclusion. Even when authors appeal to universal principles like human rights or democracy, these are used selectively and in accordance with preset goals.

Much of the discourse resembles a political rally in which competing factions yell slogans at each other from behind barriers that physically separate them. Our Chinese and Tibetan authors utilize a repertoire of historical simulacra—generally divorced from their context and stripped of the ambiguities that accompany them—that have been accepted by their respective communities as being concordant with the party line, and their conclusions follow from them. Their competing models resemble the situation Alasdair MacIntyre has described in his characterization of contemporary discourses on morality:

> The rival premises are such that we possess no rational way of weighing the claims of one as against another. For each premise employs some quite different normative or evaluative concept from the others, so that the claims made upon us are of quite different kinds. Hence it seems that underlying my own position there must be some non-rational decision to adopt that position. Corresponding to the interminability of public arguments there is at least the appearance of a disquieting private arbitrariness. It is small wonder if we become defensive and therefore shrill.[10]

Our Chinese writers begin with the premise that a strong and unified state is necessary for a people to survive in the brutal world of international relations. Each member and community of the state must subordinate personal interests and local concerns in order that the whole nation might prosper and fend off its enemies. The individual has no rights that can be asserted against the interests of the state, and the state's only real obligation to its people is to provide basic sustenance and security. Within these assumptions, the Tibetan demand for autonomy and denunciations of Chinese human rights violations by foreigners are incompatible with China's aims. Chinese widely fear that if Tibetans were to gain independence—or even significant autonomy—this would constitute a serious loss of face for their country, which has loudly proclaimed that Tibet has become "the Socialist Paradise on the Roof of the World" and that the region has made huge leaps of progress since the Chinese takeover. Outsiders are told not to worry about purported atrocities because they are merely a fiction created by China's enemies. The Tibetan people are happy and prospering under Chinese rule, and they feel intense gratitude to China for liberating them from their long period of servitude under the Dalai Lama's regime. And Chinese people want to believe this; no one wants to think of his or her nation as a brutal aggressor that has invaded a sovereign neighbor and committed atrocities. Such conclusions are generally a source of intense psychological suffering, and not surprisingly, Chinese wish to avoid them. Added to this is the cultural chauvinism to which I have referred throughout this book. The power of this myth makes it particularly difficult for Chinese to consider the possibility that the Middle Kingdom might be engaged in acts of barbarism. In addition, Tibetan autonomy might embolden other restive minorities, such as the Uighurs, and prompt them to agitate for independence. If such activities were to spread, the result would be a fatal weakening of China and a possible return to the dark days of the Century of Humiliation.

For most Tibetan exiles, Chinese concerns about territorial integrity, national solidarity, and racial pride are irrelevant. For them, the only valid concerns are the issue of Tibetan independence (*rang btsan*), the Tibetan people's right to self-determination, and the preservation of their Buddhist culture. They have adopted Western discourses of human rights and democracy—particularly in products designed for export—and use them as part of their argument for the changes they wish to see in Tibet. China generally dismisses such discourses as tools of Western hegemony that have no resonance for Chinese and other Asian peoples, who are mainly concerned with social stability and material progress.[11] While Tibetans wish to use them to argue their case, the PRC considers them invalid, and so there is no common basis of shared moral and political assumptions from which a genuine dialogue could begin. Added to this is the fact that both communities base their versions of Tibetan history on their respective communal imaginings, which derive from their educational systems, shared myths and symbols, unexamined prejudices, and cultural assumptions. The conceptual incommensurability of their respective narratives begins with incompatible premises and is supported by selective readings and overreadings of available source materials.

In this situation, it seems impossible that either side could conceivably win its argument; on the other hand, neither can lose. So we are left with a stalemate, in which the two sides shout at each other and accuse their opponents of deliberately obfuscating, while overlooking their own obfuscations. As MacIntyre notes, when two polarized sides of protestors shout at each other, their messages are primarily aimed at those who already share their imaginings, and so each faction is essentially talking to itself or shouting slogans that are ignored or rejected by the other. Thus, each group ends up talking to itself and those who already agree with it. In his discussion of the futility of competing claims about morality, he aptly sums up the situation we are faced with in debates about Tibetan history:

> The practice of morality today is in a state of grave disorder. That disorder arises from the prevailing cultural power of an idiom in which ill-assorted conceptual fragments from various parts of our past are deployed together in private and public debates which are notable chiefly for the unsettlable character of the controversies thus carried on and the apparent arbitrariness of each of the contending parties. . . . The concepts with which they work are a combination of fragmented survivals and implausible modern inventions.[12]

When I first began this study, my background in Tibetan studies mostly consisted of philosophical and doctrinal studies with refugee Tibetan lamas. During my tenure in graduate school and in subsequent research trips to South Asia, I lived in Tibetan communities and developed friendships with a number of Tibetans. In this situation, my exposure to Tibetan history was heavily conditioned by their perspective, and I implicitly assumed that the authors of Chinese versions of Tibetan history, particularly those relating to the takeover of Tibet in the 1950s, must be aware that they were lying, distorting, and fabricating and that the Tibetan case for independence was so compelling that anyone with even the slightest exposure to the facts would reach that conclusion. The deplorable human rights situation in Tibet added weight to this conclusion. But in recent years, as a result of speaking with many Chinese, both in China and overseas, and reading a wide variety of publications by Chinese authors (both inside and outside the PRC), my inescapable conclusion is that they do sincerely believe the party line. This is true of most overseas Chinese, as well as residents of Taiwan, Hong Kong, and Macau. Their commitment to its veracity is as strong as that of the Tibetans to their own paradigm, and any problematization of it is generally viewed as dangerous, the crumbling edge of a slippery slope that leads to the destruction of the certainties that sustain the Chinese worldview and the Chinese state.[13]

The certainty with which most Chinese accept their "regime of truth" with regard to Tibet should give pause even to the most passionate Tibet activist. Chinese people commonly assert that they have a valid perspective that has largely been ignored by a world that is either ignorant of the facts or deliberately misrepresents Chinese actions in Tibet. They claim that trying to present their case to pro-Tibet foreigners is like arguing with a brick wall—exactly the experience their opponents have with them. In this situation, it seems likely that both sides will continue to argue at cross-purposes, and it is difficult to imagine a resolution in light of the incommensurability of their respective premises and sources of evidence.

Notes

PREFACE

1. A more extensive listing of Chinese and Tibetan sites can be found on the Tibet Information Network's Web site: www.tibetinfo.net/admin/external.htm#Tibet.

2. See my essay, "The Free Tibet Movement: A Selective Narrative History," in *Engaged Buddhism in the West*, ed. Christopher Queen (Boston: Wisdom Publications, 2000), pp. 218–246.

3. This failure to adapt the message to Western audiences may be due to the extreme sensitivity of the Tibet issue for Chinese writers. John Israel indicates that some Chinese historical publications have been successfully translated into English, with appropriate changes in terminology and presentation. See "The December 9th Movement: A Case Study in Chinese Communist Historiography," in *History in Communist China*, ed. Albert Feuerwerker (Cambridge, Mass.: MIT Press, 1968), pp. 247–276.

CHAPTER 1

1. One issue of contention is exactly what constitutes "Tibet." The Chinese government generally limits Tibetan territory to the Tibet Autonomous Region, which consists of the central provinces of Ü and Tsang. The Tibetan government-in-exile, however, claims that Tibet includes these central provinces as well as ethnically Tibetan areas of eastern parts of the Tibetan plateau that have been made parts of other neighboring Chinese provinces by the PRC. Traditionally, the Tibetan government has claimed ownership of the "three Provinces" (Chölkhasum): (1) Ü and Tsang, which extend from Ngari Gorsum in the west to Sokla Gyao; (2) Do Dö, which extends from

Sokla Gyao to the upper bend of the Machu River and includes Kham; and (3) Do Me, which incorporates an area ranging from the Machu River to the traditional border with China, marked with a monument called the "White Chorten." Over the centuries, ownership of border areas has shifted between the Tibetan central government and China, and although Kham and Amdo, for example, were claimed by modern Tibetan governments as part of their territory prior to the Chinese invasion in the 1950s, actual control was either in Chinese hands or in those of local hegemons. In this book, the term "Tibet" is generally adopted as each side interprets it, unless otherwise indicated.

2. See the bibliography for works assigned an abbreviated designator.

3. A good example of the differences in language between publications intended for Tibetan exiles and those written for foreigners is the two versions of *Tibet: The Undying Flame* by Kunsang Paljor, a Tibetan exile who formerly worked in Chinese propaganda bodies. He is vehemently anti-Chinese in his language, but the Tibetan version is extremely polemical and is about three times the length of the English-language version. The reason for the editing is given in the introduction: the editor states, "The original Tibetan version of the work contains a fair amount of invectives and abuses directed at the Chinese." He indicates that these have been edited in the English version because the language might be offputting to non-Tibetan readers. "Editor's Note," in Kunsang Paljor, *Tibet: The Undying Flame* (Dharamsala: Information and Publicity Office of H.H. the Dalai Lama, 1977). The Tibetan version is entitled *bSregs kyang mi 'tshigs pa'i bod* (Dharamsala: Tibetan Cultural Printing Press, 1971). Another example is Tsepon Shakabpa's article "Using the Lance of Truth to Draw out the Pus of Crooked Explanations" ('Khyog bshad kyi rnag khrag 'byin byed bden pa'i gtsag bu) (Dharamsala: Office of H.H. the Dalai Lama, 1986), which was written as a rebuttal to an article by the PRC historian Tang Ke-an (Thang khre an kun dgas bsgyur) entitled "Patron/Priest Relations in Political Contexts" (Mchod yon 'brel ba'i chab srid kyi go don), *Bod 'jongs bu12* (1985): 45–60, published in Lhasa by the PRC. As the title indicates, Shakabpa's response is often vitriolic and contains a number of personal attacks on Tang Ke-an. For his part, Tang Ke-an attacks Shakabpa's credibility and integrity, accusing him of being a "splittist" who has willfully distorted history. My thanks to David Templeman for informing me about Kunsang Paljor's books.

4. See M. A. K. Halliday and Ruqaiya Hasan, *Language, Context and Text: Aspects of Language in Social-Semiotic Perspective* (Victoria, Australia: Deakin University Press, 1985).

5. A clear statement of this belief can be found on the Tibetan exile government's Web page, "White Paper: Proving Truth from Facts," www.tibet.com/WhitePaper/, p. 11.

6. In some Chinese publications the tone is distinctly paranoid, and many contain statements to the effect that various Western powers have plotted to invade and colonize China. The most extreme language I have seen in any Chinese publication is found in Huang Hongzhao's *The West Powers and Tibet* (Hong Kong: Hai Feng Publishing, 1993). The book is filled with colorful phrasings and conspiracy theories, but because it is so extreme, I have only occasionally referred to it in this book. The book

jacket indicates that Huang was born in Guangdong Province in China, graduated from the History Department at Nanjing University, and since 1965 has been teaching history there.

7. In Chinese works, the "Dalai clique" consists of the Dalai Lama and the Tibetan government-in-exile headquartered in India and its supporters. "Splittism" (*fen lie zhuyi*) refers to attempts to split the motherland of China by advocating Tibetan independence, and "reactionaries" include anyone who criticizes the Communist Revolution in China or current government policies.

8. Tsepon W. D. Shakabpa [Zhwa sgab pa dBang phyug bde ldan], *Tibet: A Political History* (New Haven: Yale University Press, 1967). See, for example, Dai Yannian, Edna Driscoll, Yan Qinghong, and Zhu Yuan, eds., *Tibet: Myth vs. Reality* (Beijing: Beijing Review, 1988), pp. 154–169.

9. A. Tom Grunfeld, *The Making of Modern Tibet* (London: M.E. Sharpe, 1996). As with the other issues discussed in this study, the two sides have diametrically opposed views on the quality of Grunfeld's work, the value of his scholarship, and his personal integrity. Scientific Buddhist Association, *Tibet: The Facts* (Dharamsala, H. P., India: Tibetan Young Buddhist Association, 1990), pp. 257–384, devotes a section to refuting him. Like much of the rest of the book, this chapter contains highly emotive language in its analysis and masses of footnotes referring to documentary evidence that the editors present to undermine his conclusions. The most vitriolic Tibetan denunciation I have seen of Grunfeld and his work is "Acme of Obscenity" by Jamyang Norbu (www.tibetanliberation.org/jnorbu82801.html). After denouncing him as a communist sympathizer and slipshod scholar, Norbu concludes that Grunfeld's book is an "open sewer. . . . If the printed word could physically emit a stink, then [it] would reek not only of dung and putrefaction but the charnel house as well. All the usual words of condemnation, scurrilous, disgusting, abominable, are inadequate to censure the man and his work." On the Chinese side, Dai Yannian et al., *Tibet: Myth vs. Reality* (pp. 10, 170) heaps praise on both Grunfeld and his work: "It is a real pleasure to read a book like *The Making of Modern Tibet*. . . . this serious, well-documented and objective study . . . throws a flood of light on the questions raised about Tibet."

10. Dai Yannian et al., *Tibet: Myth vs. Reality*, p. 7.

11. Editors of China Reconstructs Press, *Tibetans on Tibet* (Beijing: China Reconstructs Press, 1988), p. 7.

12. Ibid.

13. Wang Jiawei and Nyima Gyaincain, *The Historical Status of China's Tibet* (Beijing: China Intercontinental Press, 2001), p. 4.

14. "Tibet: Proving Truth from Facts," Tibetan government-in-exile White Paper, *www.tibet.org/WhitePaper/*, p. 1.

15. Thubten Jigme Norbu and Colin M. Turnbull, *Tibet* (New York: Simon and Schuster, 1968), p. 11.

16. Dawa Norbu, *Red Star over Tibet*, 2nd ed. (New York: Envoy Press, 1987), pp. i, iii, 10, 101.

17. Dawa Norbu, *Tibet: The Road Ahead* (London: Rider, 1997), p. ix.

18. Ibid., p. xiii.

19. Shakabpa, *Tibet: A Political History*, p. xi.

20. Scientific Buddhist Association, *Tibet: The Facts*, p. i.

21. Huang Hongzhao, *The West Powers and Tibet*, p. 8.

22. According to Mao, "These class struggles of the peasants—the peasant uprisings and peasant wars—alone formed the real motive force of historical development in China's feudal society. For each of the major peasant uprisings and wars dealt a blow to the existing feudal regime and more or less furthered the development of the social productive forces." Quoted in Albert Feuerwerker, "China's History in Marxian Dress," in *History in Communist China*, ed. Albert Feuerwerker (Cambridge, Mass.: MIT Press, 1968), p. 16. In the parlance of contemporary Chinese historiography, "peasant wars" (*nongmin zhanzheng*) are distinguished from "peasant uprisings" by their size. Peasant uprisings were localized disturbances, whereas peasant wars were armed uprisings of peasants against the landlord class. Both are presented as examples of class struggle that arose from exploitation of the masses and the contradictions of the economic system, and all are seen as leading toward the next phase of historical development.

23. Feuerwerker, "China's History in Marxian Dress," p. 26.

24. See, for example, Suzanne Weigelin-Schwiedrzik, "Party Historiography," in *Using the Past to Serve the Present: Historiography and Politics in Contemporary China*, ed Jonathan Unger (Armonk, N.Y.: M.E. Sharpe, 1993), p. 156. According to A.F.P. Hulsewé, this approach results in "an arid repetition of platitudes" and stifles real historical research. "Chinese Communist Treatment of the Origins and the Foundation of the Chinese Empire," in Feuerwerker, p. 123. There have been dissenting voices, however. An example was the Shanghai-based historian Ba Jin, who wrote several essays in 1978–1979 arguing for the "right to remember," but following Liu Binyan's expulsion from the Party in 1987 for writing history that contradicted aspects of the Party's version of events, other historians learned to toe the line or to avoid working on controversial areas.

25. Weigelin-Schwiedrzik, "Party Historiography," p. 173.

26. Wei Jing, *100 Questions about Tibet* (Beijing: Beijing Review Press, 1989), p. 27. This text, which was intended to counter Western critiques of the official Chinese view, has had a significant impact, but probably not the sort that the Chinese government intended. In addition to sparking the research that resulted in this book, it is also the basis for a book edited by Anne-Marie Blondeau and Katia Buffetrille, *Le Tibet est-il chinois? Réponses à cent questions chinoises* (Paris: Albin Michel, 2002), which addresses all 100 questions in the text and refutes most of its contentions.

27. A number of commentators on contemporary Chinese culture have noted that women often feature in representations of ethnic difference. Minority women are commonly shown in colorful and exotic native dress and are often involved in such "traditional" activities as singing and dancing. See Emily Chao, "Hegemony, Agency, and Re-presenting the Past," in *Negotiating Ethnicities in China and Taiwan*, ed. Melissa Brown (Berkeley: Institute of East Asian Studies, University of California, 1996), p. 221.

28. Hugh E. Richardson, *Tibet and Its History* (Boston: Shambhala, 1984), preface.

29. Grunfeld, *The Making of Modern Tibet*, p. 5.

30. For example, although he claims to have considered all points of view, he admits that he does not read Tibetan and has not looked at any Tibetan-language sources. Given that this is purportedly a book that presents a balanced account of Tibetan history, this is a significant omission. Moreover, although he claims in several places to be representing what Tibetans in Tibet actually believe, he gives no indication that he has ever visited Tibet (and admits that he does not speak Tibetan), and so he does not appear to have any way of ascertaining what Tibetans think. Although he claims to have a background in Chinese studies, he also does not list any Chinese-language works in his lengthy bibliography, and judging by the sources he cites, he appears to have mainly relied on outdated secondary materials.

31. Melvyn C. Goldstein, *A History of Modern Tibet, 1913–1951: The Demise of the Lamaist State* (Berkeley: University of California Press, 1989), p. xx.

32. See, for example, Melvyn C. Goldstein, *The Snow Lion and the Dragon* (Berkeley: University of California Press, 1997), p. 105–117.

33. Warren W. Smith, *Tibetan Nation: A History of Tibetan Nationalism and Sino-Tibetan Relations* (Boulder, Colo.: Westview Press, 1996).

34. Israel Epstein, *Tibet Transformed* (Beijing: New World Press, 1983), p. 7.

35. See www.china.org, "White Paper on Tibet," p. 1.

36. Western writers have been chosen for consideration in this study for either the distinctiveness of their views or as representatives of a particular approach or conclusion. Epstein's work is similar in style to Anna Louise Strong's *When Serfs Stood Up in Tibet* (Peking: New World Press, 1960), which, like Epstein's book, uses the language of Chinese propagandists and is published by a Chinese government press, and Stuart and Roma Gelder's *Timely Rain: Travels in the New Tibet* (London: Hutchinson, 1964), which, while occasionally critical of Chinese propaganda, generally follows the Chinese party line on Tibet. Grunfeld's book is a one-sidedly pro-China study of Tibetan history by a Western academic that thoroughly rejects the pro-Tibet party line. Melvyn Goldstein's books are well-researched and thoroughly documented works that take issue with the pro-Tibet side, but are also critical of key points of the standard Chinese narrative.

37. Grunfeld, *The Making of Modern Tibet*, pp. 33, 16, 129, 24. I assume that "countless" here is hyperbole, because the total population of Central Tibet was small enough to be easily counted.

38. Ibid., pp. 33, 15.

39. Ibid., p. 23.

40. Ibid., p. 149.

41. Goldstein, *The Snow Lion and the Dragon*, pp. x, 54, 52.

42. Richardson is a favorite target for attacks by our Chinese authors. Huang Hongzhao, for example, informs us that he was "a colonialist of resource astuteness. He was very sinister and also familiar with the situation in Tibet. . . . [He] gave advice and suggestions for India to invade Tibet" (*The West Powers and Tibet*, p. 248).

43. Robert A. F. Thurman, *Essential Tibetan Buddhism* (San Francisco: Harper San Francisco, 1995), p. 1.

44. Ibid., p. 39.

45. Robert A. F. Thurman, *The Tibetan Book of the Dead* (New York: Bantam Books, 1994), p. 10.

46. Smith, *Tibetan Nation*, pp. xvi, 402.

47. This term has been hotly contested in Western studies of Tibet. It translates the Tibetan *mi ser*, literally "yellow person," but opinions are strongly divided regarding its accuracy. See, for example, the debate between Goldstein and Barbara Miller in the *Tibet Journal*: (1) Melvyn Goldstein, "Reexamining Choice, Dependency and Command in the Tibetan Social System: 'Tax Appendages' and Other Landless Serfs," 11.4 (1986): 79–112; (2) Beatrice D. Miller, "A Response to Goldstein's 'Reexamining Choice, Dependency and Command in the Tibetan Social System," 13.1 (1988): 61–65; (3) Goldstein, "On the Nature of Tibetan Peasantry," 12.2 (1987): 65–67. See also Barbara N. Aziz, *Tibetan Frontier Families* (Durham, N.C.: Carolina Academic Press, 1978), where she argues that the term "serf" is inappropriate in the Tibetan context.

48. See, for example, Giuseppe Tucci, "The Validity of the Tibetan Historical Tradition," in *India Antiqua*, ed. Jean Vogel (Leyden: E.J. Brill, 1947), who examines how later Tibetan historians appropriated early dynastic chronicles, and concludes: "Tibetan historians seem to have preserved of these chronicles nothing else but the genealogical and chronological schemes; the main events which led Tibet to fight against China, the ups and downs of the struggle, the rivalry of clans, are passed unnoticed by the Lamaist chroniclers; their interest is only the Holy Law, its fortunes and propagation. The stories of its masters take the upper hand: kings are recorded chiefly as patrons and supporters of Buddhism" (p. 319).

49. Christopher Beckwith notes, "In early Oriental history [there] are not technically primary sources at all; they are mainly the surviving narrative accounts, written long after the fact." *The Tibetan Empire in Central Asia* (Princeton: Princeton University Press, 1987), p. viii.

CHAPTER 2

1. Michael Aris, preface to Dan Martin, *Tibetan Histories: A Bibliography of Tibetan-Language Historical Works* (London: Serindia Publications, 1997), pp. 9–10.

2. Wang Furen and Suo Wenqing, *Highlights of Tibetan History* (Beijing: New World Press, 1984), pp. 10–12. This is the most comprehensive English-language Chinese history of Tibet that I have seen. It attempts to impose an often tortured Marxist paradigm onto Tibetan history, which requires that the authors sometimes have to invent historical events in order to fit the model.

3. Tibetan histories generally report that the army had 100,000 soldiers, but one Tang dynasty chronicle claims that there were 200,000; see Don Y. Lee, *The History of Early Relations between China and Tibet: From Chiu t'ang-shu, a Documentary Survey* (Bloomington, Ind.: Eastern Press, 1981), p. 8. Both figures are probably highly inflated.

4. While Tibetan histories unanimously assert that the Tibetan army defeated the Chinese, the Tang annals contend that the Tibetans were defeated and that after a period of several years Tibet apologized and again begged the Tang emperor to consider a marriage alliance. See F. W. Bushell, "The Early History of Tibet from Chinese

Sources," *Journal of the Royal Asiatic Society*, n.s. 12 (1880): 444. In the *New Red Annals*, Sönam Drakpa (bSod nams grags pa, 1478–1554) emphatically states that the Chinese king was reluctant to give his daughter in marriage, and only did so because of the threat of force. See Giuseppe Tucci, *Deb t'er dmar po gsar ma: Tibetan Chronicles by bSod nams grags pa* (Rome: Istituto Italiano per il Medio ed Estremo Oriente, 1971), p. 147, in which the king's minister Gar (mGar sTong rtsan Yul zung) threatened to send a huge army against China and carry the princess away by force, following which the Chinese emperor became "much afraid." Similarly, the fifth Dalai Lama's history of Tibet reports that the king at first refused to consent to the marriage and did so only because of the threat of force: "The king . . . and his ministers were very frightened and promised to do (as requested). [He] told the princess to go (to Tibet). The princess begged not to go to that country where she would not meet her circle of friends and relatives. . . . Nevertheless . . . the lord of China could not withstand the glory of the supreme incarnate wheel-turning kingship of the King of Tibet." Zahiruddin Ahmad, trans., *A History of Tibet by the Fifth Dalai Lama of Tibet* (Bloomington: Indiana University Press, 1995), p. 27.

5. In Chinese imperial statecraft, giving royal princesses in marriage was one of the means used to pacify the barbarian tribes. This was part of the *heqin* policy, which worked to subvert the barbarians by giving them gifts from China's superior civilization and flattering them with grandiose titles. By these means, it was hoped that the barbarians would adopt Chinese culture and gradually become integrated into its polity. See Morris Rossabi, *China and Inner Asia: From 1368 to the Present Day* (London: Thames and Hudson, 1975), p. 19. In 710 another Chinese princess named Jincheng was sent by the Chinese emperor to marry the Tibetan king Tride Tsuktsen. She is said by Chinese historians to have continued Wencheng's work of civilizing the Tibetans, but she is not accorded the same importance as her predecessor.

6. Wang and Suo, *Highlights of Tibetan History*, p. 14.

7. Dai Yannian et al., *Tibet: Myth vs. Reality*, p. 16. The first phrase appears in many Chinese publications about Tibet when describing the Yarlung dynasty. The apparent implication is that the Yarlung kings were not really rulers of the country of Tibet, but rather local chieftains.

8. As Paul Demiéville has noted, both Tibetan and Chinese chronicles agree that Wencheng was not a daughter of the Chinese emperor, *La Concile de Lhasa* (Paris: Bibliotèque de l'Institut des Hautes Études Chinoises, 1952), pp. 6–7.

9. Dai Yannian et al., *Myth vs. Reality*, p. 17.

10. Wang and Suo, *Highlights of Tibetan History*, p. 16.

11. An example of this attitude is found in the *Analects* (*Lunyu*, 9.4) of Confucius, when he is questioned by one of his students regarding his stated intention to become an advisor to "barbarian" rulers. His student asks, "But could you put up with their uncouth ways?" Confucius replies: "Once a gentleman [*junzi*] settles among them, what uncouthness will there be?"

12. Bushell, "Early History of Tibet," p. 457. Wang and Suo, *Highlights of Tibetan History*, p. 19 also believe that Wencheng has become a culture hero for Tibetans, who celebrate her life and her importation of Chinese culture: "Princess Wen Cheng . . . lived in this outlying area of China for nearly 40 years. The episodes of her life

are known in the Tibetan region. It is usually with a touch of deference and gratitude that the Tibetans relate these stories as they think the Han princess did a good deal for their land. The places she is known to have stayed at or passed by are revered as holy sites. Two dates of the year have been designated as festivals in memory of her. In addition considerable space in the Tibetan annals is devoted to the description of her life and work. . . . She did a good job in strengthening the political ties between Tang and Tufan [Tibet], enhancing the economic and cultural exchanges between them and spurring the progress of Tufan society." It is true that Wencheng is revered by Tibetans, but not as an emissary of Chinese culture; rather, she is viewed as an emanation of the buddha Tārā, and she is considered to have played a key role in the "first dissemination" of Buddhism to Tibet. For Tibetans, her mission was to bring Buddhism to their land, but the sort of Buddhism that eventually prevailed was primarily derived from Indian models; however, Chinese writers assume that any contact between foreigners and Chinese must have resulted in the former adopting Han culture on the Hans' terms. For an example of the mythology of Wencheng from the "treasure text" *Maṇi bka' 'bum*, see Jacques Bacot, "Le marriage chinois du roi tibétain Sron bcan sgan po," *Mélanges chinois et bouddiques*, no. 3 (1935): 1–60.

13. See Bushell, "Early History of Tibet," p. 445.

14. Ibid.

15. See, for example, Li An-che, *History of Tibetan Religion: A Study in the Field* (Beijing: New World Press, 1994), p. 20.

16. Grunfeld, *The Making of Modern Tibet*, p. 35. Grunfeld agrees with the Chinese authors that during the dynastic period "Tibet was absorbing Chinese culture" (p. 37), and he does not even mention that India played a major role in the shaping of Tibetan culture at this time.

17. *The Emperor of Tibet* was produced by the Sing Hai Hua Cinema Company, Hong Kong. The credits indicate that it was presented by Ming Ma Chi Yen and produced by Man Shiu Kown. It was directed by G. Y. Yang and starred Jacie Don Chu and Pobo Check Ma. The date of its production was not given on the copy I viewed.

18. Shakabpa, *Tibet: A Political History*, pp. 26, 27. Giuseppe Tucci, however, considers the traditional story of a marriage to a Nepalese princess to be extremely doubtful. "The Wives of Sronbtsan sgam po," in *Oriens Extremus*, ed. Oscar Benl et al. (Hamburg: Otto Harrassowitz, 1962), pp. 121–126. He points out that according to the Tibetan chronicles Bhṛkutī is said to have been the daughter of the king Aṃśuvarman, but that in contemporaneous accounts he was described as a devout Hindu, so it is improbable that his daughter would have been a Buddhist missionary.

19. It is worth noting in this connection that several Tibetan temples are attributed to her. See Amy Heller, "Eighth- and Ninth-Century Temples and Rock Carvings of Eastern Tibet," in *Tibetan Art: Toward a Definition of Style*, ed. Jane Casey Singer and Philip Underwood (London: Laurence King Publishing, 1997), pp. 86–103.

20. See John Powers, *Introduction to Tibetan Buddhism* (Ithaca, N.Y.: Snow Lion, 1995), pp. 124–136, and Amy Heller, "Eighth- and Ninth-Century Temples," p. 90, who asserts that this identification can be traced back at least to the ninth century.

21. Dawa Norbu, *Tibet: The Road Ahead*, pp. 52, 53.

22. This emphasis on the spread of Buddhism in Tibetan histories has been

noted by Andrei Ivanovich Vostrikov in his landmark study, *Tibetan Historical Literature*, trans. Harish Chandra Gupta (Calcutta: R.K. Maitra, 1970), p. 59.

23. Similarly, the *Old Tibetan Chronicle* (*Pelliot Tibétain* 1287, a record of the early Yarlung dynasty discovered in Dunhuang that was probably composed in the late eighth or early ninth century) discusses the laws promulgated by Songtsen Gampo, but it gives no indication of Buddhist influence. As Ariane Macdonald has noted in *Une Lecture des Pelliot Tibétain 1286, 1287, 1036, 1047, et 1290; Essai sur la formation et l'emploi des mythes politiques dans la religion royale de Sronbcan Sgam-po: Études Tibetaines* (Paris: Adrien Maisonneuve, 1971), p. 256, he is described as promising to sacrifice one hundred horses on the tomb of his vassal Ba (dBa) in recognition of his oath of loyalty. Had the king really been a Buddhist convert, presumably animal sacrifice would have been anathema to him. Macdonald's conclusion is that his religion was based on indigenous beliefs, not Buddhism. His reconstruction as both a Buddhist monarch and an incarnation of Avalokiteśvara is the product of a later age, when Buddhism had become widespread throughout Tibet, and the enduring memories of Tibet's imperial past were recast in a Buddhist framework. See also Turrell Wylie, "Some Political Factors in the Early History of Tibetan Buddhism," in *Studies in History of Buddhism*, ed. A. K. Narain (Delhi: B.R. Publishing, 1980), p. 366, where he concludes that Songtsen Gampo was probably an illiterate king who adhered to the imperial cult of Bön.

24. See George Roerich, trans., *The Blue Annals* (Delhi: Motilal Banarsidass, 1979), p. 37.

25. Lama Dampa Sönam Gyeltsen (bLa ma dam pa bSod nams rgyal mtshan, 1312–1375), *rGyal rabs gsal ba'i me long*, translated as *Tibetan Buddhist Historiography: The Mirror Illuminating the Royal Genealogies* by Per K. Sørensen (Wiesbaden: Harrasowitz Verlag, 1994), p. 248.

26. See ibid., p. 249. One of several statements on Chinese attitudes toward Tibetans is the minister Gar's assertion that "Generally [we] have been treated contemptuously by the entire Chinese population. Aside from one Chinese hostess, not one single sympathetic Chinese was found. . . . Princess Kong-jo [Wencheng], how much ill-feeling have even you shown towards [Tibet]? The Chinese princess felt shame over this and was unable to utter a single word [in response]."

27. Hugh Richardson, *High Peaks, Pure Earth: Collected Writings on Tibetan History and Culture* (London: Serindia Publications, 1998), p. 212.

28. This is reflected in the popular Tibetan opera *Chinese Bride, Nepali Bride* (*rGya bza' Bal bza'*), which recounts some of the legends surrounding the deeds of Songtsen Gampo, Wencheng, and Bhṛkutī. It mainly focuses on the stories of minister Gar's trials in securing the Chinese emperor's agreement to the marriage proposal. It concludes with the popular legend that when Songtsen Gampo died, he and his two wives merged into the image of Jowo Rinpoche. This is contrary to the historical accounts of the time, which state that Songtsen Gampo actually died three years after his marriage to Wencheng and that she lived for thirty years after that.

29. Thurman, *Tibetan Book of the Dead*, pp. 6–7.

30. Thurman, *Essential Tibetan Buddhism*, p. 18.

31. See Eugene Obermiller's translation, *History of Buddhism* (Heidelberg: Otto

Harrassowitz, 1931), vol. 2, p. 188. This is also the conclusion of the *Testament of Ba* (*dBa' bzhed*); see Pasang Wangdu and Hildegard Diemberger, d*Ba' bzhed: The Royal Narrative Concerning the Bringing of the Buddha's Doctrine to Tibet* (Wien: Verlag der Österreichischen Akademie der Wissenschaften, 2000), pp. 88–89. See also the fifth Dalai Lama's history of Tibet, in which he states that the Hashang "taught meditation and led many Tibetan people astray" but was defeated and "sent back to China." When he arrived he "set fire to his body" (Ahmad, *A History of Tibet by the Fifth Dalai Lama*, p. 65). Paul Demiéville wrote a lengthy review of Obermiller's translation, in which he concluded that of all the extant accounts of the debate, Pudön's is the least likely to be correct (*La Concile de Lhasa*, p. 1 n. 2).

32. Demiéville, *La Concile de Lhasa*, p. 442. A Tibetan text associated with the "great perfection" (*rdsogs chen*) tradition, entitled *Bka' thang sde lnga*, also reports that the Chinese suddenists were victorious: see Giuseppe Tucci, *Minor Buddhist Texts II* (Rome: Istituto Italiano per il Medio ed Estremo Oriente, 1958), p. 80.

33. An overview of sources may be found in G. W. Houston, *Sources for a History of the Bsam yas Debate* (Sankt Augustin, Denmark: VGH-Wissenschaftsverlag, 1980).

34. Luis O. Gómez, "Indian Materials on the Doctrine of Sudden Enlightenment," in *Early Ch'an in China and Tibet*, ed. Whalen Lai and Lewis Lancaster (Berkeley: Asian Humanities Press, 1983), p. 396. His conclusion accords with a Chinese account of the debate that was discovered in Dunhuang by Paul Pelliot and generally referred to as PT 4646. See Demiéville, *La Concile de Lhasa*, pp. 39–40.

35. As Demiéville notes, however, according to records from Dunhuang, the Hashang traveled there after he left Tibet and became a respected teacher (*La Concile du Lhasa*, pp. 253, 254).

36. Traditional Tibetan historical works that discuss the debate are unanimous in their conclusion that the Indian side won and that the Hashang's system was declared heretical. See, for example, Sönam Drakpa's account in the *New Red Annals*, which report that after his defeat he was sent back to China and his books were hidden (Tucci, *Deb t'er dmar po gsar ma*, p. 155).

37. Tenzin Gyatso, Dalai Lama XIV, *The Buddhism of Tibet* (London: Allen & Unwin, 1975), pp. 21–22. As Matthew Kapstein notes, however, although this may be "the normative viewpoint among those educated within the tradition," the situation is considerably more nuanced and complex than this statement indicates. *The Tibetan Assimilation of Buddhism* (Oxford: Oxford University Press, 2000), p. 69.

38. Shakabpa, *Tibet: A Political History*, p. 39.

39. Thubten Jigme Norbu, *Tibet*, pp. 177, 147.

40. Li Tieh-tseng, *The Historical Status of Tibet* (New York: King's Crown Press, Columbia University, 1956), p. 11.

41. Li An-che, *History of Tibetan Religion*, p. 23.

42. L. Dongfan, " 'Cham Performance at Tashilhunpo Monastery," *China's Tibet* (winter 1993): 23. René de Nebesky-Wojkowitz reports that in some 'cham dances he is a "dignified figure," and he mentions performances at Kumbum and Tashilhunpo as examples. Nebesky-Wojkowitz also indicates that in some dances he is identified as an arhat, and in those circumstances is accorded the respect due an arhat, but in per-

formances in which he is identified as the Chinese master Hashang Mahāyāna he is an object of ridicule: "Strong Tibetan dislike of the Chinese . . . is responsible for the indignities to which Ha zhang is subject." *Tibetan Religious Dances: Tibetan Text and Translation of the 'Chams yig* (The Hague: Mouton, 1976), pp. 82–83.

43. The theme of the Hashang's propensity for self-injury is found in several Tibetan chronicles. *Nyangrel's History of the Dharma* (Nyang Nyi ma 'od zer, 1124–1196, *Chos 'byung me tog snying po sbrang rtsi'i bcud*), for example, reports that the Hashang set fire to his own head and went to the paradise of Sukhāvatī after his death and that other chroniclers asserted that he committed suicide by crushing his own genitals (reported in Sørensen, *Tibetan Buddhist Historiography*, p. 402 n. 1376). The *Statement of Ba* (*dBa' bzhed*) also contains a story of the Chinese faction threatening various forms of self-mutilation after hearing the proposed ground rules of the debate. See Pasang Wangdu and Hildegard Diemberger, *dBa' bzhed*, p. 80. These accounts, along with Pudön's version of events, probably contributed to the Hashang's reputation for self-injury among Tibetans and have apparently been incorporated into the contemporary Hashang character who appears in 'cham dances.

44. A number of Western enthusiasts of Tibetan Buddhism have opined that the fall of the Yarlung dynasty was a result of the importation of Buddhism, which they believe pacified the previously warlike Tibetans and rendered them so nonviolent that they became incapable of defending themselves against their enemies. There is little evidence to support this thesis, and in fact Tibetans continued to fight vigorously against their enemies in the following centuries (though not always very effectively, as we will see). Erik Haarh, in his landmark study of this period, also believes that Buddhism was a key factor in the demise of the Tibetan empire, but in his opinion it "was not the result of a general mollification or pacification of the Tibetan mentality, but because Buddhism became a destructive agent to the spiritual life and tradition of the Tibetan people. To the Tibetan kings, adhering to Buddhism for the purpose of making their authority independent of the ancient national traditions, which at the same time meant its very basis and its restriction, Buddhism became disastrous, ruining the Dynasty in its own defeat against the last display of strength of the aboriginal tradition." *The Yar-luṅ Dynasty* (Copenhagen: G.E.C. Gad's Forlag, 1969), p. 12.

45. The history of the demise of the Yarlung dynasty is exceedingly complex. There are various competing accounts, and details remain hazy. A useful overview of the period is Luciano Petech's article "The Disintegration of the Tibetan Kingdom," in *Tibetan Studies. Proceedings of the Sixth Seminar of the International Association for Tibetan Studies, Fagernes 1992*, ed. Per Kvaerne (Oslo: Institute for Comparative Research in Human Culture, 1994), pp. 649–659.

46. Thubten Jigme Norbu and Colin M. Turnbull, *Tibet*, p. 183.

47. In this context, "tantra" refers to texts composed in India that were called tantras and practices derived from them. These practices stress ritual and visualization as being central to the pursuit of buddhahood.

48. Li Tieh-tseng, *The Historical Status of Tibet*, p. 229 n. 16.

49. Li An-che, *History of Tibetan Buddhism*, pp. 23–24.

50. Roerich, *The Blue Annals*, p. 63. There is also a brief indication in the *Blue*

Annals that following the restoration of Buddhism in central Tibet a Chinese monk (no ethnicity is mentioned) accompanied a group of Tibetan monks, and as a result some Tibetan monks changed the way they wore their robes.

51. Quoted in Shakabpa, *Tibet: A Political History*, pp. 63–64.

52. Department of Information and International Relations, Tibetan Government-in-Exile, *The Mongols and Tibet: A Historical Assessment of Relations between the Mongol Empire and Tibet* (Dharamsala: Department of Information and International Relations, 1996), p. 9.

53. Ibid., pp. 9, 10.

54. See ibid., p. 21.

55. Wang and Suo, *Highlights of Tibetan History*, p. 57.

56. Ibid., p. 60.

57. See Lee Feigon, *Demystifying Tibet: Unlocking the Secrets of the Land of the Snows* (Chicago: Ivan R. Dee, 1996), p. 58, where he concludes that China's claim to ownership of Tibet based on Mongol conquests is "shaky."

58. See Luc Kwanten, "Tibetan-Mongol Relations during the Yuan Dynasty, 1207–1368" (Ph.D. dissertation, University of South Carolina, 1972), p. 169.

59. Dai Yannian et al., *Tibet: Myth vs. Reality*, p. 10.

60. Li Tieh-tseng, *The Historical Status of Tibet*, pp. 19–21.

61. Ibid., pp. 22, 49.

62. Shakabpa, *Tibet: A Political History*, p. 63.

63. Dawa Norbu, *Red Star over Tibet*, pp. 66–67.

64. Department of Information, *The Mongols and Tibet*, p. 21.

65. Thubten Jigme Norbu, *Tibet*, p. 195.

66. Ibid.

67. Shakabpa, *Tibet: A Political History*, pp. 63, 71.

68. Ibid., p. 70.

69. Thomas Heberer, "Old Tibet a Hell on Earth?" in *Imagining Tibet: Perceptions, Projections, and Fantasies*, ed. Thierry Dodin and Heinz Räther (Boston: Wisdom Publications, 2001), p. 113.

70. Goldstein, *The Snow Lion and the Dragon*, pp. 4–5.

71. See Rossabi, *China and Inner Asia*, p. 19. Pamela Crossley, in *A Translucent Mirror: History and Identity in Qing Imperial History* (Berkeley: University of California Press, 1999), p. 72, notes that with the more powerful chieftains of the Jurchens and Mongols the tribute system amounted to "legalized extortion" in the sense that the Chinese court effectively bribed them with valuable goods to maintain a tenuous peace.

72. June Dreyer, *China's Forty Millions* (Cambridge, Mass.: Harvard University Press, 1976), p. 17. The discourse of transformation was often appropriated by some of the groups that were conquered by the Han in order to establish themselves as having an equal standing. During the Qing dynasty some Manchu rulers also argued that their contact with Chinese culture had civilized them and that they had left behind the "barbarian" habits of their ancestors. See Crossley, *A Translucent Mirror*, pp. 255–257.

73. *Shijing*, 205: "*Pu tian zhi xia, mo fei wang tu.*" See Benjamin Schwartz, "The

Chinese Perception of World Order, Past and Present" in *The Chinese World Order: Traditional China's Foreign Relations*, ed. John K. Fairbank (Cambridge, Mass.: Harvard University Press, 1968), p. 277.

74. Yu Yu, *Tong tian*, 185.985. Quoted in Andrew March, *The Idea of China: Myth and Theory in Geographic Thought* (Melbourne: Wren Publishing, 1974), p. 18.

75. Sometimes, however, chauvinistic Chinese attitudes and assumptions about barbarian rulers led to conflicts. An example is a mission sent to Tamerlane by the first Ming emperor, led by Fu An and Liu Wei, who brought him a letter referring to him as a vassal and inviting him to acknowledge his subservience to the Chinese emperor. Tamerlane was so offended by the tone of the letter that he had the ambassador arrested. Not realizing their mistake, the emperor's advisors sent a second mission, which was also seized. The emperor died the next year and so was unable to do anything about these events, but Tamerlane decided to attack China after he quelled rebellions in other parts of his empire.

76. See Turrell Wylie's excellent article, "Lama Tribute in the Ming Dynasty," in *Tibetan Studies in Honour of Hugh Richardson*, ed. Michael Aris and Aung San Suu Kyi (Warminster, England: Aris & Phillips, 1980), p. 339, where he points out that unlike the Mongols, who patronized the Sakya hierarchs, the Ming bestowed presents and titles on lamas from all orders who were willing to come to the Ming court. He suggests that they did so not as a renewal of the priest-patron relationship, but to prevent any of them establishing such a relationship with one of the Mongol rulers, who still presented a threat to the dynasty.

77. Wei Jing, *100 Questions about Tibet*, pp. 9–10.

78. Dai Yannian et al., *Tibet: Myth vs. Reality*, p. 11.

79. Li Tieh-tseng, *Tibet: Yesterday and Today*, p. 28.

80. Shakabpa, *Tibet: A Political History*, pp. 85, 114. Department of Information, *The Mongols and Tibet*, p. 20 claims that this actually occurred when the third Dalai Lama convinced Altan Khan to refrain from military attacks on China, which "may probably have saved China from falling, once again, under Mongol rule."

81. Shakabpa, *Tibet: A Political History*, p. 73. This accords with J. K. Fairbank and S. Y. Teng's analysis of the Qing tribute system in their article, "On the Ch'ing Tributary System," *Harvard Journal of Asiatic Studies* 6.2 (1941): 135–246. They demonstrate that the fact of participation in this system cannot be taken as evidence of subordination.

82. Department of Information, *The Mongols and Tibet*, p. 30.

83. Dawa Norbu, *Red Star over Tibet*, p. 67.

84. Richardson, *Tibet and Its History*, p. 36.

85. Wang and Suo, *Highlights of Tibetan History*, p. 66.

86. Ya Hanzhang, *The Biographies of the Dalai Lamas* (Beijing: Foreign Languages Press, 1993), p. vi.

87. Shakabpa, *Tibet: A Political History*, p. 324.

88. Dawa Norbu, *Red Star over Tibet*, p. 68.

89. Dawa Norbu, "The Europeanization of Sino-Tibetan Relations, 1775–1907: The Genesis of Chinese 'Suzerainty' and Tibetan 'Autonomy,' " *Tibet Journal* 15.4 (1990): 28.

90. Cited in Zahiruddin Ahmad, *Sino-Tibetan Relations in the Seventeenth Century* (Rome: Istituto Italiano per il Medio ed Estremo Oriente, 1970), pp. 39–40.

91. Ibid., p. 183.

92. For a study of this complex and its symbolism, see Samuel M. Grupper, "The Manchu Imperial Cult of the Early Ch'ing Dynasty" (Ph.D. dissertation, Indiana University, 1979), pp. 20–48.

93. Ahmad, *Sino-Tibetan Relations*, p. 300.

94. As a minority dynasty ruling a vast empire from their capital in Beijing, the Manchus were intensely aware of the need to establish their legitimacy among its more powerful constituencies. Thus, they portrayed themselves as sagely Confucian rulers to their Chinese subjects, as successors of Genghis Khan and emanations of Mahākāla to the Mongols, and as devout Buddhists to Tibetans. See David Farquhar, "Emperor as Bodhisattva in the Governance of the Ch'ing Empire," *Harvard Journal of Asiatic Studies* 38.1 (1978): 5–34, which discusses a *thanka* of Mañjuśrī with the Qianlong emperor's face in which he holds the wheel of a universal emperor (*cakravartin*) in his left hand and the wheel of dharma in his right.

95. As Pamela Crossley (*A Translucent Mirror*, p. 341) notes, this claim is ironic in light of the fact that the Qing emphasized the notion that China was one province of their empire and differentiated themselves ethnically from their Chinese subjects.

96. Li Tieh-tseng, *The Historical Status of Tibet*, p. 130.

97. Ibid., pp. 2, 1, 215.

98. Li Tieh-tseng, *Tibet: Today and Yesterday*, pp. ii, iii.

99. Ibid., p. 52. He apparently assumes that because the ethnic Tibetan area where the Dalai Lama was born was under the control of a Chinese warlord, the people spoke Chinese instead of Tibetan.

100. Shen Tsung-lien and Shen-chi Liu, *Tibet and the Tibetans* (Stanford: Stanford University Press, 1953), p. 89.

101. Shakabpa, *Tibet: A Political History*, pp. 141, 147. Compare this last point with the statement in Dai Yannian et al., *Tibet: Myth vs. Reality* that "the Qing government lost no time in sending troops to defend the region. It drove the invaders out, secured Tibet and preserved the unification of the motherland" (p. 24).

102. Dai Yannian et al., *Tibet: Myth vs. Reality*, p. 25.

103. Li Tieh-tseng, *The Historical Status of Tibet*, p. 57.

104. See, for example, Dai Yannian et al., *Tibet: Myth vs. Reality*, p. 25.

105. Ibid., pp. 33–35.

106. Shakabpa, *Tibet: A Political History*, pp. 248, 323.

107. Tibet certainly sought to isolate itself from the outside world and succeeded in keeping most European travelers from penetrating very far beyond its borders, yet the actual extent of isolation is often overstated. Many Asian traders, merchants, pilgrims, and others were allowed into Tibet, as were Buddhist monks from Mongolian areas who came to central Tibet to study. In addition, Tibet often allowed Newari merchants from Nepal and Indian pilgrims to enter the country. The main focus of exclusion was Chinese nationals and Europeans, who were believed to have imperialist designs on Tibetan territory.

108. Li Tieh-tseng, *Tibet: Yesterday and Today*, p. vi.

109. Thubten Jigme Norbu and Colin M. Turnbull, *Tibet*, p. 314.

CHAPTER 3

1. Part of the problem was that the Europeans generally knew very little about Chinese attitudes. Their main interest in initiating contacts with China was to open the country to trade, and so they sent merchants as trade emissaries. In traditional Chinese society, however, merchants are viewed as occupying the lowest level of society and are generally scorned. Spain and Portugal, by contrast, first sent well-educated religious scholars to China, and they received a much better reception than European merchants. From the Chinese point of view, it was rather insulting that merchants would presume to initiate contacts with the Chinese court, and the fact that European countries sent such people as emissaries was considered to be in bad taste.

2. Letter from Griffith John to the London Missionary Society, in R. Wardlaw Thompson, ed., *Griffith John: The Story of Fifty Years in China* (New York: A.C. Armstrong, 1906), p. 254.

3. Lucian Pye, "How China's Nationalism Was Shanghaied," in *Chinese Nationalism*, ed. Jonathan Unger (London: M.E. Sharpe, 1996), p. 87.

4. Ibid., p. 94.

5. Following the conclusion of the war between Japan and Russia in 1905, Russia formally took control of northern Manchuria, and Japan of the south.

6. This practice was originally instituted in 1618 by the Jurchen Jin emperor Nurgaci as part of an egalitarian policy. He mandated that there should be no sartorial distinctions between the various ethnic groups that made up his empire. Although the purpose of this directive was to make everyone equal, Chinese subjects recognized that the standards of dress and fashion were those of their Manchu conquerors, and this served as a basis for resentment. It is interesting to note parenthetically that while this experience left many Han deeply resentful of their treatment under the Manchu regime—which led to massacres in Manchu quarters in some Chinese cities during the 1911 revolution—their descendants have generally failed to realize that Tibetans also resent the fact that their Han conquerors have forced them to adopt fashionable Chinese hairstyles and wear Chinese clothes, to speak Chinese, and to abandon their "backward" culture.

7. Josef Kolmas provides a useful overview of the role and status of the Manchu ambans in Tibet, along with a chronology of this institution in "The Ambans and Assistant Ambans of Tibet (1727–1912): Some Statistical Observations," in *Tibetan Studies. Proceedings of the Sixth Seminar of the International Association for Tibetan Studies, Fagernes 1992*, ed. Per Kvaerne (Oslo: Institute for Comparative Research in Human Culture, 1994), pp. 454–467.

8. Quoted in Premen Addy, *Tibet on the Imperial Chessboard* (New Delhi: Academic Publishers, 1984), p. 107.

9. For detailed accounts of the Younghusband Expedition, see Peter Fleming, *Bayonets to Lhasa* (Oxford: Oxford University Press, 1961); Alastair Lamb, *British India*

and Tibet: 1766–1901 (London: Routledge and Kegan Paul, 1960) and *The McMahon Line: A Study in the Relations between India, China and Tibet, 1904–1914* (London: Routledge and Kegan Paul, 1966). Also of interest is Younghusband's account in *India and Tibet: A History of the Relations between the Two Countries from the Time of Warren Hastings to 1910; With a Particular Account of the Mission to Lhasa of 1904* (Hong Kong: Oxford University Press, 1985).

10. Candler wrote that for the Tibetans, "the impossible had happened. Prayers and charms and mantras, and the holiest of their holy men, had failed them. I believe that they were obsessed with that one thought. They walked with bowed heads, as if they had been disillusioned by their gods." Quoted in Peter Hopkirk, *Trespassers on the Roof of the World* (Oxford: Oxford University Press, 1982), p. 175. Observers of the Chinese invasion and Tibetan military routs in the early 1950s report similar reactions. As Chinese troops were advancing deeper into Tibet, a number of prominent lamas began performing rituals that would purportedly stop an army in its tracks and used powerful mantras that they believed would destroy the Chinese force, but when they had no discernable effect, both lamas and lay Tibetans experienced a crisis of belief.

11. In 1912 Yuan Shigai, the president of the newly inaugurated Chinese Republic, issued an official edict that restored the Dalai Lama's titles and rank: "Now that the Republic has been firmly established and the Five Races united into one family, the Dalai Lama is naturally moved with a feeling of deep attachment to the mother country. Under the circumstances his former errors should be overlooked, and his Title of Loyal and Submissive Vice-Regent, Great, Good, and Self-Existent Buddha is hereby restored to him, in the hope that he may prove a support to the Yellow Church [the Gelukpa order] and a help to the Republic." "Presidential Mandate of 28 October 1912," *Government Gazette*; quoted in Eric Teichman, *Travels of a Consular Officer in Eastern Tibet* (Cambridge, England: Cambridge University Press, 1922), p. 17.

12. For an interesting alternative perspective on the Younghusband expedition and the role of the amban and the Chinese government, see Song Liming, "The Younghusband Expedition and China's Policy towards Tibet (1903–1904)," in Kvaerne, *Tibetan Studies*, pp. 789–800, which relies on Chinese records of the period. In Song's reconstruction, the amban is at the center of all negotiations and everything goes through him. Song admits that the Tibetans refused to give him transport and that they ignored his advice, but unlike the Tibetan and British accounts, in which he is completely marginalized and ignored by both sides, Song represents him as a figure of considerable influence who "was very active and effective in persuading, or rather pressing, the Tibetans to accept the terms of the convention" (p. 794).

13. In the often murky terminology of the period, Britain conceded that China had "suzerainty" over Tibet, which meant that it recognized that Tibet was a protectorate of China and that it had legitimate interests there. But Britain denied that China exercised "sovereignty" over the region, which meant that, according to Britain, the Tibetans were in control of their internal affairs.

14. Goldstein, *The Snow Lion and the Dragon*, p. 26.

15. Dawa Norbu, *Red Star over Tibet*, p. 71.

16. Thubten Jigme Norbu, *Tibet*, p. 313.

17. Shakabpa, *Tibet: A Political History*, p. 207.

18. Ibid., p. 214. See also p. 218, where he asserts that "the British army had not engaged in looting in the course of their advance and had respected the religion of the country. It paid generously for the transport and supplies it obtained from the Tibetans."

19. Ibid., pp. 215, 217.

20. Ibid., pp. 217, 218.

21. Ibid., p. 219.

22. Wang and Suo, *Highlights of Tibetan History*, pp. 122–123.

23. Ya, *Biographies of the Dalai Lamas*, pp. 200–201. See Li Tieh-Tseng, *The Historical Status of Tibet*, p. 92, which also characterizes it as a pretext, but Li thinks that You Tai's delaying tactics were a foolish attempt to enlist British help in "reasserting his authority" that ultimately failed and ended up playing into the hands of the British.

24. Wang and Suo, *Highlights of Tibetan History*, p. 123.

25. Ibid., p. 124. Ya also provides an account of "heroic" Tibetan resistance that resulted in "heavy losses," but unlike Wang and Suo he also admits that the Tibetan forces were soundly defeated by the British. See *The Biographies of the Dalai Lamas*, pp. 200–207.

26. Wang and Suo, *Highlights of Tibetan History*, p. 125.

27. Heyu, *Tibet: A General Survey* (Peking: New World Press, 1988), p. 28.

28. Wang and Suo, *Highlights of Tibetan History*, pp. 125–126.

29. Ibid., p. 126.

30. Huang Hongzhao, *The West Powers and Tibet*, pp. 104–105.

31. Wang and Suo, *Highlights of Tibetan History*, p. 128.

32. Ya, *The Biographies of the Dalai Lamas*, p. 189.

33. Quoted in Addy, *Tibet on the Imperial Chessboard*, p. 156.

34. Huang Hongzhao, *The West Powers and Tibet*, pp. 29–30, 23, 85, 103.

35. *Hong He Gu*, 1996, color, 120 min. The credits state that it was produced by the Management of Movie and Television Section, GH Pictures (China) Limited, and certified with Peoples Republic of China Censorship Board # 076. It was shot by the Shanghai Film Studio. The director was Feng Xiaoning, who also wrote the screenplay. The producers were Feng Xiaoning and Zhang Jianmin, and the supervisor was Zhuo Wu. By Chinese standards, this was a big-budget production, costing a reported $1.8 million to make, and it was enormously popular in China. It won the Excellent Picture Award in 1997 and the Hundred Flowers Award for Best Picture and Best Director.

36. Despite the fact that the Tibetans revel in physical activities like horse riding and marksmanship, in the first scene in which Hung arrives in Tibet to take Xuer back, Gasang has just won a contest involving shooting at targets hanging from a rope, but Hung rides into the middle of the field and upstages him with superior marksmanship, hitting every target. The message is that even though the wild and physical Tibetans pride themselves on such activities, the Han are still their superiors. Almaz Khan, "Who Are the Mongols? State, Ethnicity, and the Politics of Representation in the PRC," in *Negotiating Ethnicities in China and Taiwan*, ed. Melissa Brown

(Berkeley: Institute of East Asian Studies, University of California, 1996), pp. 147–148, reports that this theme is repeated in tourist literature and popular culture images of China's other minorities. He believes that such representations of the Other are used by Chinese to improve their self-image, which has been battered by contacts with more developed nations. Depicting minorities as culturally backward provides Chinese with a space in which they can assert their own superiority.

37. It is worth noting in this context that these images of Tibetans freely displaying their bodies are in stark contrast to how Tibetans actually live. Anyone who has lived among Tibetans will know that they exhibit a high level of physical modesty. Chinese images of Tibetans in this film are typical of portrayals of minorities in Chinese cinema: they are shown as displaying a lot of flesh, they are sexually promiscuous, and they are fond of singing and dancing.

38. It is not made clear in the movie, but he may be the Tibetan commander of Gyantse Fort, Dapon Tailing, recast as a Han.

39. Richardson, *Tibet and Its History*, p. 88.

40. Ibid.

41. Ibid.

42. Ibid., p. 89.

43. Ibid., pp. 89–90.

44. John Fitzgerald, *Awakening China: Politics, Culture, and Class in the Nationalist Revolution* (Stanford: Stanford University Press, 1996).

45. Liang Qichao, "A General Survey of China's Progress over the Past Fifty Years," quoted in ibid., p. 88. Liang's essay was first published in 1922.

46. Fitzgerald, *Awakening China*, p. 79.

47. Traditionally, Chinese have referred to Tibetan Buddhism as "Lamaism" (*lama jiao*), in contrast to Buddhism (*fo jiao*). Similarly, Tibetan Buddhists commonly refer to their coreligionists as "insiders" (*nang pa*), while Chinese Buddhists are thought to practice another religion (*bu ja'o*).

48. See Gray W. Tuttle, "Faith and Nation: Tibetan Buddhists in the Making of Modern China (1902–1958)" (Ph.D. dissertation, Harvard University, 2000), pp. 240, 286–287. As evidence for his contentions, Tuttle reports that in 1931 and 1934 the Panchen Lama held Kālacakra rituals in China that were attended by over 10,000 people, and over 300,000 reportedly attended his last public lecture in Shanghai in 1934. In addition, Norhla Hutukhtu performed public ceremonies for tens of thousands of people on several occasions. But in relation to China's population, these numbers are negligible, and there is little evidence that either had real influence in the government. In 1929, Norhla Hutukhtu was made a member of the Mongolian and Tibetan Affairs Commission (Meng zang Weiyuanhui), and in 1935 was named Xikang Pacification commissioner (Xikang xuanwei shi). In 1934 the Panchen lama was appointed commissioner of National Government (Minguo zhengfu weiyuan), which came with a government salary. But these were marginal positions, and the two lamas were hired as propaganda ambassadors for the Nationalist government rather than as officials with real power. Norhla Hutukhtu was captured by the Communists in 1936 while touring Kham, and he died in custody without ever realizing his dream of reclaiming his former territories. Similarly, the Panchen Lama died in

1937 on a propaganda tour of the Tibetan borderlands, and so was unable to accomplish his aim of returning to Shigatse and creating a separate state.

It is also worth noting in this context that there were many other Tibetan Buddhist lamas operating in China during this time. Based on research on the Court for Managing the Frontiers, Chia Ning reports that there were more than a hundred high-ranking Tibetan lamas in Beijing in the late Imperial period. This continued a pattern of imperial patronage that reached its apogee during the reign of the Qianlong emperor, when more than twelve hundred lamas were registered with the Court for Managing the Frontiers. The *Record of Imperial Household Ceremonies* states that in 1780 two thousand lamas were hired by the Imperial household to recite scriptures. See Chia Ning, "The Li-fan Yuan in the Early Qing Dynasty" (Ph.D. dissertation, Johns Hopkins University, 1992), p. 225. Also, Evelyn Rawski, *The Last Emperors: A Social History of Qing Imperial Institutions* (Berkeley: University of California Press, 1998), p. 271 states that 1,516 Tibetan monks were employed by the Imperial court in 1854. Most of them were probably not ethnic Tibetans, however, but were most likely Mongols, Monguors, or Chinese who had been ordained in a Tibetan tradition. See also John Blofeld, "Lamaism and Its Influence on Chinese Buddhism," *T'ien Hsia Monthly* (September 1938): 157–160, and Holmes Welch, *The Buddhist Revival in China* (Cambridge, Mass.: Harvard University Press, 1968), pp. 9–12.

49. Mao Zedong, quoted in John Bryan Starr, *Continuing the Revolution: The Political Thought of Mao* (Princeton: Princeton University Press, 1979), p. 276.

50. Michael Walzer, *Thick and Thin: Moral Argument at Home and Abroad* (Notre Dame, Ind.: University of Notre Dame Press, 1994), pp. 25–47.

51. W. J. F. Jenner, *The Tyranny of History: The Roots of China's Crisis* (London: Penguin Press, 1992), p. 3.

52. An example of this policy is Zhao Erfeng's invasion of eastern Tibet in 1905, during which he destroyed a number of monasteries and brought Kham and Lithang under direct Chinese rule. He worked to sinicize the ethnic Tibetans of the area by ordering them to wear their hair in Chinese styles and adopt Chinese names. He also forced nomadic and seminomadic people to become agriculturalists, which he believed would aid in the civilizing process. There was widespread resistance to his rule, which was brutally suppressed. As a result, he became known as "Butcher Zhao" by Tibetans. Following the 1911 revolution, he attempted to rule the area as a semi-independent warlord, but his troops were defeated by Tibetan forces and he was murdered in 1911.

53. Following the Communist Revolution, Zhang Zhiyi provided a list of minority customs that he believed were compatible with building socialism, which included "boldness, martial spirit, fondness for work, sincerity, love of singing and dancing, free choice in marital matters, and so forth." Quoted in George Moseley, *Party and the National Question in China* (Cambridge, Mass.: MIT Press, 1966), p. 117. It is significant that such core culture markers as language and religion were not part of Zhang's list of desirable qualities.

54. Chiang Kai-shek, *China's Destiny*, trans. Wang Chung-hui (New York: Roy Publishers, 1947), p. 13.

55. John Fitzgerald, "The Nationless State: The Search for a Nation in Modern

Chinese Nationalism," in Jonathan Unger, ed., *Chinese Nationalism* (London: M.E. Sharpe, 1996), p. 57.

56. Wang and Suo, *Highlights of Tibetan History*, p. 160.

57. Benedict Anderson, *Imagined Communities: Reflections on the Origin and Spread of Nationalism* (London: Verso, 1991), p. 163.

58. Jenner, *The Tyranny of History*, pp. 158–159.

59. Pye, "How China's Nationalism Was Shanghaied," p. 87.

60. Ernest Gellner, *Thought and Change* (London: Weidenfeld & Nicolson, 1964), p. 169.

61. For a classic study of the link between culturalism and modern Chinese nationalism, see James Harrison's *Modern Chinese Nationalism* (New York: Hunter College of the City of New York, Research Institute on Modern Asia, 1969).

62. Lucian Pye, *The Spirit of Chinese Politics: A Psychocultural Study of the Authority Crisis in Political Development* (Cambridge, Mass.: MIT Press, 1968), pp. 5–6.

63. James Townsend, "Chinese Nationalism," in Unger, *Chinese Nationalism*, p. 23.

64. Stuart R. Schram, ed., *The Scope of State Power in China* (Hong Kong: Chinese University Press, 1985), p. xi.

65. Ernest Gellner, *Nations and Nationalism* (Ithaca, N.Y.: Cornell University Press, 1983), p. 43.

CHAPTER 4

1. Wang and Suo, *Highlights of Tibetan History*, pp. 171–172.

2. One indication of the cultural distance between Tibet and China was the fact that when a group of Chinese monks traveled to Tibet in 1925 to study Tibetan Buddhism their work was hampered by the fact that there were no bilingual Tibetan-Chinese glossaries. See Welch, *The Buddhist Revival in China*, p. 12. The leader of this group was a Chinese monk named Taixu (1890–1947). For an account of his life and work, see Don A. Pittman, *Toward a Modern Chinese Buddhism: Taixu's Reforms* (Honolulu: University of Hawai'i Press, 2001) and Welch, p. 198.

3. Mao Zedong, *Ma'o tse tung gi gsung rtsom gces bsdus* (*Mao Zedong's Collected Works*), 1977, vol. 5, cited in Goldstein, *The Snow Lion and the Dragon*, pp. 43–44.

4. Wang and Suo, *Highlights of Tibetan History*, p. 173.

5. Quoted in Smith, *Tibetan Nation*, p. 296.

6. Tenzin Gyatso, Dalai Lama XIV, *My Land, My People* (New York: Potala Press, 1983), p. 87.

7. "Support Agreement on Measures for Peaceful Liberation of Tibet," *New China News Agency*, May 28, 1951, in *Survey of China Mainland Press* (Hong Kong: U.S. Consulate, 1951).

8. In *My Land, My People*, the Dalai Lama states, "We first came to know of it from a broadcast which Ngabo [the leader of the delegation] made on Peking Radio. It was a terrible shock when we heard the terms of it. We were appalled at the mixture of Communist clichés, vainglorious assertions which were completely false, and bold

statements which were only partly true and the terms were far worse and more oppressive than anything we had imagined" (p. 88).

9. Shakabpa, *Tibet: A Political History*, p. 304.

10. Dawa Norbu, *Red Star over Tibet*, p. 124. Several of the delegates have written
reports of their perspectives, but as far as I am aware none have been fully translated
or studied. See, for example, Hlawutara Tupden Tendar (Lha'u rta ra Thub bstan
bstan dar), "Bod zhi bas bcings 'grol byung thabs skor gyi gros thun tshan bcu bdun
la ming rtags bkod pa'i sngon rjes su," in *Bod kyi rig gnas lo rgyus rgyu cha bdam
bsgrigs* 1 (Dharamsala: Library of Tibetan Works and Archives, 1982), pp. 88–117, and
Kheme Sönam Wangdu (Khe smad bSod nams dbang 'dus), *rGas po'i lo rgyus 'bel
gtam* (Dharamsala: Library of Tibetan Works and Archives, 1982). Also of interest is
the statement by Ngabö Ngawang Jikme (Nga phod Ngag dbang 'jigs med, who
headed the delegation but who is now generally regarded by exile Tibetans as a trai-
tor), "Rang skyong ljongs mi dmangs 'thus tshogs rgyun mthud kyi kru'u rin Nga
phod Ngag dbang 'Jigs med kyis rang skyong ljongs kyi skabs lnga pa'i mi dmangs
'thus tshogs du thengs gnyis pa'i thog gnang ba'i gal che'i gsungs bshad" (Lhasa,
1989).

11. Wang and Suo, *Highlights of Tibetan History*, p. 177.

12. It is also quoted in full by Richardson, Smith, Epstein, and Goldstein.

13. Li Tieh-Tseng, *The Historical Status of Tibet*, p. 209.

14. Grunfeld, *The Making of Modern Tibet*, p. 115.

15. Goldstein, *A History of Modern Tibet*, p. 761.

16. Goldstein, *The Snow Lion and the Dragon*, pp. 46–47, 48.

17. Wei, *100 Questions about Tibet*, p. 32.

18. Wang Feng, "On the Rectification Campaign and Socialist Education among
Minorities," in *Chinese Politics Towards Minorities*, ed. Henry Schwartz (Bellingham:
Western Washington State College, 1971), p. 120.

19. Dalai Lama, *My Land and My People*, p. 128.

20. For a discussion of this group, see Tsering Shakya, *The Dragon in the Land of
Snows* (New York: Columbia University Press, 1999), pp. 144–147. As he notes, the
choice of the term "Mimang" was a reflexive move, because this is the Tibetan term
coined by the Chinese for "the people."

21. *Great Changes in Tibet* (Peking: Foreign Languages Press, 1972), pp. i–ii.

22. In Sabrine Dabringhaus, *Das Qing-Imperium als Vision und Wirklichkeit: Tibet
in Laufbahn und Schriften des Song Yun (1752–1835)* (Stuttgart: Franz Steiner, 1994),
p. 124. An even earlier characterization of this type can be found in the Tang dynasty
annals; see Lee, *The History of Early Relations between China and Tibet*, p. 5.

23. *Nongnu*, directed by Li Jun, screenplay by Huang Zongjiang (Beijing: August
First Film, 1963). The credits indicate that it was written by Huang Zongjiang, directed by Lin Jun, and produced by the Shizang Stage Company. For a description of
its conception and production, see Li Jun et al., *Nongnu: Cong Juben dao Yingpian
(Serfs: From Script to Screen)* (Beijing: China Film Press [Zhongguo Dianying Chuban-
she], 1965).

24. See Edward Said, *Orientalism* (New York: Vintage, 1979), pp. 286–314.

25. He states that the themes for *Serfs* came from the Party's article "The Tibetan Revolution and the Philosophy of Nihelu" in *People's Daily*, May 6, 1959 (*Serfs: From Script to Screen*, pp. 118–119). The book contains chapters by various people involved in the movie. There is a great deal of repetition, and most of them stress the same themes.

26. Li et al., *Serfs: From Script to Screen*, p. 119.

27. Ibid., pp. 124–125.

28. Similarly, in *Serfs: From Script to Screen*, Huang Zongjiang claims that "The characters were all drawn from real life. The conflicts between them formed a picture of class struggle" (p. 121). On p. 122 he avers that "stories like Qiangba's were very common in old Tibet." On p. 125 he states that many people have stated that the film is "more documentary than fiction," and he agrees with this assessment. He originally intended to write a documentary, but in the end decided on a film with characters who were representatives of the main classes of Tibet involved in actions typical of their classes.

29. See Edward W. Said, *Orientalism*, pp. 3, 36–40.

30. See, for example, Michel Foucault, "The Subject and Power," in *The Foucault Reader*, ed. Paul Rabinow (New York: Pantheon Books, 1984), p. 72.

31. Dai Yannian et al., *Tibet: Myth vs. Reality*, p. 41.

32. Dawa Norbu, *Red Star over Tibet*, pp. 10–11. See also Georges Dreyfus, "Tibetan Religious Nationalism: Western Fantasy or Empowering Vision," in *Tibet, Self, and the Tibetan Diaspora: Voices of Difference*, ed. P. Christiaan Klieger (Leiden: E.J. Brill, 2002), p. 54, where he refers to Tibetan intellectuals who publicly depart from the party line being "denounced, threatened and at time[s] physically abused because they were perceived to oppose the Dalai Lama and the Buddhist values that he incarnates."

33. Jamyang Norbu, "The Heart of the Matter," in *Tibet: The Issue Is Independence* (Berkeley: Parallax Press, 1994), p. 23.

34. Thubten Jigme Norbu and Colin M. Turnbull, *Tibet*, pp. 337, 336, 337; Dawa Norbu, *Tibet: The Road Ahead*, pp. xii, xiii.

35. Jamyang Norbu, *Warriors of Tibet: The Story of Aten and the Khampas' Fight for the Freedom of their Country* (London: Wisdom Publications, 1979), p. 9.

36. Dawa Norbu, *Tibet: The Road Ahead*, p. 96.

37. Shakabpa, *Tibet: A Political History*, p. 302.

38. Wei Jing, *100 Questions about Tibet*, p. 33.

39. Grunfeld, *The Making of Modern Tibet*, pp. 116, 123, 127, 149, 138; what Grunfeld quotes is from "Communiqué on the Revolt." In *Tibet: 1950–1967*, ed. Ling Nai-min (Hong Kong: Union Research Institute, 1968), p. 350.

40. Goldstein, *The Snow Lion and the Dragon*, pp. 52, 54.

41. Richardson, *Tibet and Its History*, p. 118.

42. Ibid., pp. 188, 201, 202, 204.

43. Thurman, *Essential Tibetan Buddhism*, pp. 7, 8.

44. Jamyang Norbu, *Warriors of Tibet*, p. 83.

45. Dai Yannian et al., *Tibet: Myth vs. Reality*, p. 46.

46. Hsi and Kao, *Tibet Leaps Forward*, p. 1.

47. According to the White Paper on the Chinese government's Web site, on the evening of March 17, several Khampa "rebel leaders held the Dalai Lama under duress and carried him away from Lhasa to . . . the 'base' of the armed rebel forces. When the armed rebellion failed, they fled to India" (p. 4). Huang Hongzhao contends that they kidnapped him and brought him to India, intending to "wait there for the fancied outbreak of the Third World War, when they could stage a comeback" (*The West Powers and Tibet*, pp. 256–257). In Huang's presentation, the fourteenth Dalai Lama, like the thirteenth Dalai Lama before him, is conceived as a Chinese patriot who feels intense loyalty toward his motherland but is deceived by the sinister machinations of imperialists, who poison his mind and eventually turn him against China.

48. Grunfeld, *The Making of Modern Tibet*, pp. 124, 136.

49. Zhou Enlai, *Beijing Review*, March 3, 1980, p. 19.

50. These images and their descriptions can be seen in *The Wrath of the Serfs: A Group of Life-Size Clay Sculptures* (Peking: Foreign Languages Press, 1976). Grunfeld apparently is not aware that even the PRC government has stopped trying to convince outsiders that these statues are accurate; he cites this publication as evidence for his negative portrayal of old Tibetan society (*The Making of Modern Tibet*, p. 29).

51. It should be noted in this context that according to reports from that time, much of the destruction was caused by Tibetan cadres. In addition, Tibetans were often more brutal than the Chinese, but there is no way to ascertain the extent to which their actions were motivated by sincere revolutionary fervor. Many of those who participated in looting monasteries and attacking Tibetan religious and political leaders subsequently stated that they did so only out of fear because the Chinese who orchestrated the destruction viewed anything less than enthusiastic participation as evidence of "reactionary" tendencies. Those who failed to meet their standards often became the targets of "struggle sessions" and were subjected to physical and mental torture. Despite attempts by Tibetan exiles to paint the Chinese as the sole villains of this story, however, it is clear that there were many Tibetans who did endorse Maoist doctrines and who became ardent supporters of Chinese policies in Tibet. An interesting debate on Chinese and Tibetan perspectives on this can be found in *New Left Review* 14 (March/April 2002), which has an article by Wang Lixiong entitled "Reflections on Tibet," in which he argues that many Tibetans enthusiastically embraced the Mao cult of personality and voluntarily participated in the destruction of traditional Tibetan culture. Tsering Shakya's response article, "Blood in the Snows," rebuts Wang's contentions. He claims that although some may have embraced Chinese ideas, most acted only out of fear.

52. In *The Struggle for Modern Tibet* (Armonk, N.Y.: M.E. Sharpe, 1997), Melvyn Goldstein provides some interesting insights regarding the problems involved in the collection of data by the exile government. This work tells the story of Tashi Tsering, who fled into exile but later returned to Tibet to become an educator. He indicates that the purpose of the interviews with refugees was to gather data that could be used as propaganda against the Chinese, but many of the exiles were illiterate and were unused to telling their own stories, and so they had to be prompted by the interviewers to provide the sort of accounts that would be useful to them. Many were refashioned to conform to a desired paradigm.

53. See, for example, Tibet Information Network and Human Rights Watch/ Asia, *Cutting off the Serpent's Head: Tightening Control in Tibet, 1994–1995* (New York: Human Rights Watch, 1996), pp. 25–40. See also the International Campaign for Tibet's *Forbidden Freedoms: Beijing's Control of Religion in Tibet* (Washington, D.C.: International Campaign for Tibet, 1990).

54. Quoted in *Tibetan Review*, 1968, p. 8.

55. Margaret Nowak, *Tibetan Refugees: Youth and the New Generation of Meaning* (New Brunswick, N.J.: Rutgers University Press, 1984), p. 33.

56. Heather Stoddard, "Tibetan Publications and National Identity," in *Resistance and Reform in Tibet*, ed. Robert Barnett and Shirin Akiner (London: Hurst, 1994), pp. 150, 153.

57. Tibetan Government-in-Exile White Paper, p. 7.

58. Samdhong Losang Tenzin Rinpoche, *Satyagraha* (Dharamsala: Tibetan Government-in-Exile, 1995); cited in Stoddard, "Tibetan Publications and National Identity,", p. 109.

59. Ronald D. Schwartz, *Circle of Protest: Political Ritual in the Tibetan Uprising* (New York: Columbia University Press, 1994), p. 92.

60. Eric J. Hobsbawm, *Nations and Nationalism since 1780: Programme, Myth, Reality* (Cambridge, Mass.: Cambridge University Press, 1960), pp. 78–92.

61. Ronald Schwartz, *Circle of Protest*, p. 130.

62. Ibid.

63. Dawa Norbu, *Red Star over Tibet*, p. 115.

64. An example of this is a widely used science textbook in which Tibetan children learn that they are less intelligent than the Han because the high altitude of their country has deprived their brains of oxygen.

65. Lisa Malkki, *Purity and Exile: Violence, Memory and National Cosmology among Hutu Refugees in Tanzania* (Chicago: University of Chicago Press, 1995), p. 108.

66. Robert Barnett, "Violated Specialness: Western Political Representations of Tibet," in Dodin and Räther, *Imagining Tibet*, p. 270.

67. Toni Huber, "Shangri-la in Exile: Representations of Tibetan Identity and Transnational Culture," in Dodin and Räther, *Imagining Tibet*, p. 357.

68. Quoted in Richard Bernstein, "Behind U.S. Celebrities' Love Affair with Tibet," *New York Times*, March 19, 1977.

CONCLUSION

1. James Hilton, *Lost Horizon* (London: Macmillan, 1933).

2. See Donald S. Lopez Jr., *Prisoners of Shangri-la: Tibetan Buddhism and the West* (Chicago: University of Chicago Press, 1998), pp. 181–207.

3. Tsering Shakya, "Who Are the Prisoners?" *Journal of the American Academy of Religion* 69 (2001): 185–186.

4. See Pico Iyer, *Video Night in Kathmandu* (New York: Knopf, 1988), pp. 280–290.

5. The copy I viewed (which was three videotapes long) said that it was produced

by Theg mchog rnam grol bshad sgrub dar rgyas gling and that the producer was H.H. Pema Norbu Rinpoche. It was directed by Tulku Ngedon Rinpoche and Lama Ogyen Wangdu. The title of the video is *The Drama of the Three Dharma Masters [Padmasambhava, Trisong Detsen, and Śantarakṣita] (Mkhan slob chos gsum gyi zlos gar)*, and it is mainly a reading of the traditional popular biography of Padmasambhava. No date was given.

6. Huber, "Shangri-la in Exile," pp. 358–359.

7. Tsering Shakya, *The Dragon in the Land of Snows*, p. xii.

8. See Anderson, *Imagined Communities*, p. 6; Claes Corlin, "The Nation in Your Mind: Continuity and Change among Tibetan Refugees in Nepal" (Ph.D. dissertation, University of Göteborg, 1975), p. 153.

9. Walker Connor, "Ethnonationalism," in *Understanding Political Development*, ed. Myron Weiner and Samuel Huntington (Boston: Little, Brown, 1987), p. 203.

10. Alasdair MacIntyre, *After Virtue: A Study in Moral Theory* (London: Duckworth, 1985), p. 8. My thanks to Joseph Walser for pointing out the relevance of MacIntyre's analysis in an insightful response to an early version of this study presented at the American Academy of Religion conference in Denver, Colorado in November 2001.

11. I have discussed the Chinese government's claim that it champions "Asian values" and rejects human rights and democracy language as tools of Western hegemony, along with its conceptual ramifications, in "Human Rights and Cultural Values: The Dalai Lama versus the People's Republic of China," in *Buddhism and Human Rights*, ed. Damien V. Keown and Charles Prebish (Richmond, Va.: Curzon Press, 1998), pp. 175–202.

12. MacIntyre, *After Virtue*, pp. 71, 256.

13. Holding on to beliefs in the face of conflicting evidence is not, of course, a unique feature of either Chinese or Tibetan thought. There is an interesting and growing body of psychological research on this phenomenon. A number of studies have found that people generally seek to hold on to cherished beliefs and avoid changing them, even when they are counterproductive. In "Accepting Threatening Information: Self-Affirmation and the Reduction of Defensive Biases," *Current Directions in Psychological Science* 11.4 (2002): 119–123, for example, David K. Sherman and Geoffrey L. Cohen conclude that such behavior is often motivated by a desire to maintain a sense of self-worth and "integrity of the self." They also state that it is easier for "self-affirmed individuals," that is, people who are secure in their sense of individual and social identity, to consider competing information that challenges their beliefs. A consideration of this literature lies outside the scope of this study, but it suggests possible reasons for why these two communities hold on to their respective beliefs so passionately. In the Tibetan case, we have a refugee community whose traditional way of life was abruptly transformed and whose culture was destroyed. Large numbers of people died, and many went into exile in unfamiliar lands. In this situation, it is hardly surprising that retaining traditional beliefs would assume a high level of significance and that there would be a strong resistance to change. For contemporary Chinese, their society has also undergone radical change, and the country faces serious crises of unemployment, environmental degradation, population growth, and so on.

Coupled with this are bitter memories of the Century of Humiliation and deeply entrenched attitudes of suspicion of foreigners and cultural superiority. Both groups exhibit a distinct lack of "self-affirmation," and current psychological studies of belief persistence would predict that they would strenuously reject competing information and hold on to their beliefs, even in the face of compelling counterevidence. My thanks to Cynthia Powers for providing a sampling of the current research on this subject and explaining it to me.

Bibliography

TEXTS ANALYZED IN THIS STUDY

Chinese Sources

Dai Yannian, Edna Driscoll, Yan Qinghong, and Zhu Yuan, eds. *Tibet: Myth vs. Reality*. Beijing: Beijing Review, 1988. (C1)

Editors of China Reconstructs Press. *Tibetans on Tibet*. Beijing: China Reconstructs Press, 1988. (C2)

Great Changes in Tibet. Peking: Foreign Languages Press, 1972. (C7)

Hsi Chang-hao, and Kao Yuan-mei. *Tibet Leaps Forward*. Peking: Foreign Languages Press, 1977. (C3)

Li An-Che. *History of Tibetan Religion: A Study in the Field*. Beijing: New World Press, 1994.

Li Tieh-Tseng. *The Historical Status of Tibet*. New York: King's Crown Press, Columbia University, 1956. (C4)

———. *Tibet: Today and Yesterday*. New York: Bootman Associates, 1960. (C5)

Ling, Nai-min. *Tibetan Sourcebook*. Hong Kong: Union Research Institute, 1964. (C6)

Shen Tsung-Lien and Shen-Chi Liu. *Tibet and the Tibetans*. Stanford: Stanford University Press, 1953. (C9)

Tibet Today. Peking: Foreign Languages Press, 1974. (C8)

Wang Furen and Suo Wenqing. *Highlights of Tibetan History*. Beijing: New World Press, 1984.

Wang Jiawei and Nyima Gyaincain. *The Historical Status of China's Tibet*. Beijing: China Intercontinental Press, 2001. (C10)

Wei Jing. *100 Questions about Tibet*. Beijing: Beijing Review Press, 1989. (C11)

Ya Hanzhang. *The Biographies of the Dalai Lamas*. Beijing: Foreign Languages Press, 1993 (Chinese: *Dalai Lama zhuan*. Beijing: Renmin chubanshe, 1984). (C12)

Zhou Jin, ed. *Tibet: No Longer Mediaeval*. Beijing: Foreign Languages Press, 1981. (C13)

www.china.org/WhitePaper (C14)

Tibetan Sources

Dakpa, Rinchen, and B. A. Rooke. *In Haste from Tibet*. London: Robert Hale, 1971. (T1)

Department of Information and International Resources, Tibetan Government-in-Exile. *Tibet under Communist China: 50 Years*. Dharamsala: Department of Information and International Resources, 2001. (T2)

Dhondup, K. *The Water-Horse and Other Years*. Dharamsala: Library of Tibetan Works and Archives, 1984. (T3)

Gyaltsen, Sakyapa Sonam. *The Clear Mirror: A Traditional Account of Tibet's Golden Age*. Trans. McComas Taylor and Lama Choedak Yuthok. Ithaca, N.Y.: Snow Lion, 1996. (T4)

Norbu, Dawa. *Red Star over Tibet*. New York: Envoy Press, 1987. (T5)

———. *Tibet: The Road Ahead*. London: Rider, 1997. (T6)

Norbu, Jamyang. *Warriors of Tibet: The Story of Aten and the Khampas' Fight for the Freedom of Their Country*. London: Wisdom Publications, 1979. (T7)

Norbu, Thubten Jigme, and Colin M. Turnbull. *Tibet*. New York: Simon and Schuster, 1968. (T8)

Scientific Buddhist Association. *Tibet: The Facts*. Dharamsala, H. P., India: Tibetan Young Buddhist Association, 1990. (T9)

Shakabpa, Tsepon W. D. *Tibet: A Political History*. New Haven: Yale University Press, 1967. (T11)

Tibetan Government-in-Exile. *Tibet: Proving Truth from Facts*. White Paper, www.tibet.com/WhitePaper/. (T12)

Tsarong, Dundul Namgyal. *In the Service of His Country*. Ithaca, N.Y.: Snow Lion, 2000. (T13)

Western Sources

Epstein, Israel. *Tibet Transformed*. Beijing: New World Press, 1983. (W1)

Goldstein, Melvyn C. *A History of Modern Tibet, 1913–1951: The Demise of the Lamaist State*. Berkeley: University of California Press, 1989. (W2)

———. *The Snow Lion and the Dragon: China, Tibet, and the Dalai Lama*. Berkeley: University of California Press, 1997. (W3)

Grunfeld, A. Tom. *The Making of Modern Tibet*. London: M.E. Sharpe, 1996. (W4)

Richardson, Hugh E. *Tibet and Its History*. Boston: Shambhala, 1984. (W5)

Schwartz, Ronald D. *Circle of Protest: Political Ritual in the Tibetan Uprising*. New York: Columbia University Press, 1994. (W6)

Smith, Warren W. *Tibetan Nation: A History of Tibetan Nationalism and Sino-Tibetan Relations*. Boulder, Colo.: Westview Press, 1996. (W7)

Thurman, Robert A. F. *Essential Tibetan Buddhism*. San Francisco: Harper San Francisco, 1995. (W8)

———. "Tibet, Its Buddhism, and Its Art." In *Wisdom and Compassion: The Sacred Art of Tibet*, ed. Marylin M. Rhie and Robert A. F. Thurman. New York: Abrams, 1991. (W9)

———. *The Tibetan Book of the Dead*. New York: Bantam Books, 1994. (W10)

———. "Tibetan Buddhist Monastic and Intellectual Culture." In *White Lotus: An Introduction to Tibetan Culture*, ed. Carole Elchert. Ithaca, N.Y.: Snow Lion, 1990. (W11)

GENERAL SOURCES

Ahmad, Zahiruddin, trans. *A History of Tibet by the Fifth Dalai Lama of Tibet*. Bloomington: Indiana University Press, 1995.

———. *Sino-Tibetan Relations in the Seventeenth Century*. Rome: Istituto Italiano per il Medio ed Estremo Oriente, 1970.

Anderson, Benedict. *Imagined Communities: Reflections on the Origin and Spread of Nationalism*. London: Verso, 1991.

Barnett, Robert, ed. *Resistance and Reform in Tibet*. London: Hurst, 1994.

Beckwith, Christopher. *The Tibetan Empire in Central Asia: A History of the Struggle for Great Power among Tibetans, Turks, Arabs, and Chinese during the Early Middle Ages*. Princeton: Princeton University Press, 1987.

Bishop, Peter. *Dreams of Power: Tibetan Buddhism and the Western Imagination*. London: Athlone Press, 1993.

———. *The Myth of Shangri-La: Tibet, Travel Writing and the Western Creation of Sacred Landscape*. London: Athlone Press, 1989.

Blondeau, Anne-Marie, and Katia Buffetrille. *Le Tibet est-il chinois? Réponses à cent questions chinoises*. Paris: Albin Michel, 2002.

Bourdieu, Pierre. *Outline of a Theory of Practice*. Trans. Richard Nice. Cambridge, England: Cambridge University Press, 1977.

Braudel, Fernand. *On History*. Chicago: University of Chicago Press, 1972.

Bushell, F. W. "The Early History of Tibet from Chinese Sources." *Journal of the Royal Asiatic Society*, n.s. 12 (1880): 434–541.

Cayley, Vyvyan. *Children of Tibet: An Oral History of the First Tibetans to Grow Up in Exile*. Balmain, NSW: Pearlfisher, 1994.

Chiang Kai-shek. *China's Destiny*. Trans. Wang Chung-hui. New York: Roy Publishers, 1947.

Chiu, Hungdah, and June Teufel Dreyer. *Tibet: Past and Present*. Baltimore: School of Law, University of Maryland. Occasional Papers/Reprints Series in Contemporary Asian Studies 4, 1989.

Clifford, James. "Diasporas." *Cultural Anthropology* 9.3 (1994): 302–338.

Corlin, Claes. "The Nation in Your Mind: Continuity and Change among Tibetan Refugees in Nepal." Ph.D. dissertation, University of Göteborg, 1975.

Crossley, Pamela Kyle. *A Translucent Mirror: History and Identity in Qing Imperial Identity*. Berkeley: University of California Press, 1999.

Department of Information and International Relations, Tibetan Government-in-Exile. *The Mongols and Tibet: A Historical Assessment of Relations between the Mongol Empire and Tibet.* Dharamsala: Department of Information and International Relations, 1996.

Deutsch, Karl. *Nationalism and Social Communication.* Cambridge, Mass.: MIT Press, 1966.

Devoe, Dorsh Marie. "Keeping Refugee Status: A Tibetan Perspective." In *People in Upheaval,* ed. Scott Morgan and Elizabeth Colson. New York: Center for Migration Studies, 1987, pp. 54–65.

———. "Survival of a Refugee Culture: The Longterm Gift Exchange between Tibetan Refugees and Donors in India." Ph.D. dissertation, University of California, Berkeley, 1983.

Dikötter, Frank. "Culture, 'Race,' and Nation: The Formation of National Identity in Twentieth Century China." *Journal of International Affairs,* no. 2 (1996): 590–605.

———. *The Discourse of Race in Modern China.* London: Hurst, 1992.

Dirlik, Arif. *Revolution and History: The Origins of Marxist Historiography in China, 1919–1937.* Berkeley: University of California Press, 1978.

Ditfurth, Jutta, and Colin Goldner. "Ahnungslose Schwärmerei. Tibet Politik: Die Dalai Lama-Verehrung in Deutschland." *Die Tageszeitung,* February 17, 1996.

Dittmer, Lowell, and Samuel S. Kim, eds. *China's Quest for National Identity.* Ithaca, N.Y.: Cornell University Press, 1993.

Dodin, Thierry, and Heinz Räther, eds. *Imagining Tibet: Perceptions, Projections, and Fantasies.* Boston: Wisdom Publications, 2001.

Dreyer, June. *China's Forty Millions.* Cambridge, Mass.: Harvard University Press, 1976.

Dreyfus, Georges. "Proto-nationalism in Tibet." In *Tibetan Studies. Proceedings of the 6th Seminar of the IATS, Fagernes 1992,* ed. Per Kvaerne. Oslo: Institute for Comparative Research in Human Culture, 1994, pp. 205–218.

———. "Tibetan Religious Nationalism: Western Fantasy or Empowering Vision?" In *Tibet, Self, and the Tibetan Diaspora: Voices of Difference,* ed. P. Christiaan Klieger. Leiden: E.J. Brill, 2002.

Elvin, Mark. *The Pattern of the Chinese Past: A Social and Economic Interpretation.* Stanford: Stanford University Press, 1973.

Fairbank, John K., ed. *The Chinese World Order: Traditional China's Foreign Relations.* Cambridge, Mass.: Harvard University Press, 1968.

———. *Trade and Diplomacy on the China Coast.* Cambridge, Mass.: Harvard University Press, 1969.

Feigon, Lee. *Demystifying Tibet: Unlocking the Secrets of the Land of the Snows.* Chicago: Ivan R. Dee, 1996.

Fitzgerald, John. *Awakening China: Politics, Culture, and Class in the Nationalist Revolution.* Stanford: Stanford University Press, 1996.

Gelder, Stuart, and Roma Gelder. *Timely Rain: Travels in the New Tibet.* London: Hutchinson, 1964.

Gellner, Ernest. *Nations and Nationalism.* Ithaca, N.Y.: Cornell University Press, 1983.

————. *Thought and Change*. London: Weidenfeld & Nicolson, 1964.

Gladney, Dru C. "Representing Nationality in China: Refiguring Majority/Minority Identities." *Journal of Asian Studies* 53.1 (1994): 92–123.

————. "Tian Zhuangzhuang, the Fifth Generation, and Minorities Film in China." *Public Culture* 8.1 (1995): 161–176.

Haarh, Erik. *The Yar-luṅ Dynasty*. Copenhagen: G.E.C. Gad's Forlag, 1969.

Hansen, Peter H. "The Dancing Lamas of Everest: Cinema, Orientalism, and Anglo-Tibetan Relations in the 1920s." *American Historical Review* 101 (1996): 712–747.

Harrell, Stevan, ed. *Cultural Encounters on China's Ethnic Frontiers*. Seattle: University of Washington Press, 1995.

Harrison, James. *Modern Chinese Nationalism*. New York: Hunter College of the City of New York, Research Institute on Modern Asia, 1969.

Heberer, Thomas. *China and Its National Minorities: Autonomy or Assimilation?* Armonk, N.Y.: M.E. Sharpe, 1989.

Heyu. *Tibet: A General Survey*. Peking: New World Press, 1988.

Hobsbawm, E. J. *Nations and Nationalism since 1780: Programme, Myth, Reality*. Cambridge, England: Cambridge University Press, 1992.

Houston, G. W. *Sources for a History of the Bsam yas Debate*. Sankt Augustin, Denmark: VGH Wissenschaftsverlag, 1980.

Huang Hongzhao. *The West Powers and Tibet*. Hong Kong: Hai Feng Publishing, 1993.

Huber, Toni, ed. *Amdo Tibetans in Transition: Society and Culture in the Post-Mao Era*. Leiden: E.J. Brill, 2002.

Imeda, Yoshiro. "Documents tibétains de Touen-houang concernant le concile du Tibet." *Journal Asiatique* 263 (1975): 125–146.

Information and Publicity Office of H.H. the Dalai Lama. *Tibet under Chinese Rule: A Compilation of Refugee Statements 1958–1975*. Dharamsala: Information and Publicity Office of H.H. the Dalai Lama, 1976.

————. *Tibetans in Exile*. Dharamsala: Information and Publicity Office of H.H. the Dalai Lama, 1981.

Jackson, Roger. "Sa skya Paṇḍita's Account of the bSam yas Debate: History as Polemic." *Journal of the International Association of Buddhist Studies* 5 (1982): 89–99.

Jagchid, Sechin, and Van Jay Symons. *Peace, War, and Trade along the Great Wall: Nomadic-Chinese Interaction through Two Millennia*. Bloomington: Indiana University Press, 1989.

Jenner, W. J. F. *The Tyranny of History: The Roots of China's Crisis*. London: Penguin Press, 1992.

Johnson, Chalmers. *Peasant Nationalism and Communist Power: The Emergence of Revolutionary China, 1937–1945*. Stanford: Stanford University Press, 1962.

Kapstein, Matthew T. *The Tibetan Assimilation of Buddhism: Conversion, Contestation, and Memory*. Oxford: Oxford University Press, 2000.

Kau, Michael Y. M., and John K. Leung, eds. *The Writings of Mao Zedong*. Armonk, N.Y.: M.E. Sharpe, 1986.

Kerr, Blake, and John Ackerly. "Witness to Repression." *Utne Reader* (March/April 1989).

Klieger, P. Christiaan. "Accomplishing Tibetan Identity: the Constitution of a National Consciousness." Ph.D. dissertation, University of Hawai'i, 1989.

———. *Tibetan Nationalism: The Role of Patronage in the Accomplishment of a National Identity*. Meerut, India: Archana Publications, 1992.

Knaus, John Kenneth. *Orphans of the Cold War: America and the Tibetan Struggle for Survival*. Washington, D.C.: Public Affairs Press, 1999.

Korom, Frank J., ed. *Constructing Tibetan Culture: Contemporary Perspectives*. Quebec: World Heritage Press, 1997.

———. ed. *Tibetan Culture in Diaspora: Papers Presented at a Panel of the 7th Seminar of the International Association for Tibetan Studies, Graz 1995*. Wien: Verlag Oder Österreichischen Akademie der Wissenschaften, 1997.

Kunsang Paljor. *bSregs kyang mi 'tshigs pa'i bod*. Dharamsala: Tibetan Cultural Printing Press, 1971.

———. *Tibet: The Undying Flame*. Dharamsala: Information and Publicity Office of H.H. the Dalai Lama, 1977.

Kvaerne, Per, ed. *Tibetan Studies: Proceedings of the Sixth Seminar of the International Association for Tibetan Studies, Fagernes 1992*. Oslo: Institute for Comparative Research in Human Culture, 1994.

Lee, Don Y. *The History of Early Relations between China and Tibet: From Chiu t'ang-shu, a Documentary Survey*. Bloomington, Ind.: Eastern Press, 1981.

MacIntyre, Alasdair. *After Virtue: A Study in Moral Theory*. London: Duckworth, 1985.

March, Andrew L. *The Idea of China: Myth and Theory in Geographic Thought*. Melbourne: Wren Publishing, 1974.

Malkki, Lisa. *Purity and Exile: Violence, Memory and National Cosmology among Hutu Refugees in Tanzania*. Chicago: University of Chicago Press, 1995.

Martin, Dan. *Tibetan Histories: A Bibliography of Tibetan-Language Historical Works*. London: Serindia Publications, 1997.

Namkhai Norbu. *The Necklace of gZi: A Cultural History of Tibet*. Dharamsala, H. P., India: Narthang Publications, 1981.

Norbu, Jamyang. "Dances with Yaks: Tibet in Film, Fiction and Fantasy of the West." *Tibetan Review* 33.1 (1998): 18–23.

Nowak, Margaret. *Tibetan Refugees: Youth and the New Generation of Meaning*. New Brunswick, N.J.: Rutgers University Press, 1984.

Palakshappa, T. C. *Tibetans in India: A Case Study of Mundgod Tibetans*. New Delhi: Sterling Publishers, 1978.

Petech, Luciano. *China and Tibet in the Early 18th Century*. Westport, Conn.: Hyperion Press, 1973.

Powers, John. "The Free Tibet Movement: A Selective Narrative History." In *Engaged Buddhism in the West*, ed. Christopher Queen. Boston: Wisdom Publications, 2000, pp. 218–246.

———. "Human Rights and Cultural Values: The Dalai Lama versus the Peoples' Republic of China." In *Buddhism and Human Rights*, ed. Damien V. Keown and Charles Prebish. Richmond, Va.: Curzon Press, 1998, pp. 175–202.

———. *Introduction to Tibetan Buddhism*. Ithaca, N.Y.: Snow Lion, 1995.

Pye, Lucian. *Asian Power and Politics*. Cambridge, Mass.: Harvard University Press, 1985.

―――. *The Spirit of Chinese Politics: A Psychocultural Study of the Authority Crisis in Political Development*. Cambridge, Mass.: MIT Press, 1968.

Ran, Cheng. *Why Tibet Is an Integral Part of China*. Beijing: New Star Publishers, 1991.

Richardson, Hugh E. *Adventures of a Tibetan Fighting Monk*. Bangkok: Tamarind Press, 1986.

―――. *High Peaks, Pure Earth: Collected Writings on Tibetan History and Culture*. London: Serindia Publications, 1998.

Rossabi, Morris. *China and Inner Asia: From 1368 to the Present Day*. London: Thames and Hudson, 1975.

Ruegg, David Seyfort. *Buddha-nature, Mind, and the Problem of Gradualism in a Comparative Perspective: On the Transmission and Reception of Buddhism in India and Tibet*. London: School of Oriental and African Studies, 1989.

Rustow, Dankwart. *A World of Nations: Problems of Political Modernization*. Washington, D.C.: Brookings Institution, 1967.

Sahlins, Marshall. *Historical Metaphors and Mythical Realities*. Ann Arbor: University of Michigan Press, 1981.

Said, Edward W. *Orientalism*. New York: Vintage Books, 1979.

Saklani, G. "Tibetan Refugees in India: A Sociological Study of an Uprooted Community." *Tibet Journal* 3.4 (1978): 41–46.

Sautman, Barry. "Tibet: Myths and Realities." *Current History* 100. 647 (September 2001): 278–283.

Schell, Orville. *Virtual Tibet: Searching for Shangri-la from the Himalayas to Hollywood*. New York: Metropolitan Books, 2000.

Schram, Stuart R. ed. *The Scope of State Power in China*. Hong Kong: Chinese University Press, 1985.

Schrempf, Mona. "From 'Devil Dance' to 'World Healing': Some Representations, Perceptions and Innovations of Contemporary Tibetan Ritual Dances." In *Tibetan Culture in the Diaspora*, ed. Frank J. Korom. Wien: Verlag der Österreichischen Akademie der Wissenschaften, 1997.

Schwartz, Benjamin. "The Chinese Perception of World Order, Past and Present." In *The Chinese World Order: Traditional China's Foreign Relations*, ed. John K. Fairbank. Cambridge, Mass.: Harvard University Press, 1968.

Schwartz, Ronald D. "Buddhism, Nationalist Protest, and the State in Tibet." In *Tibetan Studies: Proceedings of the Sixth Seminar of the International Association for Tibetan Studies, Fagernes 1992*, ed. Per Kvaerne. Oslo: Institute for Comparative Research in Human Culture, 1994, pp. 728–738.

Scofield, Aislinn. "Tibet: Projections and Perceptions." *East-West Film Journal* 7 (1993): 106–136.

Shakabpa, Tsepon W. D. "Using the Lance of Truth to Draw out the Pus of Crooked Explanations" ('Khyog bshad kyi rnag khrag 'byin byed bden pa'i gtsags bu). Dharamsala: Office of H.H. the Dalai Lama, 1986.

Shakya, Min Bahadur. *The Life and Contributions of the Nepalese Princess Bhrkuti Devi to Tibetan History*. Delhi: Book Faith India, 1997.

Sørensen, Per K. *Tibetan Buddhist Historiography: The Mirror Illuminating the Royal Geneologies, An Annotated Translation of the XIVth Century Tibetan Chronicle: rGyal-rabs gsal-ba'i me-long*. Wiesbaden: Otto Harrassowitz, 1994.

Spence, Jonathan D., and John E. Wills Jr., eds. *From Ming to Ch'ing: Conquest, Region, and Continuity in Seventeenth-Century China*. New Haven: Yale University Press, 1979.

Sperling, Eliot. "Review of *The Myth of Shangri-la*." *Journal of the American Oriental Society* 112.2 (1992): 349–350.

Starr, John Bryan. *Continuing the Revolution: The Political Thought of Mao*. Princeton: Princeton University Press, 1979.

Stoddard, Heather. "Tibetan Publications and National Identity." In *Resistance and Reform in Tibet*, ed. Robert Barnett and Shirin Akiner. London: Hurst, 1994, pp. 121–156.

Strong, Anna Louise. *When Serfs Stood Up in Tibet*. Peking: New World Press, 1960.

Subba, T. B. *Flight and Adaptation: Tibetan Refugees in the Darjeeling-Sikkim Himalaya*. Dharamsala: Library of Tibetan Works and Archives, 1990.

Teichman, Eric. *Travels of a Consular Officer in Eastern Tibet*. Cambridge, England: Cambridge University Press, 1922.

Teng, S. Y., and J. K. Fairbank, eds. *China's Response to the West: A Documentary Survey, 1839–1923*. Cambridge, Mass.: Harvard University Press, 1979.

Tenzin Gyatso, Dalai Lama XIV. *My Land, My People*. New York: Potala Press, 1983.

Thurman, Robert A. F. "Tibet: Mystic Nation in Exile." *Parabola* 10. 2 (1985): 56–69.

Trimondi, Victor, and Victoria Trimondi [Herbert and Mariana Röttgen]. *Der Schatten des Dalai Lama*. Düsseldorf: Patmos, 1999.

Tsering Dorje Gashi. *New Tibet: Memoirs of a Graduate of the Peking Institute of National Minorities*. Dharamsala: Information Office of H.H. the Dalai Lama, 1980.

Tsering Gyalbo, Guntram Hazon, and Per K. Sørensen. *Civilization at the Foot of Mount sham-po: The Royal House of Ha Bug-pa-can and the History of g.Ya'-bzang*. Wien: Verlag der Österreichischen Akademie der Wissenschaften, 2000.

Tsering Shakya. *The Dragon in the Land of Snows: A History of Modern Tibet Since 1947*. New York: Columbia University Press, 1999.

Tucci, Giuseppe. *Deb t'er dmar po gsar ma: Tibetan Chronicles by bSod nams grags pa*. Rome: Istituto Italiano per il Medio ed Estremo Oriente, 1971.

Tuttle, Gray Warren. "Faith and Nation: Tibetan Buddhists in the Making of Modern China (1902–1958)." Ph.D. dissertation, Harvard University, 2000.

Ugen Gombo. "Tibetan Refugees in the Kathmandu Valley: A Study in Socio-Cultural Change and Continuity and the Adaptation of a Population in Exile." Ph.D. dissertation, State University of New York at Stony Brook, 1985.

Unger, Jonathan, ed. *Chinese Nationalism*. London: M.E. Sharpe, 1996.

———. *Using the Past to Serve the Present: Historiography and Politics in Contemporary China*. Armonk, N.Y.: M.E. Sharpe, 1993.

Van der Kuijp, Leonard. J. "Miscellanea to a Recent Contribution on the Bsam-yas Debate." *Kailash* 11.3–4 (1984): 149–184.

———. "Tibetan Historiography." In *Tibetan Literature: Studies in Genre*, ed. José Ignacio Cabezón and Roger R. Jackson. Ithaca, N.Y.: Snow Lion, 1996.

Vostrikov, A. I. *Tibetan Historical Literature*. Trans. Harish Chandra Gupta. Calcutta: R.K. Maitra, 1970.

Walker, Connor. "Ethnonationalism." In *Understanding Political Development*, ed. Myron Weiner and Samuel Huntington. Boston: Little, Brown, 1987.

Wei Jing. *Is Tibet An Independent Country?* Beijing: New Star Publishers, 1991.

The Wrath of the Serfs: A Group of Life-Size Clay Sculptures. Peking: Foreign Languages Press, 1976.

Wylie, Turrell. "Lama Tribute in the Ming Dynasty." In *Tibetan Studies in Honour of Hugh Richardson*, ed. Michael Aris and Aung San Suu Kyi. Warminster, England: Aris & Phillips, 1980.

Ya Hanzhang. *Biographies of the Tibetan Spiritual Leaders Panchen Erdinis*. Beijing: Foreign Languages Press, 1994. (Chinese: *Banchan E'erdeni zhuan*. Lhasa: Xizang Renmin chubanshe, 1987. Tibetan: *Pan chen sku phreng rim byon gyi mdzod rnam*. Trans. Blo bzang phun tshogs, 'Brug grags. Lhasa: Bod ljongs mi dmangs dpe skrun khang, 1992.)

Index

Page numbers in italics refer to figures.

45 cenobitic